CHINA COLLECTING IN AMERICA

by ALICE MORSE EARLE

ILLUSTRATED

CHARLES E. TUTTLE COMPANY
Rutland, Vermont

Representatives

Continental Europe: BOXERBOOKS, INC., *Zurich*

British Isles: PRENTICE-HALL INTERNATIONAL, INC., *London*

Australasia: PAUL FLESCH & CO., PTY. LTD., *Melbourne*

Canada: M. G. HURTIG LTD., *Edmonton*

*...blished by the Charles E. Tuttle Company, Inc.
of Rutland, Vermont & Tokyo, Japan
with editorial offices at
Suido 1-chome, 2-6, Bunkyo-ku, Tokyo, Japan*

Copyright in Japan, 1973, by Charles E. Tuttle Co., Inc.

Library of Congress Catalog Card No. 78-142764

International Standard Book No. 0-8048-0958-5

*First edition published 1892
by Charles Scribner's Sons, New York
First Tuttle edition published 1973*

PRINTED IN JAPAN

TO

THE COMPANION OF MY CHINA HUNTS

MY SISTER

FRANCES CLARY MORSE

TABLE OF CONTENTS

Table of Contents

LIST OF ILLUSTRATIONS

PUBLISHER'S FOREWORD

"China-collecting is not a mere fancy—it is a complete education," an English collector wrote. To Alice Morse Earle, famous for her popular and authoritative books dealing with various phases of early American life and customs, it was an edification as well as an education. She was a connoisseur, first, whose love of the old, quaint, and historical prompted her to collect and convert these treasures into life-long friends.

Her china hunting also revealed to her many ghosts of the past—visions and dreams that never became realities, the inexorable fate, the sad kismet of New England life. She liked to think that the china she loved had been warmly loved before—in much the same friendly affection that she felt for an old well-read, half-worn book; the unknown hands through which it had passed, the unseen eyes which had gazed on it, endearing it to her. The same can be said of this book, which will endear itself to the reader, and it is a pleasure indeed to bring it back into print for a new generation of collectors.

I.

CHINA HUNTING

Y dearly loved friend, Charles Lamb, wrote, in his "Essays of Elia," "I have an almost feminine partiality for old china. When I go to see any great house, I inquire first for the china-closet, and next for the picture-gallery. I have no repugnance for those little lawless azure-tinted grotesques that, under the notion of men and women, float about uncircumscribed by any element, in that world before perspective —a china teacup." In that partiality for old china I humbly join, and it is of the search through New England for such dear old china loves, and of the gathered treasures of those happy china hunts, that I write.

China hunting is a true "midsummer madness." When grass grows green and "daffodils begin to peer"

my fancy lightly turns to thoughts of china. Hot waxes the fever as crawls up the summer sun; fierce and fiercer rages the passion and the hunt, till autumn touches with her cold though glorious hand the trees and fields. Then doth my madness wane, and chase grow dull, and icy winter finds me sane and calm, till charming spring returns to witch me to "mine old lunes" once again. Thus is every china captive of that mad summer chase aglow to me with summer suns and beauty—not a dull lifeless clod of moulded painted clay, but a glorious idealized token of long warm halcyon days too quickly passed, of "yesterdays that look backward with a smile."

Were the possession of old or valuable specimens of porcelain and pottery, or even of happy memories of "days of joyance," the only good things which came from the long hours of country ranging and farm-house searching spent in our china quests, Philistines might perhaps scoff at the waste of time and energy; but much else that is good have I found. Insight into human nature, love of my native country, knowledge of her natural beauties, acquaintance with her old landmarks and historical localities, familiarity with her history, admiration of her noble military and naval heroes, and study of the ancient manners, customs, and traditions of her early inhabitants have all been fostered, strengthened, and indeed almost brought into existence by the search after and study of old china. How vague and dull were my school-day history-lesson memories of Perry, of Lawrence, of Decatur, until I saw their likenesses on some hideous Liverpool pitchers! then I read eagerly every word of history, every old song and ballad about them. How small was my knowledge of old "table manners" and table furnishings until I discovered, through my china studies, how our ancestors ate and served their daily meals! How little I knew of the shy romance and the deep-lying though sombre sentiment in New England country life, until it was revealed to me in the tradition of many a piece of old china. How entirely powerless was I to discover the story of human nature as told in the countenance until my inquiries after old china made me a second Lavater in regarding the possibilities of successful purchase in case the questioned one chanced to own any old porcelain heirlooms! How few of our noble wood and valley roads had I seen until I drove through them searching for old farm-houses that might contain some salvage of teacups or teapots! And not only do we learn of America through our china hunts, but of England as well; for nearly all of our old table-ware was English, and the history of the production of English china can be traced as easily in New England as in old England. Few of the more costly pieces came here, but humbler specimens show equally well the general progress of the manufacture.

Let me be just and honest in my tale; though all is ideal happiness in the hours of the china chase, the counting of the spoils is sometimes vastly disappointing.

> " As high as we have mounted in delight
>   In our dejection do we sink as low."

There is no hobby of so uncertain gait, none other
fancy in the pursuit of which one meets with so many
rebuffs as in china collecting. I mean in real china collecting by individual search and pursuit, not in china
buying at high prices at a fashionable china-shop. For
such Crœsus buyers, who know not the sweet nor the
bitter of true china hunting, these pages are not written.

Sad, sad failures does your china hunter often make,
but there is a blessed delight and pride when a long
search is at last successful which rewards him and makes
him, or rather her, forget the cruel blows of the past,
and makes hope spring eternal in her breast, undying,
and undimmed. Disappointments were few in early
china-collecting days in America; friendly farm-wives
then gladly brought out their precious and plentiful
stores, and eagerly sold them for silver to buy a new
cotton gown or a shell-comb, and attics and pantries
were ransacked and depleted with delight. Now can
the china hunter drive for days through the country,
asking for old crockery at every house which is surmounted by a gambrel roof, has a great square chimney,
or an old well-sweep, without even hearing of one old
teapot; and yet such is the power of china-love, she
will start out again the next week, cheerful, hopeful,
and undaunted, "to fresh woods and pastures new."

Nor will it always prove clear sailing should she discover the home of the sought-for treasure. She may
learn from friendly and loquacious neighbors that "old
Miss Halsey" or "John Slade's widder" has stores of
old crockery in barrels in the attic, or on the top shelf of

the pantry, or even " up over the woodshed," but she cannot obtain one glimpse of the hidden hoards—far less can she purchase them.

We have visited again and again one gray old farm-house in Massachusetts, a farm-house with moss-covered " lean-to," which we know contains enough old English pottery and porcelain to found a museum; but cajoleries, flatteries, persuasions, open demands, elaborate explanations, and assumptions of indignant and hurt astonishment at refusals—one and all are in vain; not even one old plate have we ever seen. The farmer's wife greets us most cordially, gives us doughnuts and milk in summer, and apples and cider in the winter, maple-sugar in the spring, and hickory-nuts and butter-nuts in the fall, but in aggressively modern pitchers and dishes; and when we leave she urges us hospitably and warmly to " come again." We know well where her precious china is hidden. High up on either side of the great mantel-pieces in " living room " and " best room " are cupboards, so high that one would have to climb upon a chair to see into them; and from the good wife's frequent and furtive glances—speaking though silent—at her locked cupboard-doors, we know well what treasures are stored therein.

At that china-hiding abode we often have concocted for us an old-time country drink, composed of water flavored with molasses and ginger, which was in Revolutionary times called " beveridge." Gallons of that vile fluid have I drunk with the hostess, hoping that the joys of the flowing bowl might loosen her tongue and

unlock her cupboard doors, but I have risked my diges-
tion in vain. Still I sit "smiling with millions of mischief in the heart," for life is short, and I am waiting,
wickedly waiting; the farmer and his wife are old, very
old, and when they depart from this life they cannot
take their keys and crockery with them.

More complete and mortifying routs sometimes,
though rarely, have befallen us. We were driving quietly along one day on the outskirts of the town, when
we saw at the door of a shabby modern house, a vine-
gar faced woman, who sat energetically mixing chicken-
dough in one of the most beautiful old blue and white
Nankin bowls that ever was seen. As each blow of the
heavy iron spoon came down on the precious antique, it
struck an echoing and keener blow to our china-loving
hearts, and we hastened to ask the owner of the bowl to
sell it ere it was broken. Sell it? not she. She didn't
know where it came from, nor who had owned it—and
she didn't care, but she wouldn't sell it for any money;
and if a tin pan was just as good to mix the meal in, she
would use this "old crockery thing" if she wanted to;
and she walked into the shabby house, and "slammed"
the door before our abashed and sad faces. The thought
of that bowl at the mercy of that fierce iron spoon has
made us very unhappy; scores of times have we driven
past the house glancing furtively in, at the wood-shed,
the hen-house, the kitchen door, ready almost to steal
the poor prisoner if we found it unguarded; but we do
not dare attempt an honest rescue lest we suffer a still
more ignominious and mortifying defeat.

Strange answers are sometimes made to our inquiries
and requests ; strange objects presented to our china-
searching eyes. In farm-houses, presided over by deaf
old housewives we have had shown to us crackers for
crockery, pitchforks for teapots, tubs for cups, and once,
by some strange and incomprehensible twist of the poor
deaf ears, or our own dull tongues, were cheerfully offered
buckwheat flour when we asked to see a Washington
pitcher. We also drove several miles at the sea-shore,
in high spirits and with great expectations, to see some
very old teapots, " all kinder basket work," and were
confronted by a strange machine of seafaring appearance,
which proved to be an eel-pot, and was truly an ancient
one. Other kindly country souls, knowing well what
we want, offer us as far more desirable and artistic treasures, faded samplers, worsted flowers, crocheted tidies,
preserved wreaths, wax fruit, hair jewelry, and Parian
busts, and look at us with commiseration when we
cling to our strange idiosyncrasy—our preference for old
china. Sometimes the kindly intention to guide and
help us to our goal is evident and powerful enough, the
desire to inform us is rampant, but power of expression
is lacking, or even a modicum of memory; the narrow
limits of country vocabulary are painful to witness and
the expressions of its poverty are painful to hear, and
suggestions only lead the speaker farther astray in his
attempted descriptions. He is also color-blind, and has
vague remembrance of size and nomenclature. He can't
describe the china, he can't date it, he can't name it,
sometimes—though he vaguely remembers that he has

seen it—he can't place it, he simply knows that somewhere he has seen something that he fancies may be
somewhat like what we want; and too often when we
try to follow his vague and jejune clue, we go upon a
" thankless arrant."

We once addressed to an old Yankee farmer, who had
brought a load of apples into town, the stereotyped inquiry which we have asked, ah! how many hundred
times, and received this drawling answer, " No-o I donow
as I know anyone as has got any old furnitoor or chayner
she wants ter part with. My wife haint got any anyway. My Aunt Rebecca's got one curous old plate
and I guess she'd sell it—she'd sell her teeth if anybody'd buy 'em an' pay enough ter suit her." We finally extracted from him (after much parrying of our direct questions) that, " she got it in Washington more'n
fifty year ago," that " the folks set great store by it,
and said it came from Mount Vernon and belonged to
Marthy Washington," that it had the names of the States
around it, " it was blue and perhaps green too, and it
had stars sure and he guessed they were gilt." Now we
had seen pieces of the Martha Washington tea-set, and
we knew that it was decorated in blue and green with
the names of the States in the links of a chain, and the
initials M. W. in the centre in a great gilt star. We
knew at once that Aunt Rebecca's plate must be one of
that set. What a discovery!

To the benighted and narrow-lived souls who have
never hunted for old china it may seem strange that we
knew at once that it was one of those rare plates ; but I

am sure every china hunter, whose path is always illumined by the brilliant possibilities which form such an encouragement in the pleasures of the china chase, will fully comprehend our confidence and anticipation. We figured our plate in all the loan collections, marked with our names in large letters as joint owners; we planned a velvet silver-bound box to safely hold our "heavenly jewel" after we had caught it; we even hesitatingly thought that we might make our joint will and leave it to the Mount Vernon Association— and then we drove eighteen miles to

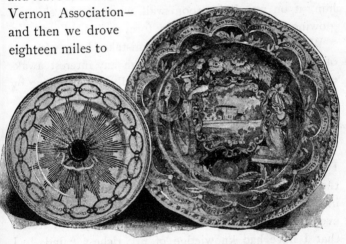

The Plate we Hoped to Find and the Plate we Found.

secure it. I shall never forget the sickening disappointment I felt when I saw the Martha Washington plate. There were the names of the States; and stars there were, but not a gilt one. And where were the touches of verdant color? All was blue—deeply, darkly, vilely blue. At any other time we should have hailed the fine " States " plate which was shown us with keen delight, but now we could hardly speak or bear to look at it. At last, in sullen disparagement, we offered a dollar for it, had our offer accepted, carelessly took it, threw it on the carriage-seat and drove away. I reviled the farmer and his villainous memory and vocabulary, and would not look at the deep-dyed " States " impostor for a month, but when I heard that a collector had paid twenty dollars for a similar plate in New York, I unwrapped it and hung it on my dining-room wall, where it now shines a glowing bit of dark color, a joy forever.

Warned by many such dreary mistakes I am very shy of having china sent to me through any interest awakened by its description, and am equally shy of buying by proxy.

> " Let every eye negotiate for itself,
>   And trust no agent."

I have learned also to listen with attention, not placing the slightest confidence in what I hear, and yet always to investigate with cheerfulness and alacrity. It is not, however, from elaborately detailed and willingly told stories that I have had knowledge of my richest " finds." I have learned to " take a hint " — a maxim which should be eternally impressed on every china hunter. Learn to " grasp the skirt of happy chance ; " let your motto be, " Semper paratus." Let no suggestion of old people or old house-furnishings, no glimpse of blue color or sprigged surface, even on a broken sherd of crockery by the wayside, no hint of distant and out-of-the-way farms, no prospect of country sales, of " New England dinners," no news of refurnishing old houses, no accounts of the death of old inhabitants fall on unheeding eye or ear. For myself, I never hear the words " old china " but my heart is moved, more than " with sound of a trumpet." I breathe the battle afar and hurry to the fray, to return at times victorious with dainty trophies of war, and sometimes, alas, empty-handed, with the hanging head of sore disappointment and defeat. Sometimes the scent is poor and broken and you must ferret out the way to the lair; even with much trouble and diligence you cannot always learn at once and definitely the lurking-place of the porcelain treasures; you meet with reserve and a disinclination to reveal. Then comes stratagem to the fore. Learn to wheedle, to hint, to interrogate slyly, to blandly let the conversation drift— " muster all wiles with blandished parleys, feminine assaults, tongue batteries "—in short, vulg. dict., to "pump" —and work that pump with judgment, with craft, and with thoroughness. Moments of quickly repented expansiveness come to all mortals in country and in town, and in those rare moments of telling all they know, even reticent and secretive country people will give you many a china clue to follow.

I have not found, as did the members of the China Hunters' Club, that country housekeepers would, as a rule, rather have money than china; my country people will not sell their china willingly—they prefer china to silver. Times have changed since 1876; a fancied knowledge, an exaggerated estimate of the value of old "crockery" now fills many a country soul, and a high monetary value is also placed on family relics, on "storied urns" and on the power of association. I will confess that, as a last resort in times of direst stress, when you really cannot go without that Pilgrim plate, when you positively need it—if you take your money out and lay it on the table in full sight of the plate-owner, you wield a powerful lever to work the transfer; nor do I consider such a statement at all derogatory to the character of my New England neighbors, nor is the trait peculiar to them.

But do not make too aggressively prominent the money part of the transaction. Be courteous and careful even to extremes in addressing your country people for purposes of china purchase. Never ask them to sell their china—*sell* is a most offensive and brutal word—ask them if they are "willing to part with it." Never hint, by word or deed, that you fancy they really need the money. Never disparage the desired articles, the shrewd country wives would see through your pretence at once—"Why, if it be so common-place, do you wish it?" A base and deceitful, though clever, china hunter of my acquaintance declares that she has found it invariably to her advantage to say that the coveted article matched exactly, either in shape or decoration, something which she had at home. The staid country mind, liking to see things in "sets," always appeared to be most immoderately and unaccountably influenced to sell by this disingenuous assertion.

We have many times during the past five years crossed the trail of a collector who appears to have wholly depleted of china the old farm-houses of the Connecticut Valley. We have found, through comparing the accounts of his visits, that he has a little slyness too. He always desires to purchase his particular bit of china simply to form a link in a chain. He either has a specimen of the entire succession of production of a factory except the very piece the farm-wife has, or he has a perfect list of historical plates except the very plate she owns, or he has a choice bit of every known color of lustre except her special pitcher. The satisfaction of supplying the long missing link, and the value that link will give to a history the purchaser is going to write of such china, seem to prove a powerful lever to effect the transfer to his catenulate collection.

The men are, as a rule, always willing to sell china— when did man ever reverence the vessels of his household gods? I always delight to ask a Yankee farmer, in field or road, whether he has any old crockery that he would be willing to part with. How he will skurry home " cross-lots," over the ploughed fields, or through the rows of growing corn, eager to pull out and sell his wife's pantry treasures! Not that he can sell them if " Mother " isn't willing—in her realm she reigns supreme. Even in the midst of my sore disappointment I have thrilled with malicious satisfaction and delight to see the calm and authoritative way in which " Father " is turned out of the " butt'ry " when he tries to pull down from the shelf an old blue bowl or plate to sell. " Mother" has kept her cinnamon-sticks and nutmegs for her apple-pies in that "Blue Dragon" bowl for forty years, and she isn't going to sell it now to please anyone. To hail the farmer in advance with china questions is not, therefore, so underhanded and despicable a proceeding as might be thought, nor so dangerous to the family peace ; he really is a poor, uninfluential, unpowered vassal in kitchen and pantry, his advice is not asked, his word is not heeded, nor if he attempt to be at all bumptious will his presence be tolerated. I have found it to be an unvarying rule that the farmer is always willing and eager to sell his wife's mother's china, while the wife is always openly disparaging, and cares little for his mother's china; and when once the source of inheritance is discovered, the rule of action and plan of attack are plainly defined.

It may be argued that it is neither very courteous nor very kind to walk into a stranger's house and ask him to sell you his household goods and chattels. To such argument may be offered the reply that one can hardly judge a farm home by the same rule as one does a city home. The visit of a stranger is regarded with widely different eyes ; it is a pleasure, a treat, to most farm-wives to receive such a visit, and the farmer will come plodding home from the distant fields, in order not to lose the chat with the stranger and the pleasant diversion. Who would attempt to enter and to lodge over night in a stranger's house in the city ? A police-station or a lunatic asylum would probably quickly shelter your intruding head. There is hardly a farm-house where such a suggestion would be unwelcome or resented, provided you look not like a bandit or horse-thief. Then, too, farmers and even farm-wives do not generally regard their old furniture and furnishings with quite the same feeling that we do ours. The old blue Staffordshire ware they consider almost worthless, and are often glad to sell it for ready cash ; but their lilac-sprigged china, a wedding-gift or a purchase with their few hard-earned dollars, they often value and cherish as we do Sèvres. A farmer handles very little money—his wife still less, and ofttimes the money paid by china hunters is a godsend in country homes. Much good is done, much comfort conferred by exchanging money for crockery. Carpers say: "But you do not pay city prices." Sometimes, alas, we do, fired by our china mania, "the insane root that takes the reason prisoner," though we never should. The farmer does not pay city rents, he has not the risk and expense of transfer to the city, he pays no salesman. If he could sell all his farm products as easily, profitably, and safely as he sells his china, lucky would he be. Sometimes the discovery that the "old blue pie-plates" are of any value is a delight and a surprise to him, but he sees at once that when they are worth so much he cannot afford to keep them. Hence he is far from being offended at the easy means of sale offered to him.

One piece of advice I give to china hunters—advice, the wisdom and advantage of which I have learned at the cost of much unpleasant and disappointing experience. Do not hurry prospective china sellers : bustling city ways annoy them, fluster them, and worry them, and in sheer bewilderment they say "No" to get rid of you.

Be tentative and gentle in your approach. Do not—as we did—rush in upon a deaf and timid old lady and frighten her, by the bouncing and bustling inquiries we made, into vehement denials of china-possession and simultaneous refusals to sell anything. This dear old "Aunt Dolly" lived in the sole new house in a village of old colonial dwellings, and we rather contemptuously thought to pass by the brand-new French roofed intruder, but decided "just to ask"—and "just to ask" and receive a frightened negative answer was all we did do, and we left with self-important assurance, to hunt elsewhere. A tin-peddler (a "china runner" perhaps in disguise), with quieter voice and more truly well-bred manners, carried off her rare treasures about a week later—a canopy-topped mirror with Washington and Franklin mirror-knobs, a "Boston State House" pitcher, four "Valentine" plates having Wilkie's design, half a dozen Staffordshire plates with the "cottage" pattern, and two Wedgwood teapots; and Aunt Dolly took as payment two shining new tin milk-pans and a cheap wringing-machine that wouldn't wring. We knew her well in after years when it was too late, and she confessed to us that at our first meeting we talked so fast, and talked together, and "hollered so she couldn't hear," and that she did not understand what we meant or what we wanted, and said "No" to obtain peace.

And oh! what an enviable advantage the ubiquitous tin-peddler, that "licensed vagrom," has over every convention-trammelled china hunter! What a delight, what a dream it would be to go a-china hunting with a tin-peddler's cart; what lonely out-of-the-way roads and by-lanes I would take, careless where I went, since wherever I wandered I should be welcome. How I would sit on my lofty seat and view the lovely country o'er, in the " sessions of sweet, silent thought," with my strong and willing and safe horse to pull me up hill and down dale; with my stock of shining tin-ware, my brooms and notions and gaily painted pails, all ready for advantageous exchange; with my big, red, roomy wagon, in whose mysterious cavernous interior I could store in safety unwieldy china treasures, such as tureens and bowls and pitchers; with my air of ready assurance, of intimate familiarity with the family, my jovial raillery, my opportunities of kitchen and pantry investigation, my anxious health inquiries and profound medical advice, backed up by bottles of patent medicines which I should sell at half-price to curry favor and china; or, better still, exchange, giving a bottle of liniment for a " Landing of Lafayette," or a box of pills for a Pilgrim plate—oh! next to being a gipsy living under the greenwood tree, who would not be a Yankee tin-peddler a-china hunting? But perhaps the farm-wife might wish me to take in exchange for my wares, eggs, or butter, or rolls of wool—what should I do with a pail of butter in summer-time on a tin-peddler's cart? Or, worse still, old rags—just fancy it —instead of old china! I should then answer her with an air of deep and sombre mystery: " Madam, I would gladly take your readily exchangeable merchandise an' I could; the old rags are particularly desirable and attractive, but I have sworn a vow—I have a secret which I cannot now divulge—it must be crockery or naught, especially dark blue crockery with American designs, else I and my glittering and uncommonly cheap wares must pass wearily on, homeless, chinaless, a wanderer on the face of the earth." Alack-a-day! such happy peaceful joys are forbidden to me, not because of lack of inclination or capacity, but—thrice bitter thought—because I am a woman. Tin-peddlering is not for me, it is not "woman's sphere." Perhaps when I am old, too old to clamber up and proudly sit on that exalted driver's seat (though never too old to go china hunting), perhaps when women have crowded into every other profession, calling, and business in the land, some happy, bold feminine soul will taste the pleasures of "advanced life for women," the pleasures forbidden to me, and dare to go tin-peddlering, though there will then be no old china left in the country to buy.

Though I have never been china hunting with a tin-peddler I have been on the trail with a Yankee china dealer, and his unique method of management was delightful. He worked upon the most secretive, the most furtive plan. He never would have shared with us his coverts nor taken us to his haunts, save for this reason: he had run down a noble prey, an entire set of fine old English ware, and to his dismay the owner refused to let him enter the house. Again and again had he essayed to come to some terms, even to see the china, but without success. He felt sure, however, that if any woman asked she would not plead in vain, hence his divulgement as a favor to us. We made several stops at farm-houses on the road to our goal, and his way of carrying on his business of china buying deserves to be told as a matter of interest and instruction to amateur china hunters, for he was a professional, a star. He never, by any chance, told the truth about himself, and above all never gave his correct name and place of residence, nor drove away from the house in the way he really intended to go. He represented himself as an adopted son, this seeming to be more mysterious than ordinary family con-ditions; never gave twice alike the name of his adopted father, but had a series of noble parents, the most prom-inent and influential men in the country around. The reasons he assigned for wishing to buy the china were so ingenious and so novel that we listened to him in de-light and amazement, and with keen anticipation as to what he would next invent; the glamour of romance was added to the delightful madness of china hunting. He was at one farm-house a tender-hearted, indulgent hus-band, whose delicate invalid of a wife had expressed a wish for a set of old china and he was willing to spend days of search in order to satisfy her whim. It is need-less to add that he was a bachelor. At another time his adopted father was losing his mind and would eat off nothing but old-fashioned china; hence he was hunting to find a set to carry dutifully home. Again he was fit-ting out a missionary-box for the Western wilds, and wanted to buy a little old-fashioned crockery to send out to the minister to remind him of his New England home. At the next door he assumed an air of solemnity and dignity and announced that he was founding a museum, and was forming a collection of old New England house-furnishings as a nucleus. At another place he swelled with paternal kindliness, and wanted to get a few plates to give to his three little children to show them the kind of crockery he used to eat from at his grandfather's. Once he boldly announced that he was a china manufacturer and was dissatisfied with the quality of his ware and wanted some old china to grind up and thus learn the correct ingredients. Then he was collecting china for the Columbian Exhibition. At another door his wife turned into an accomplished china-painter who wanted these plates for patterns. He curried warm favor and won much china at one house by stating that his mother's china set had been badly broken by her daughter-in-law and he wished to replace the broken pieces. An aged couple who were living with their son and his wife were easy victims to this specious invention. He bargained for hay, for potatoes, for a whole farm; we seemed at one time in imminent danger of being forced to buy a cow and to depart leading her behind the wagon. Let me be just to this inventive soul; his dishonesty lay in words only. He paid good prices for all the china he bought, neither undervalued nor disparaged it; and showed a thoughtful kindliness toward the dwellers in every house he visited. After a prolonged stay within one shabby kitchen he appeared with two little copper lustre saucers which he rather shamefacedly acknowledged having paid two dollars for. We extracted from him that he had found a bed-ridden old woman alone, shivering, thirsty; that he had built a fire for her, pumped water, and paid for her only pieces of old china double their value because he pitied her so.

We suggested at one house that he should say plainly that he was a dealer and wanted to buy the china to sell. He scorned our dull, commonplace suggestion, and said it wouldn't be any fun, and that they wouldn't let him within their doors. " Half the places I go to anyway they look out the window afore they answer me to see if I aint got a sewing-machine in the wagon, and if they don't see any, then they think I must have a cyclopedy." China hunting was to him the romance of his life, his tournament, his battle-field. He told us of several narrow escapes he had had from detection, and exposure of his fables. In addition to vending old china, he sold old junk and farming tools; and thrice farmers of whom he had bought china recognized him within his own doors. But with the active imagination of a Dumas, he had an instant explanation. He had either just gone into the business, or else they were mistaken: he had a twin brother who had been adopted, etc. He developed to us a plan of action which we were to pursue at the special farm-house that contained the set of china. He would stop at the foot of the hill and lurk out of sight while we climbed to the door. Then we were to represent ourselves as relatives of the Republican candidate for Governor, as it was within a week of election and the farmer was a Republican. We were to tell little anecdotes of the candidate's private life, to hint that it was to please the Governor-elect that we wished this china, and that it would be used in the gubernatorial mansion in Boston. He told us exactly how we were to work up the conversation and lead up to the purchase, what to pay and what to offer at first. All was well and carefully arranged when a dire suspicion seized him that Farmer Rice was a Democrat after all. This depressed him much, and he decided to sound a neighbor on this important point ere we committed ourselves within doors. His conversation with the guileless neighbor held us spellbound, he represented himself as a political census taker and hinted darkly that we were to be the candidates for high offices on the Woman's Rights ticket at the next election. He found that farmer Rice was a bitter Democrat. This was a sharp blow, for neither he nor we knew one thing about the private life of the Democratic candidate—not even where he lived, nor indeed on our part one thing about politics anyway. Nothing daunted, he searched a newspaper which he chanced to have, and invented an imaginary home for the Democratic Governor, which would doubtless have answered every purpose, with the strong points on Free Trade and Protection which he drilled into us. We very prosaically, however, preferred our old honest plan, and whether because of our suspicious appearance on foot at such a great distance from any village, or because we made an extremely inauspicious entrance, awakening a very deaf old lady from a very sound nap, we could not buy the china either, but we saw it, a whole chest full, and the sight was well worth the long journey.

Thus it may be seen that china hunting, like many another hobby, is not a wholly ennobling pursuit. Strange and petty meannesses develop in you, envious longings, you have "an itching palm," you learn to be secretive and dissembling, "to smile and smile and be a villain." You learn to hide your trail, to refuse to give information to other sportsmen, to conceal the location of your hunting-grounds, to employ any wile to gain attention and entrance. Two worthy young men, without a fault, save an overweening and idolatrous love for old china, can attribute their fall from the paths of honesty and truthfulness to china hunting. Searching one day in a country town, one of these china hunters descended from the carriage and pounded the knocker of a fine but somewhat dilapidated country mansion. A pompous and repelling old gentleman of extreme deafness and reticence opened the door. What was the amazement and mortification of the waiting friend in the carriage to hear the bold intruder roar in his loudest and most persuasive voice, "I have come to see whether you have any old china, or know of anyone who has old china to sell," and as the door was about to be slammed, he added, "My friend, the late Judge V——, of Worcester, told me that if anyone in the country knew of old china and relics it was you."

The way that proud and shy old man rose to that transparent bait was wonderful to behold. He ushered in the young deceiver, with Chesterfieldian bows of welcome. The "late Judge V——" had been a man well known and honored throughout the county, though he knew so little and thought so little of china that he might have dined off pewter and never known it—but he was dead, and could never be brought up as a refuting witness, which was a great point. The lonely watcher in the carriage sat shamefacedly waiting, cringing at the thought of his companion's wickedness. He listened to the loud roars into the deaf old ears as the twain walked

Millennium Plate.

from room to room while "glozed the tempter," and the specious sounds were wafted out on the summer air; he thought of possible treasures within, he listened and wondered and yielded —such is the contamination of wicked example— walked into the

house, and added to the lie tenfold. As a result of their duplicity, and since the flattered one was a widower with no woman to say nay, they captured and brought away four Millennium plates, two Wedgwood pickle-leaves, a silver-lustre teapot, and a glorious great flip-mug. But "things ill-got had ever bad success;" as they lifted the large and knobby newspaper parcel from the carriage, it slipped from their contaminating grasp, and all the pieces were broken save the flip-mug, which, being specially protected, escaped. Though warned by this plain rebuke, they persevere; and so hardened are they now become in their base habits of deception, that they have worked that " late Judge V——" scheme, with some slight variations, in a score of country homes. They always tell that abominable falsehood whenever they have a man to deal with, not only adding deception to deceit, but showing a most despicable lack of originality—a " most damnable iteration."

They cringingly allege their intention to change the name of the imaginary recommender as soon as any one of sufficient note and widespread fame in the county dies, and thus through his death becomes eligible to the position in the fable. I only wish the wraith of the late Judge V——, a man of portentous ugliness in real life, such abnormal ugliness that the thought of the sight of his dematerialized ghost is really appalling—I only wish his indignant wraith would appear before them at the lintel of the door, at the portal of some china-besieged house, and demand, in the loud roars which character-ized him in his lifetime, the meaning of this unwarrant-able and presumptuous use of his name.

In the meantime, unchecked and undiscovered, this simple and transparent scheme invariably works to a charm—how proud the man always is to learn that the late Judge V—— recommended him as a connoisseur of anything! he hastens to sell his china, if his wife be will-ing and have any to sell, and he manages to think of someone else who will probably sell, should he chance to have none himself. The flip-mug has been filled many a time to the old-time toast, " Success to Trade"—and yet the base china hunters are really honest fellows enough in every-day life. Alas! that greed for things so beautiful should so deform the soul!

Such duplicity is, however, rare. I tell of it only to express my abhorrence, my condemnation. Dissimulation is seldom necessary. You are sometimes falsely accused of it when your motives are as open as the light of day. After telling with exact truth precisely what I intended to do with some pieces of china, I was answered, with an angry toss of the head, " Why didn't ye tell me first-off ye didn't want me 'to know."

We are sometimes, in our china hunts, brought into close contact with baser crimes than falsehood and duplicity. We have a number of daintily-shaped pieces of sprigged china, with a graceful ribbon border, which are known to us by the name of " Beach ware," but which would be generally and more correctly called " cottage china." These six-legged teapots and cream-jugs of " Beach ware " received their descriptive and pretty title from the simple folk of whom they were bought, not from the name of their maker nor from their place of manufacture. " Beach ware " was found in crates or boxes along the beach on the shores of Barnegat Bay at the beginning of this century. It was part of the cargo of a great English ship laden with china, which was lured to destruction and robbed by a notorious family of Barnegat " wreckers," one of whose members died not many years ago at the age of ninety years, having served in his youth a well-deserved term

" Beach Ware."

of twenty years' imprisonment in State Prison, the sentence received at his trial for cruel robbery and murder through "wrecking."

At that time, though vessels and their cargoes were insured, the underwriters frequently did not make their appearance down the coast at the scene of the wreck for many days and even weeks after the ship broke up or came ashore. And when the tardy officials did arrive, Barnegat natives, even from far inland—honest men and knavish rogues alike—had always managed to capture everything of value that came ashore or could be taken from the vessel. In order to conceal their stolen salvage, indestructible merchandise or articles that were not affected by the action of the soil and water were frequently buried until after the baffled insurance company and the ship's owners had left the scene. The arrest and sentence of the leader of this gang of wreckers caused much apprehension and excitement in every Barnegat home, and much fine china was pounded up or thrown into the water, as well as buried, lest its presence seem proof of complicity in the convict's guilt. Our pieces of " Beach ware " remained under ground for years—it is said until the wicked old convict served out his term in prison, since he alone could find the spot where he had buried it. The green-ribboned and pink-sprigged teapots and teacups look too innocent to have known aught of such wickedness and violence, but bear no more guileless face than did the patriarchal old wrecker in the peaceful prosperous days of his later years when he unblushingly and unwincingly sold to us this " Beach ware," of which his gossiping neighbors had told to us the tale.

Shall I have the dire name of " fence " applied to me when it is told that I am the receiver of stolen goods ?

The best piece of Wedgwood jasper ware that I own was bought from an old Englishman of mild appearance and junk proclivities. A second visit to his den found it closed. A friendly plumber in the adjacent shop explained with effusion that the junk-man was a wretched old thief, and no one but thieves sold to him or bought of him (I winced at the accusation) ; that "he broke into a museyum in England and stole a lot of china and brought it over here to sell, and had kep' stealin' ever sense," and he (the plumber) was "glad the perlice had chased him out, for he was a disgrace to the neighborhood." Was not my pretty Flaxman-designed piece of Wedgwood stolen from that English collection?

A beautiful cup and saucer of old Worcester in the "Japan taste," rich without and within in red and gold and blue, has long been regarded by me with intense suspicion of my honest and legal right to its possession. It was sold to me with the assurance that it had belonged

Old Worcester in "Japan Taste."

to Lucien Bonaparte; I did not doubt that part of the story, for I had seen its sister in the possession of a family who I knew inherited it through a gift of that Bonaparte. But how should my cup and saucer have been offered for sale to anyone? By a curious chain of circumstances, too tedious to repeat, I discovered that the pretty cup and saucer had been stolen by a servant, and sold long ago to an old merchant in New York, who should have and doubtless did know better, but who loved old china.   Shall I tell his name ?   Shall I hunt up the lawful heir and owner of my Worcester teacup ?

Only one possibility mars the pleasure of a day's china hunt—the necessity of obtaining a midday meal " upon the road," in any chance farm-house you may be within at high noon.   The old hunter fights shy of such repasts by carrying her lunch with her, but when a drive of several days is taken this course is not very attractive or possible.   She must then succumb to fate, accept the hospitality which is invariably and cordially offered to her, and eat, or, at least, try to eat.   I think June is the most trying month for such ventures.   Spring vegetables are unknown in the land of their supposed birth. Fruits and berries are not ripe.   You are given a mysterious repast, flavored throughout with sour milk and smelling of sour milk, which reaches its highest and sourest point in the bread.   I always plead dyspepsia and cling to a milk diet, thus eliciting much sympathy, and hygienic and medical advice.   Doubtless in late fall or in winter, country fare might be more endurable, but, with keen and most vivid fancy, I cannot imagine going china hunting in the country in the winter time. Even glorious sleighing or the promise of vast treasure trove could not englamour it with an enticing charm. Think of shivering over snow-blocked roads under leaden skies, through dreary, wind-wailing, naked woods, struggling up icy, snow-swept, and blast-beaten hills to that lonely hill-top home, a New England farm-house ! Hope would perish on the road.   Think of entering that drear abode; of sitting, while you unfolded your wishes and went through the stereotyped china questions with the stereotyped china smile, with bursting veins and flushed face, in a stuffy, torrid, unaired room, in front of a red-hot, air-tight stove, for there are no glorious open wood fires nowadays in the great chimneys of country houses in New England. Think of going from that super-heated, stifling atmosphere to a frigid pantry or icy best room to look at china! How the congealed plates would clatter in your trembling stiffened fingers; how you would hurry through the repelling ordeal; never, as in summer, climbing upon chairs to peer on upper shelves, never exploring in old window-seats, never lingering to examine separately and lovingly each plate in a great pile. Above all, think of ransacking a farm-house garret, "in cobwebbed corners, dusty and dim," with the thermometer below zero—it is beyond my power of fancy to fathom such a scene. A fellow china hunter tells me a tale of a lonely drive and Arctic exploration, and of riding gayly home therefrom in the winter twilight, warming the cockles of her heart with four Baltimore & Ohio plates pressed closely to her side, with two Lafayette pepper-boxes and half a dozen Lowestoft custard-cups packed snugly in her muff, and with a Pennsylvania Hospital platter in the fur robe at her feet. I never believed her; it could not be true. China does not grow in winter, 'tis a fair summer flower, and must be gathered under summer suns.

But to what out-of-the-way, simple, rustic scenes has our china hunting led us through the long summer days, scenes to be painted by Miss Wilkins or Mrs. Slosson. To country auctions—not the ill-ventilated, Hebrew-jostled, bawling arenas of city life, but auctions in country villages, on old farms, where the auctioneer, if the day be warm, stands outside the house on a door taken from its hinges and laid across two barrels on the green, or among the beds of flowering phlox and marigolds ; where the lots for sale, unnumbered, uncatalogued, and unclassified are handed out, a heterogeneous company, to the presiding seller through the open windows behind him ; where every small parcel of value is neatly tied up and labelled with the names of past owners—Aunt Hepsy, Mrs. Catey Doten, Old Job Greening; where every queer-gowned and queer-coated neighbor for miles around has driven over in every kind of vehicle to look at, if not to buy, the scattering house treasures. At these country auctions, china and ancient underclothes, or pewter porringers with feather pillows, may form a single "lot," and you must buy all or none. If you purchase you pay your money at once to the auctioneer, with much friendly change-making by hard-fisted old farmers on either hand ; the china is delivered to your eager hands, the underclothes are thrown to you or at you by the auctioneer over the heads of the audience ; the hay-rakes, or churns, or quilting-frames, or whatever addenda may have been tacked to your porcelain, are brought around and piled in a little heap by the side of your chair, or if you have "backed up" your country wagon, are placed therein. I once bought six large bundles of neatly labelled pieces of woollen cloth, pieces of all the old petticoats and breeches and greatcoats that had been worn in that house for forty years, just to get one India china plate. A rug-making—or I should say, " mat-braiding "—dame at my left, seeing my dismay at my unsought treasures and noting my love of china, offered to give me a modern match-box for the tidy bundle of pieces, which kindly exchange I gladly accepted as being less cumbersome, if not more beautiful.

Surely the summer sunlight never flickered down on a more typical New England scene than a country auction. Sad are the faces around, quiet reigns ; no one smiles, no one jests as the hoarse-voiced auctioneer holds up, explains, and extols some very mirth-provoking "lots." This breaking up and disbanding of a home has no droll side to country minds. The last country auction I attended was at an old house in Rutland. At it were sold the effects of an ancient lady of ninety years, who had just died. Her nephew, a lively lad of eighty, carried away by the excitement of the sale, or by the sight of so much ready money, recklessly handed out to the auctioneer, as he stood under the dusty lilac bushes, a large number of articles of furniture and tableware which had been temporarily stored in the house by the old lady's housekeeper, an equally ancient matron. The unconscious theft was discovered late in the afternoon, just as we were about to drive off, and the old man, overcome with horror at his unwitting crime, or dread of the results of its discovery, tearfully forced us to disgorge half a dozen McDonough's Victory plates and several mugs and pitchers which we had eagerly purchased and gleefully packed away. He "comforted us with apples," however, pressing upon us a peck of red-streaked, spicy Sapsons to console us for our evident disappointment—and our sorrow that we had not sensibly and cannily departed at an earlier hour.

But do not fancy that every gathering of country wagons in country door-yards, every row of patient horses hitched at barn doors and along the fence, denotes an auction within the doors of the farm-house. Draw no such rash conclusion, and make no hasty and unheralded entrance within, else you may find yourself, with china smiles on your lips and china inquiries on your tongue, an impetuous and mortified intruder at the saddest of all sad scenes, a country funeral. I cannot resist telling that, after one such impertinent intrusion on that solemn function, we returned in a few hours, when on our way home, to apologize and explain our infelicitous and uninvited entrance at so unfitting a time. When we stated that we were hunting for old-fashioned china, a gleam of comprehension entered the faces of the two elderly women who sat rocking by the fireside in the lonely kitchen, and as a result a china-closet was raided, and we bought a number of pieces of unusually fine Canton and Lowestoft china. At the time of purchase, we innocently fancied that we gained this treasure honestly from the new-made heirs, but have since then had harassing suspicions that the china was sold to us by temporary care-takers who remained to "redd the house," while the mourning relatives had driven to the country grave-yard, and who thus snatched from the jaws of death a most dishonest penny.

Nor can you be over-confident that all auctions held in the country are true country auctions. The ways of " antique men " are past finding out. A sale of the household furnishings of an old farm-house in the heart of the White Mountains, attracted a vast number of summer travellers, and brought forth purchase sums that bewildered the farm residents for miles around. Ere the sun went down on the day of the sale, a thrifty dealer who happened to be present had had a conference with the farm-wife, and as a result it was announced that she had a reserve stock of furniture and china in her garret, which would be sold the following week. Back to town sped the dealer, packed up a vast collection of unsalable débris which he chanced to have on hand, and an " assorted lot " of modern willow pattern ware, freshly imported Canton china, new copper lustre and painted teasets, with a sparse sprinkling of old pieces. He sent the entire lot by rail to the New Hampshire town ; conveyed it by dead of night to the farm-house ; placed the crockery in the cupboards, the brand-new brass candlesticks on the mantels, and the flimsy new andirons in the old fireplaces, arranged all the furniture in judicious shadow, and had a successful auction of " rare old colonial furniture and family china."

A famous starting-point, or rather rallying-point, on a china hunt is the district school. Driving along the quiet country road, you chance, in some barren and unlovely spot, often at some lonely cross-roads, upon a small unshaded, single-storied building, whose general ugliness and the beaten earth of whose door-yard tell to you its purpose and character without the proof of the high-pitched and precise chorus of monotonous three-syllabled words that vibrates shrilly out through the open window. Hitch your steed to a tree, a fence, by the roadside, and enter one of the twin portals of the abode of learning, passing by the low-hanging rows of ragged straw hats, gingham sun-bonnets, and chip "Shakers," over the "warping floor," in front of the "battered seats, with jack-knife's carved initial." "Teacher" is glad to see you, the children are gladder still. She sends a grinning barefooted boy out to draw a pail of fresh well-water. You are asked, as a distinguished visitor, to address the scholars. If you are a man, and thus of course an orator, you do so with fluent tongue. If you are a woman, and thus tongue-tied in public, you can ask for "recess" to be given, and make your address informally to each little freckled face. You are, of course, anxious to refurnish a house like the one in which you lived when you attended the village school in the days of your youth. Do the children know of any old blue china plates with trees and houses on them? Have their mothers or grandmothers any pitchers with pictures of soldiers, or sailors, or ships? Of course the children know; they know everything—far more than grown people. You soon have an exact ceramic report from every house in town whose little sons and daughters are in the school, and of the homes of all their neighbors too. You have extracted an unbiassed account from a set of little ready-tongued and keen-eyed spies, whose penetration is acute, and whose memory is active. If you can draw you can quickly show the children with chalk and blackboard the kind of china you wish, and can depart with a long list of houses which will repay you to visit.

But why do I longer tell the story of the chase, or vainly try to give advice and rules for china-finding ? I can only " pay you my penny of observation," knowing well that " Gutta fortunæ præ dolio sapientiæ." Nor can I fitly paint the pleasures. nor tell the pains of the search, more than I could mould and shape the treasures it has brought to my home. Nor can I hope to fire in other veins the fever that burns in mine; I must be content to say with Olivia, " 'Tis a most *extracting* frenzy of mine own."

II

TRENCHER TREEN AND PEWTER BRIGHT

THE history of the use of china as tableware in America would be incomplete and ill-comprehended, without some reference to the preceding forms of table furnishings used by the earliest colonists, the dishes of wood and pewter, which so long influenced the form and even the decoration of their china successors. As in the "Life of Josiah Wedgwood" we are given an account of the pottery and porcelain of all times, so in my story of china in America I tell of the humble predecessors that graced the frugal boards of our ancestors.

In a curious book, Newbery's "Dives Pragmaticus," written in 1563, a catalogue of English cooking-utensils and tableware is thus given by a chapman :

> "I have basins, ewers of tin, pewter, and glass,
>   Great vessels of copper, fine latten, and brass,
>   Both pots, pans, and kettles such as never was.
>   I have platters, dishes, saucers, and candlesticks,
>   Chafers, lavers, towels, and fine tricks ;
>   Posnets, frying pans, and fine pudding pricks ;
>   Fine pans for milk, trim tubs for souse."

These were practically the table and kitchen furnishings brought by the Pilgrims to New England, and for similar furnishings they sent to old England for many years.

The time when America was settled was the era when pewter ware had begun to take the place of wooden ware for table use, just as the time of the Revolutionary War marked the victory of porcelain over pewter. Governor Bradford found the Indians using " wooden bowls, trays, and dishes," and "hand baskets made of crab shells wrought together." Both colonists and Indians used clam-shells for plates, and smaller shells set in split sticks as spoons and ladles.

The Indians made in great quantities for their white neighbors, even in the earliest days, bowls from the knots of maple-trees that went by the name of " Indian bowls," and were much sought after and used. One large bowl taken from the wigwam of King Philip is now in the collection of the Massachusetts Historical Society. The settlers also established factories for dish-turning. One thrifty New England parson eked out his scanty and ill-paid salary by making wooden bowls and plates for his parishioners. Wooden " noggins," low bowls with handles, are often mentioned in early inventories, and Mary Ring, of Plymouth, thought in 1633 that a " wodden cupp " was quite valuable enough to leave " as a token of friendship."

In Vermont bowls and plates of poplar wood were used until Revolutionary times, and fair white dishes did that clean hard wood make. Sometimes the wooden plates used by the poor planters were only square blocks slightly hollowed out by hand—whittled, without doubt.

Wooden trenchers, also made by hand, were used on the table by the colonists for more than a century. I find them advertised for sale with pewter and china in the *Connecticut Courant* of May, 1775. These trenchers were either square or oblong. From an oblong trencher two persons, relatives or intimate friends, sometimes ate in common, just as they had done in old England. Two children frequently ate from the same trencher, thus economizing table furnishings. In earlier times man and wife ate from a single trencher or plate. Walpole relates that the aged Duke and Duchess of Hamilton, in the middle of the last century, sat upon a dais together at the head of their table and ate from the same plate— a tender tribute to unreturnable youth, a clinging regard for past customs, and a token of present affection and unity in old age.

A story is told of a Connecticut planter, that having settled in a quickly-growing town and having proved himself to be a pious God-fearing man, his name was offered to his church for election or ordination as a deacon. Objection was made to him, on the ground that he had shown undue pride and luxury of living in allowing his children each to use and eat from a single plate at the table, instead of doing as his neighbors did—have two children eat from one trencher. He apologized for his seemingly vain manner of living, and gave in excuse the fact that previous to his settlement near New Haven he had been a dish-turner, so it had not then been extravagant for the members of his family to have a dish apiece; and having grown accustomed to that manner of "feeding," he found it more peaceable and comfortable; but he was willing to change his ways if they considered it desirable and proper, as he did not wish to put on more airs than his neighbors.

But wooden trenchers, even in the first half of the first New England century, gave place to pewter, and the great number of pieces of pewter table-ware still found in New England country homes would alone prove to how recent a date pewter utensils were universally used. The number would doubtless be much larger if it were not deemed by metal-workers that new pewter is of much better substance if the metals composing it are combined with a certain amount of old pewter. Hence old pewter always has commanded a good price, and many fine old specimens have been melted up to mould over again for the more modern uses for which pewter is employed by printers and lapidaries.

The trade of pewterer was for two centuries a very respectable and influential one. The Guild of Pewterers in London was a very large and powerful body, and English pewterers, men of worth, came with other tradesmen at once to the Colonies. Richard Graves was a pewterer of Salem in 1639, and Henry Shrimpton, an influential merchant who died in Boston in 1666, made large quantities of pewter ware for the Massachusetts colonists. The pewterers rapidly increased in numbers in America, until the War of Independence, when, of course, the increasing importation of Oriental and English china and stone ware, and the beauty and interest of the new table-ware, destroyed forever the pewterer's trade. Advertisements of pewter table-furnishings appear frequently, however, in American newspapers until well into this century.

Nor was it different in England at the same date. Englishmen and Englishwomen clung long to pewter. In a poem written in 1828 by J. Ward, of Stoke-upon-Trent, upon the Potter's Art, he says :

> "The housewife, prim in days we know ourselves,
> Display'd her polished pewter on her shelves ;
> Reserv'd to honour most the annual feast,
> Where ev'ry kinsman proved a welcome guest.
> No earthen plates or dishes then were known,
> Save at the humble board as coarse as stone,
> And there the trencher commonly was seen,
> With its attendant ample platter treen." (Wooden.)

It is a curious fact that in the inventory of the household possessions of Thomas Wedgwood, the potter, made at Burslem in 1775, we find that he had forty-four pewter plates worth seven pence half penny each, and twenty-four pewter dishes worth two shillings each, though the inventory of the goods at his factory at that time included two hundred and ninety-five dozen table plates of best white ware.

At a very early date all well-to-do colonists had plenty of "latten ware," which was brass, as well as pewter. All kinds of household utensils were made, however, of the latter metal ; even "pewter bottles, pints, and quarts," were upon a list of goods to be sent from England to the Massachusetts Colony in 1629. I have never seen an old pewter bottle, even in a collection or museum, and they must soon have been superseded by glass.

In the Boston *Evening Post* of July 26, 1756, appeared this advertisement: " London pewter dishes, plates, basons, porringers, breakfast bowls, table spoons, pint and quart pots, cans, tankards, butter cups, newest fashion teapots, table salts, sucking bottles, plates & dish covers, cullenders, soop kettles, new fashion roased plates, communion beakers and flagons, & measures." A vast number of names of other articles might be added from other lists of sales of pewter at that time—" quart & pint jacks," " bottle crains," " ink pots," " ink chests," " ink horns," " ink standishes," and " ink jugs."

Pewter " cans for beer, cyder, and metheglin," were in every household ; pewter mugs and pewter " dram-cups with funnels," pewter " basons," cisterns, and ewers graced the " parlour," which contained also the best state bed, with its " harrateen " or " cheney " curtains. Pewter candlesticks held the home-made, pale-green candles of tallow and spicy bayberry wax. " Savealls," too, were of pewter and iron. " Savealls " were the little round frames with wire points which held up the last short ends of dying candles for our frugal ancestors.

Salt-cellars and spoons were of pewter, while extremely elegant people had spoons of alchymy, or occonny, alcaney, alcamy, occomy, ackamy, and accamy, as I have seen it spelt, a metal composed of pan brass and arsenicum. Forks were almost unknown, and fingers played an important part in serving and eating at the table. A lady traveller, in 1704, spoke with much scorn of Connecticut people, because they allowed their negro slaves to sit and eat at the same table with themselves, saying that "into the great dish goes the black hoof as freely as the white hand."

"The porringers that in a row
Hung high and made a glittering show."

Pewter porringers, or "pottingers," of every size were much prized. One family, in 1660, had seven porringers, while another housewife was proud of owning nine, and one silver queen porringer. The smaller porringers were called posnets, a word now obsolete. Posnet was derived from a Welsh word, *posned*, a little round dish. In these posnets posset was served, and they were also used as pap-bowls for infants. Posnets and porringers, when not in use, were hung by their handles on the edge of the dresser shelf. The porringers with flat pierced handles are of English or American make, while the "fish-tail" handles are seldom found in New England, being distinctly Dutch.

Plates and platters were much valued. Governor Bradford, of Massachusetts, left to his heirs fourteen pewter dishes and thirteen platters, three large plates and three small ones, one pewter candlestick and one pewter bottle—a most luxurious and elaborate household outfit. Governor Benedict Arnold, of Jamestown, R. I., and Mr. Pyncheon, of Springfield, Mass., bequeathed their pewter plates and dishes in the same list, and with as much minuteness of description, as the silver tankards and bowls, and the humble pewter was as elaborately lettered and marked with armorial devices as was the silver. Miles Standish left to his heirs sixteen pewter dishes and twelve wooden trenchers.

Pewter was not thought to be too base a metal to use for communion services. In 1729, the First Church of Hanover, Mass., bought and used for years a full communion service and christening basin of pewter ; and the bill of purchase and the old pieces are still preserved by the church as relics. The pewter communion service of the Marblehead Church is now in the rooms of the Essex Institute, and until this century advertisements of " Pewter Communion Flagons " appeared in New England newspapers.

These pewter dishes and plates were a source of great pride to every colonial housekeeper, and much time and labor was devoted to polishing them with " horsetails " (*equisetum*), or "scouring rush," till they shone like fine silver; and dingy pewter was fairly counted a disgrace. The most accomplished gentleman in Virginia, of his time, gave it as a positive rule, in 1728, that "pewter bright" was the sign of a good housewife.

In some old country homes, either lack of money, the power of habit, or the strong love of ancient articles and associations, caused the preservation of the old pewter utensils, and they now form the cherished ornaments of the kitchen and dining-room. In the lovely old town of Shrewsbury, which stands so high on Massachusetts hills that the railroad has never approached its lonely beauty, there stands on the edge of the "Common" a house, in which everything that is good and old has been preserved, and appears as when the house was built, in the year 1779.

The old fireplaces have cranes and iron "dogs," are festooned with ears of yellow seed-corn, and are surmounted by the old fire-arms, while by the chimney sides are hung old-fashioned brooms of peeled birch. These brooms are made of birch splints, carefully split and peeled, and tied in place with hempen twine on the strong handle; and many a farmer's boy, years ago, earned his first spending-money by making them, for six cents apiece, for the country stores. Old settles, chairs, and tables stand on the white-scoured floors; and in the "living-room" is a piece of furniture seldom seen in New England, though common enough in Pennsylvania, New York, and New Jersey in olden times—a "slaw bank." The word is a corruption of *sloap bancke*, or sleeping bench, and the slaw bank was the great-grandfather of our modern cabinet folding-bed. At one end of the room are doors apparently belonging to cupboards, which, upon being swung wide open, disclose the oblong frame of a bed with a network of ropes to serve as springs. This bed-frame is fastened at one end to the wall with heavy hinges, and was hooked up against the wall in the day-time, and at night was lowered to a horizontal position and supported on heavy wooden turned legs, which fitted into sockets in the frame; and it was thus ready for use. This bed is still kept made up as of old, with hand-spun linen sheets, hand-woven "flannel sheets," a "rising-sun" patchwork quilt, and blue and white woollen bedspread.

But in the dining-room and kitchen of this old Shrewsbury homestead are the greatest treasures—corner cupboards and shallow dressers full of pewter dishes, which greet their owner with "shining morning faces" at breakfast, and reflect in a hundred silvery disks the goodly cheer on his table at midday and night. Round plates and platters are there of every size, up to the great round shield on which was placed of old the enormous Thanksgiving turkey. All are round, for oval platters seem to have been then unknown.

The deep bowls, in which vegetables were served, stand there in "nests" of various sizes. Teapots, too, and cream-pitchers and sugar-bowls, or sugar-boxes, but no pewter teacups. I believe the little handleless teacups were among the earliest pieces of porcelain imported from China, and were often used when the rest of the " tea equipage " was of pewter. Pewter salt-cellars, mustard-pots, flip-mugs, and syrup-cups are interspersed among the larger pieces on the dresser.

Some of these articles are marked with initials and dates, not engraved, but stamped, as with a die, J. S. and B. K., 1769. Doubtless these were wedding gifts, and I doubt not that a set of shining pewter plates and platters was as graceful and welcome a gift to Betsey Sumner in 1769, as is a set of Royal Worcester porcelain to her great-granddaughter Bessie, in 1892.

Some of the teapots are really beautiful in shape, and are decorated with a quaint engraved design of leaves and round flowers. These were undoubtedly of Dutch manufacture, and are identical in shape and ornamentation with teapots authentically known to have been imported from Holland. These teapots were probably used for company " tea drinkings " and such state occasions, and thus the engraving on the soft metal was not worn by daily use.

Pewter spoons, too, are there in every size, though Betsey Sumner surely had silver teaspoons, for were they not inherited from her by her son, the old parson? As these pewter spoons were liable to be quickly bent, worn, or broken, every thrifty household had its various sized spoon moulds of heavy metal, into which the melted pewter was poured and came out as good as new, or, according to the apparent law of pewter, better than new. Button moulds, too, were common enough, containing deep holes to form half a dozen buttons at once. And perhaps Betsey Sumner turned her old spoons into buttons to adorn John's coat, and polished them till they shone like the silver and cut-steel buttons of the French Court.

Many of the pewter articles in this homestead have had recently engraved upon the underside various commemorative dates, and the names of past owners, and the outlines of any eventful story connected with the dish, if story there fortunately be remembered to tell. And every owner of pewter plate or porringer, who knows by tradition the story of his old relic, should have the statement engraved now upon the back of the piece, for even in one generation these facts are forgotten, and the article is rendered valueless as an historic record.

In the kitchen of the great colonial house at Morristown, N. J., now owned and occupied by the Washington Association of New Jersey, may be seen a fine collection of old pewter table and cooking utensils; while at Indian Hill, at Newburyport, still is shining in cupboard and dresser the rare pewter collected by Ben Perley Poore.

To a day well within the remembrance of many now living, round pewter meat platters were used in farmhouses, long after the other pewter dishes had vanished; for it does not dull a carving-knife to cut upon pewter as it does upon porcelain or crockery, and old farmers cling stubbornly to usages and articles that they are acquainted with; and no " boiled dinner " ever could taste quite the same to them unless all heaped together on a great shining pewter platter.

Another pewter piece often found, and often still used, is the hot-water jug with its wicker-covered handle. This was brought every night, in colonial and Revolutionary times, well filled with boiling water, to the master of the house, for him to mix the hot apple-toddy or sangaree for the members of his household, who drank their share out of pewter cups or heavy greenish glasses. I know of two of these pewter jugs which have been in daily use for certainly forty years (though in the more temperate vocation of hot-water jugs to carry shaving-water to the bedrooms), and still retain, sound and firm, the old wicker coverings on the handles, which may have been woven upon them a hundred years ago. Truly, our grandfathers made things for use, not for sale.

Strange hiding-places have these old forsaken and forgotten pewter dishes. They lurk in tall and narrow cupboards by the side of old chimneys, or in short and deep cupboards over the mantel. They lie in disused fireplaces, hidden from view by gaudy modern fire-boards. They are at the bottom of deep boxes under wide window-seats, and are shoved under the dusty eaves of dark attic-lofts. On the highest pantry shelves, under cellar stairs, in old painted sea-chests, in the woodhouse, are they found. From the floor of hen-houses have they been rescued, where they have been long ignominiously trodden under foot by high-stepping and imperious fowl.

Let us take them from these obscure corners, and preserve them with care, for though they have no intrinsic value like silver, no brilliancy like glass, no beauty of color or design like china, they are still worthy our interest and attention, for they were the first table ware used by our ancestors. We are a young nation of few years and few relics, let us then reverently preserve the old pewter plates and platters, remembering that these simple dishes of inexpensive metal illustrate the frugal home-life of the men and women who were the founders of the Republic.

III.

EARLY USE AND IMPORTATION OF CHINA IN AMERICA

THE knowledge and use of porcelain in England did not long antedate the departure of the Pilgrims for the New World. As early as 1506, one exceptional importation of Chinese porcelain bowls is spoken of; but even in 1567—half a century later—one of Queen Elizabeth's valued gifts was a " poringer of white porselyn and a cup of green porselyn," and the notice paid such intrinsically valueless and small articles by their mention proves their rarity. Great ignorance of the processes of porcelain manufacture existed; even that learned, that marvellously well-informed man, Lord Bacon, wrote of " mines of porcelain," and had the queer idea that china was developed in the earth, out of the common clay, by some strange and mysterious process of purification. Another universal belief was, that porcelain was a sovereign detector of poison, that it instantly showed the presence of poison in any draught that came in contact with it. Shakespeare speaks once of china, in his " Measure for Measure," " a dish of some three-pence, your honors have seen such dishes, they are not china dishes, but very good dishes." Ben Jonson refers more frequently to porcelain.

" *Broker*.   'Tis but earth
                      Fit to make bricks and tiles of.
  Shunfield.   'Tis but for pots or pipkins at the best
                      If it would keep us in good tobacco pipes—
  Titus.   Or in porc'lane dishes."

Again he says :

        " The earth of my bottles which I dig
          Turn up and steep, and work, and neal, myself,
          To a degree of porc'lane."

By the time of Pope and Dryden, china had become
more widely known in England, and these writers and
their contemporaries frequently refer to it. It is not
probable that much china came to England until 1650,
when the English East India Trading Company was
established, though the Dutch had even then a large
trade with China. Doubtless tea and china became
plentiful in Europe together.

Addison wrote in 1713, " China vessels are playthings
for women of all ages. . . . I myself remember
when there were few china vessels to be seen that held
more than a dish of tea; but their size is so greatly enlarged that there are many capable of holding half a
hogshead."

It is asserted that pieces of Delft ware were brought to
America by the first English and Dutch settlers. It
had been manufactured since the fifteenth century; but
when our Pilgrim Fathers made their night-trip through
Delft, no plebeian persons had Delft ware on their tables;
hence the Pilgrims could have brought few pieces to

New England on the Mayflower. Nor is it probable that those frugal souls owned any India china. The earliest Dutch settlers of New Netherlands were not likely either to have brought to the new land any pieces of the aristocratic Delft ware, though I have seen many Delft plates and tea-pots that bore the reputation of such ownership.

"Blew & white ware" is however not an infrequent item on early inventories of the last half of the century. John Betts, of Cambridge, Mass., had before his death, in 1662, "Som duth earthen platters & Som other Earthen ware," valued at 6s. 8d. A citizen of Salem had in 1664 "17 pieces of blew & white earthen ware" worth 8s. 6d. John Cross, of Ipswich, left behind him in 1650 his "Holland jugs." All these were doubtless Delft or the early imitations of Delft.

The oldest and most authentic piece of stone ware in the country is the fine jug preserved in the collection of the American Antiquarian Society, at Worcester. It was the property of Governor Winthrop, who died in 1649, and was given to the Society by a descendant, Adam Winthrop. It stands eight inches in height and is apparently of German Gres-ware, and is richly mounted in silver. The lid is engraved with a quaint design of Adam and Eve with the tempting serpent in the apple-tree. Estienne Perlin, writing in Paris in 1558, says, "The English drink beer not out of glass but from earthern pots, the cover and handles being made of silver for the rich. The middle classes mount them with tin." Another writer, in 1579, spoke of the

English custom of drinking from " pots of earth of sundry colors and moulds, whereof many are garnished with
silver or at leastwise with pewter." Such is this " beer
mug " or tankard of
Governor Win-
throp's, which is cer-
tainly three hundred
years old. Other
Massachusetts colo-
nists had similar beer-
mugs. Jacob Leager,
of Boston, left in 1662
a " stone judg tipt
with silver ; " Henry
Dunster had a " tipt
jugg " in 1655; and
Thomas Rix had in
1678 " 3 fflanders
jugs."

Lisbon ware, which
was earthen ware, was
left by will in Massa-
chusetts in 1650; and
Spanish platters and

Winthrop Jug.

painted platters are mentioned in an inventory in 1656.
Peter Bulkeley, of Concord, Mass., had in 1659 " ten
paynted earthen dishes " valued at ten shillings. In the
lists and inventories of the town of Stamford, from 1650
to 1676, only two shillings worth of earthen ware is entered, and Stamford planters were far from poor. In

the *Boston News Letter* of February 9, 1712, six hogs-heads of earthen ware, including teapots, were advertised for sale. These early teapots are said to have been of black earthen ware.

One of the earliest mentions of china in America is in the inventory made in 1641, of the property of Thomas Knocker, of Boston, " 1 Chaynie Dish." In 1648, in the estate of President Davenport, of Harvard College, was, " Cheyney, £4." This was doubtless India china. Governor Theophilus Eaton had a " cheny basen." In the list made in 1647, of the possessions of Martha Coteymore, a rich widow (who afterward married Governor Winthrop), is seen this item, " One parcel cheyney plates and saucers, £1." Katherine Coteymore had " 3 boxes East India dishes," valued at £3. As early as October, 1699, John Higginson wrote to his brother with regard to importations from India, that " china and lacker-ware will sell if in small quantity," and with-out doubt some small importations from India were made.

After the first decade of the century many rich Bos-tonians, such as Elizur Holyoke, had china. Isaac Caillo-well's estate in 1718 contained " Five China Dishes, One Doz. China Plates, Two China Muggs, a China Tea-pott, Two China Slopp Basons, Six China Saucers, Four China Cupps, and One China Spoon Dish."

The earliest mention of the sale of china table ware which I have seen is not in 1732, as given by Mr. Felt in his " New England Customs." There are several notices of sales of china of earlier dates. In the *New*

England Weekly Journal of April 15th of the year 1728, were advertised for sale, at the Sun Tavern in Boston, "Chainey Bowles Dishes Cups Saucers and Teapots;" and "china cups & saucers" on June 17th. This "chainey" was probably all India china. In 1729, William Welsteed, a Boston merchant, had a large number of plates and "pickle caucers" for sale. In 1731, Andrew Faneuil announced that he had for sale at his warehouse "All sorts of Dutch Stone and Delf ware just imported from Holland." In 1730 John Buining and Mrs. Hannah Wilson both advertised in the *Boston News Letter*, that they had "several sorts of china for sale;" and another Boston shopkeeper announced at the same time that he was going to sell out everything he owned, including china ware, and that his fellow-townsmen had better flock to his shop, for "buyers have reason to Expect good Bargains for this will be the Packing Penny," which I suppose was the colonial slang expression for "bottom price." At a later date the "Packing Penny" became "to buy the pennyworth." It was not till 1737 that china ware was sold by "Publick Vandoo or Outcry," or by "Inch of Candle," in Boston, thus showing that it was being imported in larger quantities. In September of that year there was sold on Scarlett's Wharf, with spices and silks and negro slaves,

"A Rich Sortment of China Ware. A Parcel of fine large Enamel'd Dishes. Ditto of divers Sizes of Bowles burnt & Enamel'd. Ditto of all Sorts of Plates. Sundry Complete Setts of Furniture for the Tea Table. Blue & White Bowles; Blue & White Cups & Sawcers. Several sorts of small Baskets, &c."

By this time Boston milliners and mantua makers, and fan mounters, and lace menders, had all begun to announce the sale of " chayney " in their show-rooms and shops. Fair Boston dames picked their way along the narrow streets, or were carried in stately sedan chairs, to " Mistress Alise Quick's, over against the Old Brick Meeting House on Cornhill, at the sign of the Three Kings," or to " Widow Mehetable Kneeland's," to see her " London baby drest in the latest fashioned Hooped Coat and lac'd Petty Coat with ppetuna hood ; " or to " Mrs. Hannah Teatts, Mantua Maker, at the head of Summer Street, Boston," who charged five shillings for showing her " Baby drest after the Newest Fashion of Mantues and Night Gowns and everything belonging to a Dress, latilly brought over on Captain White's ship from London "—these bedizened doll-babies being the quaint colonial substitutes for fashion plates. These modish New-English dames first pulled over and tried on the " rayls and roquilos and cardinals," and admired the ivory and cocoa paddle stick-fans ; and peeped at their own patched faces and powdered hair in the lacquered looking-glasses ; and then, perhaps, selected some flower. seeds for their prim little gardens—their pleasaunces, " blew and yellow lewpin, double larkin-spur, sweet feabus, Love lies bleeding, Queen Margrets, Brompton flock, and sweet-scented pease ; " and then they turned, unwearied and unsated, to the " Choise Sortment of Delph, Stone, Glassware, and China, viz., Bowles of Divers Sizes, Plates of all Sorts, and Dishes, Teapots, Cups & Saucers, Strayners, Mugs of Divers Sorts and Colors, Creampots pearl'd &

plain, Bird Fountains, Tankards," and they held up the tiny china teacups to the light and examined the painting, and perhaps sipped a little of the mantua maker's Orange Pekoe or Bohea. And I doubt not many a china teapot or teacup stood cheek by jowl with quoyfs and ciffers on colonial milliners' bills, and many a feathered " Kitty Fisher Bonnet," or silver shape, or peaked Ranelagh cap was sent home to the daughters of the Puritans, packed with " cat-gut," and " robins," and " none-so-prettys," in an India china punch-bowl.

Of the prices paid for these colonial ceramic luxuries we know but little.   The enterprising outcrier, who cried out and vandooed at the " Blew Boar, at the South End of Boston," announced in February, 1749, in the *Boston Independent Advertiser*, that he had " Fine blue & white and Quilted China Plates at Eleven Pounds the Dozen, or Six Pounds the Half Dozen."   So the shades of our ancestors can hardly cry out to us for extravagance. These quilted china plates were, I think, from subsequent references to them, plates impressed in the paste with a basket design, as we often see now on Chinese porcelain ; or possibly with a larger, a truly quilted design, such as I have seen on rare old Oriental porcelain. In the inventory of the estate of John Jekyll, of Boston (made in 1732), we learn that " 2 Burnt China Bowls were worth £2, 6 Chocolate Bowls £2, 1 Pr China Candlesticks Tipt with Silver £4, 12 Coffe cups with handles £1 7s."   In many inventories such a number of pieces are " crackt " or " mendid," and so little hint of quality or decoration is given, that it is impossible to compare justly the values assigned with those of the present day. John Jekyll also had a "sett of burnt china." The first mentioned sale of a "set" of china is in the *New England Weekly Journal* of April 19, 1737— "A Fine Double Sett of Burnt China for sale, Enquire of the Printer." Until then the precious porcelain had been sold only in single pieces, or in small numbers. The wills and inventories of the times speak of no sets of china, though the lists of the possessions of all persons of wealth, the advertisements of sales of estates, contain many items of china ware. Governor Burnet, who died in 1729, owned much china—three hundred pieces—as became a man who had £1,100 spent on his funeral; and his friend and neighbor, Peter Faneuil, had a bountiful supply of china and glass, as he had of other luxuries.

There are far more frequent mentions and advertisements of china in old New England newspapers than in other American papers of the same years. The southern publications of colonial times that I have seen contained no announcements of the sale of china. None appeared bearing date until after the Revolutionary War. And it is plain, from the evidence of inventories, "enroulments," wills, and newspapers of the eighteenth century, that porcelain was far more plentiful in New England than elsewhere in America at the same date. Mr. Prime says, "Few of the people of Revolutionary times had seen porcelain;" but when it had been advertised in every New England newspaper; had been sold in grocers', milliners', chemists', dry-goods, saddlers', and hardware shops; had been displayed at the printers' and book-shops and writing-schools in every town of any size throughout New England; and sold in considerable quantities by all the little Boston shopkeepers—the Amorys, Waldos, Brimmers, Adamses, Sheaffes, and Boylstons, I fancy all New England good wives must have owned a few pretty pieces.

Doubtless the wealthiest Virginians of colonial times also had some china. It is not, however, named in Baltimore inventories until after the year 1700. Nor was it plentiful in New York; one of the earliest mentions of china in New York is in the list of the possessions of wealthy Cornelius Stienwerck, " Ten pieces of china dishes or porcelain £4." In August, 1748, the *New York Weekly Journal* contained its first announcement of the sale of china—" A choice parcel of China Ware just imported to be sold at Wholesale. Enquire of the Printer." Now, the " Printer " at that date was a woman, the Widow Zenger, wife of the former owner of the newspaper, and with her assumption of the printing and editing business came various feminine advertisements such as this of china ware, others of mantuas and hair-powder, and of " bonnet-papers," which she cut and made and sold in large numbers; but this china sale was certainly exceptional in New York at that date.

China did not abound in New York, either in Dutch or English families, until after the Revolutionary War. Nor did advertisements of it frequently appear in ante-Revolutionary New York newspapers. In an inventory made at that time of the contents of a house on the Neutral

Ground in Westchester County, there were such wealth-evincing items as twenty-six horses, thirty-six table-cloths, rich and abundant furniture, bed-linen, and clothing, large quantities of fine silver ; and of pewter, " 1 Coffee Kettle, 1 Teapot, 27 Dishes, 12 Plates, 12 Soup Plates, 6 Butter Plates, 3 Mugs, 2 salons, 5 basons, 6 Spoons, 3 Measures ; " and not one piece of china. This list of household belongings is not exceptional. China is seldom mentioned. But few pieces of porcelain or pottery are named in the inventories of the possessions of the New Jersey farmers whose houses were burned, and whose household goods were either destroyed or stolen by the soldiers in the Revolutionary War, and who expected to receive indemnity from the Government for their losses. We discover therein that each family seldom owned more than three or four china cups and saucers. These records are extremely valuable for reference, as they are true and faithful lists of the entire household belongings of well-to-do people at that time ; they indicate that china was far from plentiful in New Jersey at that date. Watson says in his " Annals," " When china was first introduced into America, it was in the form of tea-sets ; it was quite a business to take in broken china to mend. It was done by cement in most cases, but generally large pieces, like punch-bowls, were done with silver rivets or wire." An advertisement in the *Boston Evening Post* in 1755 reads : " This is to give Notice to all Them that have any Broken China, at the Lion and Bell on Marlboro Street, Boston, they may have it mended by Riveting it together with a Silver & Brass Rivets it is first put together with a Cement that will stand boiling Water and then Riveted."

China appears to have been more plentiful in Philadelphia than in New York. Benjamin Lay, the "Singular Pythagorean Cynical Christian Philosopher," to show his hatred of the use of tea, brought in 1742 all his wife's china into the market-place at Philadelphia, and began to break it piece by piece with a hammer; "but the populace, unwilling to lose what might profit them, overset him, scrambled for the china, and bore it off whole." As the "Singular Pythagorean Philosopher's" wife was dead, this wanton destruction of her dear china was not so cruel as at first appears. An old lady wrote in 1830, about things as they were before the War of Independence—"Pewter plates and dishes were in general use. China on dinner tables was a great rarity. Glass tumblers were scarcely seen. Punch, the most common beverage, was drunk from a silver tankard. China tea-cups and saucers were half their present size, and china tea-pots and coffee-pots with silver nozzles were a mark of superior finery. Where we now use earthen ware they then used Delft ware imported from England, and instead of queen's ware (then unknown) pewter platters and porringers made to shine along a dresser were universal. Some, especially country people, ate their meals from wooden trenchers."

That frugal and plain-living man, Benjamin Franklin, though he constantly impressed upon his wife, as well as upon the public, the wisdom and necessity of great economy, and the propriety and good taste of simplicity in all modes of living, still could find time and money to pick out for her, when he was in England, and to send to her many a piece of china for her beaufet in Philadelphia. He writes thus from London, in February, 1758, to his Deborah: " I send you by Captain Budden a large case and a small box containing some English china, viz: melons and leaves for a dessert of fruit and cream or the like; a bowl remarkable for the neatness of the figures, made at Bow, near this city; some coffee-cups of the same; and a Worcester bowl, ordinary. To show the difference of workmanship, there is something from all the china workers in England; and one old true china basin mended; of an odd color. . . . I also forgot among the china to mention a large, fine jug for beer, to stand in the cooler. I fell in love with it at first sight, for I thought it looked like a fat, jolly dame, clean and tidy, with a neat blue and white gown on, good-natured and lovely, and put me in mind of—somebody. Look at the figures on the china bowl and coffee-cups with your spectacles on, they will bear examining." This was certainly a very tender attention on the part of Franklin, and one particularly grateful, doubtless, to his good dame, if she loved china as do others of her sex. In 1765 she wrote to her " dear child " (of over three score years) while he was in France, and thus describes a room that she had been furnishing: " The blue room has a set of tea-china I bought since you went from home, a very handsome mahogany stand for the tea-kettle to stand on, and the ornamental china." This latter clause refers doubtless to the fine English pieces which he had sent her eight years previously. In spite of all this fine array, Mrs. Bache wrote thus to her father, on October 30, 1773 : "We have no plates or dishes fit to set before your friends, and the queen's ware is thought very elegant here, particularly the spriged. I just mention this, as it would be much cheaper for you to bring them than to get them here." Let us hope her father took this broad hint and brought the "spriged" dishes to his daughter; and as there still exist among

her descendants, pieces of a set of china bearing little sprigs, I choose to think that they are parts of this very set.

A very interesting pitcher of English ware of yellowish paste, with a raised design of vine leaves in varicolored lustres, is

Province House Pitcher.

known to us by the name of the Province House Pitcher, because it was found, with two tall pewter drinking-cups, hidden behind a panel in the wainscoting of the historic old Province House in Boston. I fear it is not old enough to have been held by the fair hands of gentle Agnes Surriage, but I doubt not some romance attended its imprisonment.

By Revolutionary times a change appeared in the character and quality of the china that was imported to America. In the *Connecticut Courant* of September, 1773, we read in the advertisement of the " Staffordshire and Liverpool Warehouse," on King Street, Boston, that they have " for little more than sterling cost, a fine sort-ment of Crockery Ware, consisting of almost every kind of China, Glass & Delph : Cream color, white, blue & white, black, brown, agot, tortoise, melon, pineapple fruit pattern, enaml'd, and many other kinds of Stoneware. A few complete table services of very elegant printed and painted and guilt ware ; " and at a later date " Cream Color Pyramids, Candlesticks, Inkstands, & Chamber Lamps." The advertisements of this importing house are found in the files of New England papers for many years. Every notice of " English goods " arrived from Eng-land for Jolley Allen, for Hopestill Capen, for Cotton Barrell, three thrifty Boston shopkeepers, contained items of English and of India china. " Large & Neat Sort-ment of India China Dishes of Various forms & sizes, viz : Pudding, Soup, Mackrel, round, oval, Octagon, ribb'd, scallop'd. Also a variety of table & Butter Plates ; Patty Pans, Bowls & Sauceboats." Even in war times there still was china in many shops outside of poor be-sieged, war-swept Boston, though often only " a few crates well Sortid considering the Scarsity." By 1778 china began to pour into other ports than Boston. In New Haven were sold in August of that year (and strange to tell, were advertised to be sold at the very highest price) " Oval Dishes of Several Different Sizes, small Cream coloured Plates, Punchbowles, cream colour'd Teapots, Red ditto, Blue ditto, Colliflower ditto, Cream colour'd coffee cups & sausers, Tortoise shell bowles, enamel'd flat bottom cups." The cream-colored wares of Wedgwood and of Liverpool make, were evidently just beginning to be fashionable, though the latter had been named in the *Boston Gazette* as early as 1749. In 1780 we first see the advertisement of Queen's ware in the *Providence Gazette*, the *Connecticut Courant*, the Boston newspapers. In October, 1783, "An Assortment of Yellow ware such as cups, saucers, mugs," was advertised in the *Providence Gazette*, and again "Yellow ware both flat and hollow," meaning plates and pitchers. Yellow ware was Liverpool ware, and is still so called by country people on the sea-coast. In 1783 there came into Baltimore, on the ship Brothers, from Liverpool, "Queen's ware & Liverpool ware," and on the ship Yungfrau Magretha, from Copenhagen, more Queen's ware; and on the ship Pacifique, from France, "boxes and barrels of china ware;" and on the ship Candidus, from Amsterdam, "Delph ware"—and these vessels with their cargoes were all advertised at the same date, bewildering Baltimore housewives with the array of "richness." Then came announcements of "burnt china"—as if it were not all burnt! In May, 1785, "Beautiful Pencil Chinney Tile," and then frequent announcements of "Pencil China," "Pencil ware," "Pensil'd Yellow ware," all of which were one and the same—Liverpool ware printed with engraved designs. "Enameled ware" doubtless meant glazed ware, and was so called to distinguish it from the unglazed wares of Wedgwood. The "Amiled Milk Pots" in the *Boston Evening Post* of 1749 were doubtless also enamelled. In 1784 and 1785, in all American newspapers of note appeared announcements of sales of Nottingham

ware, a favorite importation before the war. Soon, with
the growth of ship-building and Oriental trade, came the
vast influx of Oriental porcelain direct from China, and
advertisements of Canton china crowded the columns
of every American newspaper.

It is interesting to note the various shapes of china and
the names of the pieces that were imported in colonial
and Revolutionary times, as well as the variety of wares.
In the *Boston News Letter* of 1742 I find "china boats
for spoons." In the *Boston Evening Post* in 1749, "china
mugs, pitchers, and Turk caps," which latter mysterious
articles were, I am sure, china also. What are "Mint
Stands in delph," or rather what were they in 1751? In
1753 they had "custard-dishes" for sale; and did they
have "terines" or "terreens" before 1760? I do not find
them named at an earlier date. A year later came "sal-
lade bowls" and the first "china handle coffee-cups,"
though John Jekyll had had handles on his cups in 1732.
Not until 1772 do I find "Enamel'd Tea cups & Saucers,
with handles to the cups." In 1763 china patch-boxes
and china sweetmeat boxes came to New England.
China stoves were advertised, but I think they were rare.
"China tumblers, with covers," seem strange to us.
What were the "yellow klinckers and Red glaz'd pantils"
advertised in the *South Carolina State Gazette* in 1787?
China "sweetmeat and pickle saucers" came in 1773, and
"half pint blue & white enameled Basons with Sawsers."
China milk-jugs, milk-pots, milk-cups, milk-ewers, and
creamers, all antedated the milk-pitcher. We had sugar-
boxes, sugar-basons, sugar-pots, and sugar-dishes before

we had sugar-bowls. "Twifflers" were of porcelain also
—pudding-dishes we call them now.

"China voiders" also are advertised for sale. These
colonial ceramic articles of nomenclature most unpleasing
in sound to modern ears, were really only an ancient type
of what are known to dealers nowadays as "crumb-trays."
Into a voider fragments of food remaining on the table—
bones and the like—were gathered after a meal by a void-
ing-knife. Pewter voiders abounded, and "china baskets
and voiders" appear in newspaper lists in 1740.

Doubtless many of these voiders and Turk caps,
twifflers, and mint-stands have descended to us, but are
known now by the uniform and uninteresting name of
dishes.

IV.

EARLY FICTILE ART IN AMERICA

IN all our wanderings and searchings we have never found any specimens of old American china, for one author says that, like the snakes in Iceland, there are none. The history of the early manufacture of porcelain in this country is so meagre that it is quickly written, and records of early pottery-works are not plentiful, and specimens are comparatively unobtainable, and frequently far from beautiful or instructive. Still I believe that America deserves a fuller ceramic history, and has had a larger manufacture of pottery and porcelain than is generally known.

One class of pottery relics should not be neglected by collectors—those of the North American Indians. When our Pilgrim Fathers landed on the bleak shores of New England they found the red man using rough bowls and pans of coarse earthen ware as cooking utensils. Gookin wrote of them thus : "The pots they seethe their food in are made of clay and earth almost in the form of an egg with the top broken off." Bradford wrote that the colonists also found great pottery vessels buried in the earth, containing stores of maize. Perfect specimens of the work of New England savages are rare, and are usually in a simple bowl shape. In the fragments found in the Connecticut Valley mica is mingled with the clay, as in the old Celtic wares of Ireland. Wherever the white man landed, to whatever spot he penetrated, he found Indians, and he also found the Indians using coarse pottery vessels, " akeeks," of their own manufacture. The early accounts of the country—Spanish, Portuguese, French, and English—all tell of the use and manufacture of pottery among the Indians. In the " Brevis Narratio" of Le Moyne de Morgues, written in the sixteenth century, we are given illustrations purporting to be of some forms of pottery used by the Florida Indians at that time. Father Hennepin, writing about 1680, asserts that before the arrival of Europeans in North America, " both the Northern and Southern Salvages made use of, and do to this day use, Earthen Pots, especially such as have no Commerce with the Europeans from whom they may procure Kettels and other Moveables." It is the fashion among antiquaries to place no confidence in Father Hennepin, but I think we may believe this statement of his, since we have so much additional evidence, both through past writers and present discoveries.

In Hariot's " Virginia," of the date 1590, we learn that the Virginian Indians " cooked their meate in earthen pottes. Thier women know how to make earthen vessels with special Cunninge, and that so large and fine that our potters with thoye wheles can make no better ; and they Remoue them from place to place as easeleye as we can doe our brassen kettles."

The Cherokee Indians, having fine clays of various

colors to work with, made a good class of pottery, far better than any made by northern Indians, some of the vessels being of large size. Lieutenant Timberlake, who visited them in 1765, says he saw one at a "physic-dance" that would hold twenty gallons. Adair, writing in 1775, says that they made "earthen pots of very different sizes, so as to contain from two to ten gallons, large pitchers to carry water, bowls, platters, dishes, basons, and a prodigious number of other vessels of such antiquated forms as would be tedious to describe and impossible to name. Their method of glazing them is, they place them over a large pit of smoky pitch pine which makes them smooth, black, and firm. Their lands abound with proper clay and even with porcelain, as has been proved by experiment." A description of the vessels of "antiquated forms" would, of course, have made his account of far more use and interest to us nowadays. William Bartram, that intelligent observer, writing in 1773, confirms the accounts of other travellers among the Indians in South Carolina and Georgia, and tells of the discovery of a very interesting earthen pot found in an Indian mound on Colonel's Island, in Liberty County, Ga. He says "it was wrought all over the outside representing basket-work, and was undoubtedly esteemed a very ingenious performance by the people at the age of its construction." This burial urn (for such the pot proved to be) was indeed a very good piece of work for an Indian potter, and is still preserved. It is about fifteen inches in height and ten in its greatest diameter, of graceful outline, and is covered with an impressed design of fine basket-work. It was made with an admixture of gravel and powdered shell, which rendered it strong enough to resist the disintegrating influences of the soil by which it was surrounded. It was enclosed in two outer vessels of ruder workmanship, which crumbled into fragments upon exposure to the air. Within the inner vessel were the bones of a young child. Too young to own any earthly possessions to be buried with him, this little Indian baby was interred in the tumulus of shell and clay, in his earthen coffin alone.

In the burial mounds of grown persons vast amounts of broken vessels and ashes of other burnt property are discovered. All peoples have at some period of their history had the custom of burying articles of use or value with their dead, or of burning these possessions at the time of the burial of the dead owner. To this custom, which existed among the North American Indians, we owe the preservation of nearly all the specimens of their poorly baked, fragile cooking utensils and burial urns that we now possess. Many filled with food and drink were whole when placed in the mound, but were quickly destroyed and crushed by the sinking earth, or disintegrated by the moisture. Many also remain, and sherds of Indian pottery are constantly being brought to light by our civilized ploughshares. It has been erroneously thought by some students that Indian pottery was only sun-dried; had it been so, no specimens would have withstood for so many years the action of the soil and elements, but would have returned ere this to their old clayey consistency.

In examining this Indian pottery it is easy to see the natural way in which the earliest forms were developed. The gourd, the shell, the basket, the square box of bark—all these primitive shapes of vessels were copied in the pottery. The ornamentation, too, was compassed in a simple fashion ; the vessel was sometimes modelled within a rush basket or frame of reeds—thus the impressed design remained upon it. Rude dyes were applied. One indented design is said to have been formed by the finger-nail of the Indian potter ; other designs have been impressed by twisted thongs. All these methods and forms of ornamentation were also used by the Celtic potters. Little pieces of mica or shell were inserted in the wet clay pot, and were fired in as a further ornament.

The earthen vessel was either baked in a rude kiln or inverted over coals of burning wood. We have several very good descriptions of the methods of manufacturing and firing of Indian potters at a later date. Dumont writes in 1848, of the Louisiana Indians : " After having amassed the proper kind of clay and carefully cleaned it, the Indian women take shells which they pound and reduce to a fine powder ; they mix this powder with the clay, and having poured some water on the mass, they knead it with their hands and feet and make it into a paste of which they form rolls six or seven feet long, and of a thickness suitable to their purpose. If they intend to fashion a plate or a vase, they take hold of one of these rolls by the end, and fixing here with the thumb of the left hand the centre of the vessel they are about to make, they turn the roll with astonishing quickness around this centre, describing a spiral line; now and then they dip their fingers into water and smooth with the right hand the inner and outer surface of the vase they intend to fashion, which would become ruffled or undulated without that manipulation. In this manner they make all sorts of earthen vessels, plates, dishes, bowls, pots, and jars, some of which hold from forty to fifty pints."

This is a prettier and more domestic picture of the Indian wife than many we have of the draggled, over-worked squaw digging in the fields, or carrying the tent-poles on her back like a pack-horse. The whirling coil of clay, the growing earthen jar, the deftly-shaping hand, are certainly picturesque and homely. The Indian women were potters in all the tribes, it being deemed unmanly work for a lordly brave.

The Indians of the Mohawk Valley, the Iroquois, made much and varied pottery. In the fine collection of Indian relics owned by A. G. Richmond, Esq., of Canajoharie, N. Y., are some very interesting pieces of pottery which have been taken from Indian mounds—among them two jars of so delicate and friable a character that one wonders how they have ever escaped disintegration and destruction; also a rare fragment wrought with a representation of the human figure.

Another form of Indian pottery must not be forgotten, for the significance of the pipe in the early history of our country cannot be over-rated. The calumet was a moral, religious, and political influence; on its manufacture and

ornamentation the Indian expended all his skill and his
best labor; and to its suited and significant use he gave
his deepest thought. The use of the pipe was a devotion-
al service—the Great Spirit smoked His pipe, and his fol-
lowers did likewise in His honor; it was a political signal
—no war was declared, no treaty of peace was signed
without the accompaniment and symbolical use of the
pipe. Lieutenant Timberlake says that the Cherokees
made pipes " of the same earth they made their pots with,
but beautifully diversified," and he pathetically records
that he was forced to smoke so many pipes of peace with
them that he was made very unpleasantly sick thereby.
This special tribe of Indians had such fine blue clay, and
knew so well how to mix and prepare it, that they made
better pipes than their neighbors, and thus pipes became
a medium of exchange—Indian money. The strong clay
pipes of the English settlers were, as soon as imported,
eagerly sought for and quickly purchased by the Indians.

Fine and varied specimens of the pottery vessels and
pipes of the various Indian nations may be found in the
cabinets of the Smithsonian Institution, in the rooms of
the various State historical societies, in the buildings of
our colleges and natural history associations, and may be
studied to advantage by the student of ceramics. A full
or worthy history of the fictile art of the North American
Indians has yet to be written.

I doubt if the colonists ever used the Indian pottery,
for at an early date they began to manufacture bricks and
earthen ware, and having wheels to help them in shap-
ing their pots, could far outdo the Indians. They made

laws to protect such manufacture. The General Court of Massachusetts ordered, as early as 1646, that "tyle earth to make sale ware shall be digged before the first of 9 mo and turned over in the last or first before it be wrought." John Pride, of Salem, was registered as a potter in 1641. He may have helped to establish a pottery in Danvers, then a suburb of Salem, for the manufacture of earthen ware in that town was coeval with the existence of the settlement; and the Danvers potworks were, I believe, the first to be established in America by any of the colonies. Higginson, writing from Salem in 1629, said, " It is thought here is good clay to make bricks & tyles and earthen pot as may be. At this instant we are setting a bricke kill to worke to make brickes and tyles for the building of our houses."

William Osborne was the first Danvers potter, and his descendants carried on the business in that immediate vicinity for about two centuries. Mr. Joseph Reed then took charge as the successor of the house of Osborne. At the end of the eighteenth century the production of "Danvers ware" was extensive. Morse's *Gazetteer* of 1797 says, "Large quantities of brick and coarse earthen ware are manufactured here." A resident of the town wrote thus in 1848, "Table ware of Danvers China brought a high price during the late war." To call the common red pottery "china" is certainly flattering, but may be pardoned on account of the local pride of the writer.

At the "time of the late war"—the war of 1812— there were no less than twenty-six of these pottery works where now there is only one. The situation of the residence and pot-works of William Osborne is still known, and the manufacture of earthen ware has gone on in the same place without interruption ever since. Simple forms only have been made—often lead-glazed— bean-pots, jugs, pitchers, milk-pans, jars, etc. We must except, of course, the table ware of war times. This Osborne kiln is situated in what is called Peabody, but in the town of North Danvers there was discovered a few years ago the foundation of an old forgotten kiln, which had been owned by a potter named Porter. There is no finer quality of clay than is still found in large quantities within a quarter of a mile of this old Porter kiln. This clay is, however, carried to Boston and elsewhere instead of being manufactured where it is dug. Potters make good citizens. Staffordshire men say, "working in earth makes men easy-minded," and a community of potters is always orderly, law-abiding, thrifty, and industrious. A larger and constantly increasing manufacture of Danvers ware should have been encouraged.

An enthusiastic local minstrel sings thus of Danvers pottery and patriots :

> " Here plastic clay the potter turned
>   To pitcher, dish, jug, pot, or pan,
> As in his kiln the ware was burned,
>   So burned the patriot in the man,
> Into persistent shape, which no
> Turning could change back to dough.
> It might be broken, ground to dust,
> But ne'er made ductile as at first."

The Quakers kept up with the Puritans in the attempt to establish home manufactures and home industries. Father Pastorius wrote in 1684, " Of brick kilns and tile ovens, we have the necessary number." Gabriel Thomas found in Pennsylvania, in 1696, both brick-kilns and pot-works. He writes thus to encourage emigration from England, and to show the high wages in the new land. " Brick-makers have twenty shillings per thousand for their bricks at the kilns, and potters have sixteenpence for an earthen-ware pot that may be bought in England for fourpence."

In New Jersey, at Burlington, Governor Coxe, of " West Jersey," established in 1690 a pottery of considerable size and pretension. The Virginians kept pace with the Quakers and Puritans. As early as 1649 there were several pot-works in Virginia.

Potteries were also established on Long Island in the eighteenth century. On March 31, 1735, " The widow of Thomas Parmynter offers for sale her farm at White-stone, opposite Frogs Point. It has twenty acres of clay ground fit for making tobacco pipes. For sale also two negroes, with utensils and other conveniences for carry-ing on that business." On July 3, 1738, the same farm, with its " beds of pipe-making clay," was again sold. On May 13, 1751, this advertisement appeared : " Any persons desirous may be supplied with vases, urns, flow-er-pots to adorn gardens and tops of houses, or any other ornament made of clay, by Edward Annely at White-stone, he having set up the potter's business by means of a German family that he bought (?), who are supposed

by their work to be the most ingenious that arrived in
America. He has clay capable of making eight different
kinds of ware." This was evidently quite a pretentious
start in the pottery manufacture, and with the assistance
of the ingenious family of German potters, and the ad-
vantages of convenient beds of clay, Edward Annely
should have succeeded; but no record remains to indicate either his success or failure.

Upon the old farm of John Lefferts, in Flatbush, Long
Island, there exists a large pond called by the apparently incongruous name of Steenbakkery. This pond was
formed by the removal of clay for use in a steenbakkery
or pottery upon the place, and from the size of the ex-
cavation vast numbers of bricks and coarse stone ware
must have been made. The ruins of the racks for the
bricks remained standing within the memory of persons
now living. This pond having, of course, no outlet
through its clay bottom, has in our present age of sani-
tary drainage been ordered to be filled in. In New
York City, near "Fresh Water Pond," back of the City
Hall, a German potter named Remmey established
works, but his descendants were crowded out by the
growing city, and removed to South Amboy.

In 1748 the State of Massachusetts offered bounties to
encourage the manufacture of earthen ware, and many
new pot-works were established. "Mangness" for the
use of potters was offered for sale in the newspapers, and
the would-be purchaser was to inquire of the printer,
who in colonial days seemed literally to have a finger in
every pie. One of the oldest of these colonial potteries

was started previous to the year 1765, by a man whose descendants of the same name still conduct the pottery works known as the factory of A. H. Hews & Co., in North Cambridge, Mass. The record of this family firm is so remarkable for America that it should be told at some length. Not only has the company continued in the same business in an uninterrupted line of the same firm name, but it possesses a record of a century and a third of unspotted integrity in business dealings. It has passed through times of foreign and civil wars, through business crises and depressions, in an even career of honor and fair-dealing, and now has earned a deserved and independent position, having the largest manufactory of flower-pots in the world—making many millions yearly—as well as a large and varied line of art pottery. When Abraham Hews was pottering around in his little pottery in Weston, in 1765, making milk-pans and bean-pots, and jugs and teapots, and exchanging them for general merchandise, in which New England rum and molasses took no inferior part, he little foresaw the vast business enterprise that would be carried out by his great-grandson in 1891. The clay used by him in Weston was brought from Watertown, and later from Cambridge, and the firm did not move their works to Cambridge until 1870. Abraham Hews, second, lived to be eighty-eight years old (being post-master for fifty-one years), and his son lived to be eighty-one years old, dying in 1891—the good old Puritan stock showing in long life as well as in honest life. Thus does a chain of only three lives reach to ante-

Revolutionary times, and an ante-Revolutionary pottery.

In the *Norwich Gazette* of September 15, 1796, we find this advertisement of a pottery: " C. Potts & Son inform the Public that they have lately established a Manufactory of Earthen ware at the shop formerly improved by Mr. Charles Lathrop, where all kinds of said Ware is made and sold either in large or small quantities, and warranted good." This pottery was on Bean Hill. It is referred to in Miss Caulkin's " History of Norwich," Dr. Peters's " History of Connecticut," and in Morse's *Gazetteer*.

At the commencement of the Revolutionary war a man named Upton came from Nantucket to East Greenwich, R. I., and there manufactured earthen ware. The pottery when made was baked in a kiln which stood at the corner of King and Marlboro Streets. He made pans, bowls, plates, cups, and saucers of common red clay, a little finer than that now used in the manufacture of flower-pots. As little porcelain was imported from Europe during the War, people used willingly, and even eagerly, the coarse plates, and drank their " Liberty Tea" from the coarse cups and saucers. The clay came from Goold's Mount, now owned by Mr. Henry Waterman, of Quidneset. After the war was ended Potter Upton went back to his safety-assured home on Nantucket, and the Greenwich pottery was closed.

In 1793 there was a flourishing pottery in Quasset, Windham County, Conn., and the pottery carts of

Thomas Bugbee, the proprietor, were well known throughout the county. He made inkstands, bean-pots, jugs, jars, and many other common shapes, and the demand for milk-pans alone always kept his kiln running all summer. There was at this time another similar pottery in Stonington, owned by Adam States, who made gray jugs and pots and jars with salt-glaze. Another firm at Norwalk manufactured red ware with a lead glaze. There is a specimen in the Trumbull-Prime collection. Mr. Prime says they manufactured mugs, teapots, jars, and milk-pans at this Norwalk pottery. In 1794 a Mr. Fenton, of New Haven, set up in Lynn Street, Boston, a pottery where "all manner of stone vessels were made after the manner of imported Liverpool ware and sold at a lower rate." The clay for this manufacture was brought from Perth Amboy, N. J.

An article in the *American Museum* in 1791, on the existing state of American manufactures, said, "Coarse tiles and bricks of an excellent quality, potters' wares, all in quantities beyond the home consumption, a few ordinary vessels of stone mixed with clay, some mustard and snuff bottles, a few flasks or flagons, a small quantity of sheet glass, and of vessels for family use, generally of inferior kinds, are now made." Dr. Dwight, in 1822, gave among his list of Connecticut factories and manufactures, " potteries twelve," " value of earthen and stone ware $30,940;" and for Massachusetts, "earthen ware, $18,-700."

Though nothing but coarse earthen ware was made in America in these colonial days, the new land played no unimportant part in the first steps toward porcelain manufacture in England in the middle of the eighteenth century. It was the custom, when English vessels had discharged their freights in southern American ports, for them to take samples of the alluvial deposits of North and South Carolina, of Georgia and Florida, to carry back to England for English potters and chemists to experiment upon. The Bow china-works began to manufacture porcelain about the year 1744. In that year a sample of china-clay being brought from America, a patent was taken out by Thomas Frye, of West Ham, Essex, and Edward Heylyn, of Bow, for the production of porcelain, of which one of the ingredients was " an earth, the product of the Cherokee nation in America, called by the natives '*unaker*.'" When this patent was renewed in 1794, no mention was made of " unaker."

In Plymouth a shrewd old Quaker, William Cookworthy, also had his eye upon the American china-clay. He wrote to Mr. Hingston on May 30, 1745, saying that kaolin and petuntse had been discovered in America, and that he had seen specimens said to have been manufactured from the American materials. One letter of his on the subject runs thus : " I had lately with me the person who hath discovered the china-earth. He had with him several samples of the china ware of their making which I think were equal to the Asiatic. 'Twas found on the back of Virginia, where he was in quest of mines, and having read Du Halde, he discovered both the petuntse and the kaolin. 'Twas this latter earth which he says is essential to the success of the manufacture. He is going for a cargo of it, having bought from the Indians the whole country where it rises. They can import it for £13 per ton, and by that means afford their china as cheap as common stone ware. The man is a Quaker by profession, but seems to be as thorough a Deist as I ever met with." In 1768 Cookworthy established the Plymouth china works, but no further mention is made of the deistical Quaker and his promised cargo of china-earth.

In 1655 a box of "porcelain-earth from the internal parts of the Cherokee nation, four hundred miles from hence (Charleston) on mountains scarcely accessible," was consigned to another English potter, Richard Champion, who founded the Bristol china works. This box of clay was sent by Champion's brother-in-law, Mr. Caleb Lloyd, of Charleston, to be forwarded to the Worcester china works to be used there in experiments. At the same time another box was sent to Champion for a relative of his, the Earl of Hyndford, who desired Champion to open it and make experiments with it, or to give it to Mr. Goldney, "who is a very curious gentleman." The curious Mr. Goldney declined using the clay, and Champion experimented unsuccessfully "on the principle of Chinese porcelain," and then decided to use clay from Cornwall, which was "not so fine as the Cherokee; however, there can be no chance of introducing the latter as a manufacture when it can be so easily procured from Cornwall."

In 1766 the English Society for the Encouragement of Arts, Manufactures, and Commerce gave a gold medal to Mr. Samuel Bowen, with the inscription that it was given to him " for his useful observations in china and industrious application of them in Georgia." It was doubtless the industrious Mr. Bowen's china that was referred to in Felix Farley's *Bristol Journal*, in the issue of November 24, 1764. " This week some pieces of porcelain manufactured in Georgia was imported ; the materials appear to be good, but the workmanship is far from being admired." Though this china venture was of enough importance to be-medal its projector, all traces of its location, progress, and fate have been lost.

Other and more pretentious pot-works were brought into life by the Massachusetts bounties. In the *Boston Evening Post* of October 30, 1769, we read, " Wanted immediately at the new Factory in New Boston, four Boys for Apprentices to learn the Art of making Tortoise-shell Cream and Green Colour Plates, Dishes, Coffee and Tea Pots, Cups and Saucers and other Articles in the Potter's Business, equal to any imported from England. Any Persons inclined to Bind out such Lads to the aforesaid Business is desired to apply immediately at the said Factory or at Leigh's Intelligence Office."

It is very evident, from many advertisements at about this date, that a strenuous and well-directed effort was made to establish and maintain pot-works in Boston. Thus on May 12, 1769, there appeared in the *Boston Evening Post* this notice : " Wanted Samples of different clays and fine White Sand. Any Person or Persons that will send about 5 lbs. of Clay and a Pint of fine white Sand to Leigh's Intelligence Office, in Merchants'

Row, Boston, if it is the sort wanted the Proprietors will have advantage of Proposals made to them to supply a quantity." Good wages, too, for the times, were offered to workmen, practised potters. "Twenty Dollars per Month with Victuals Drink Washing and Lodging given to any persons Skill'd in Making Glazing and Burning common Earthen ware who can be well recommended. Enquire of the Printer."

All this applying and experimenting and establishing, and the fact that a Quaker named Bartlam, an unsuccessful English master-potter, had started a pottery in Camden, S. C., in the very heart of the clay supply —all this seriously alarmed that far-seeing and shrewd business man, Josiah Wedgwood. He had once before lost his foreman, Mr. Podmore, who left him with the intention of establishing pot-works in America. Mr. Chaffers, a Liverpool manufacturer, had caught the intending emigrant during his pre-embarking stay in Liverpool, and finding that Podmore showed so much intelligence and practical knowledge of the business, had made him sufficiently liberal offers to induce him to remain in England. English potters had also emigrated in large numbers.

Wedgwood wrote thus at that time to his patron, Sir W. Meredith : " Permit me, Sir, to mention a circumstance of a more public nature, which greatly alarms us in this neighborhood. The bulk of our particular manufactures are, you know, exported to foreign markets, for our home consumption is very trifling in comparison to what is sent abroad ; and the principal of these markets

are the Continent and Islands of North America. To
the continent we send an amazing quantity of white
stone ware and some of the finer kinds, but for the islands we cannot make anything too rich and costly.
This trade to our colonies we are apprehensive of losing
in a few years, as they set on foot some pot-works there
already, and are at this time amongst us hiring a number of our hands for establishing new pot-works in South
Carolina, having got one of our insolvent master-potters
there to conduct them. They have every material there,
equal if not superior to our own, for carrying on that
manufacture ; and as the necessaries of life and conse-
quently the prices of labour amongst us are daily ad-
vancing, it is highly probable that more will follow them
and join their brother artists and manufacturers of all
classes who are from all quarters taking a rapid flight indeed the same way."

Wedgwood did not intend to be left out or left behind
in the "flight" into the benefits and resources of the New
World ; Pensacola clay was brought to him in 1766; and
in 1767, from Ayoree (or Hyoree as he spelt it), other
clays were fetched, and the canny potter at once attempted to secure a patent right to the exclusive use of
them. A man named Griffiths, who had owned in South
Carolina a one-third share in three thousand acres of land,
where he had "attempted the manufacture of maple-sugar after the manner of the Indians," now became Wedgwood's agent in America, under heavy bonds. Griffiths,
the owner of the ill-situated maple grove and sugar factory, went to the Cherokee country and sent home clay to

Wedgwood to experiment upon. The growing and free use of the Cornish clays, however, rendered the importation of American clays as superfluous as it was expensive and inconvenient; and the interference of the Revolutionary war destroyed all fear of American competition in the manufacture of pottery. The vicinity near Camden, S. C. (where the Bartlam pottery had been established), was particularly devastated, many fierce battles being fought around it.

In 1784, Richard Champion, who was always an enthusiastic lover of America, and who had unsuccessfully experimented in England with the Cherokee clays, left Bristol and came to live on a plantation named Rockybranch, near Camden. Wedgwood must have felt many apprehensions and fears when Champion took this step, for he knew well the energy and determination of the emigrant to America, who had in previous years completely routed him in a long-contested and bitter lawsuit over the use of certain English clays in the manufacture of china. Wedgwood knew, too, Champion's ability and capacity as a potter, and without doubt dreaded lest the man who had done such good work at Bristol should do more and better still when in the land of the Cherokee clay, at Camden. His fears (if they existed) were destined never to be realized, for Champion became a planter, filled several public offices in the State, died in 1793, on the seventh anniversary of the day he left England, and was buried near Camden.

In the year 1770 china-works were in operation in Philadelphia. They were established by Gousse Bonnin and George Anthony Morris. On December 20, 1769, an advertisement was printed in a Philadelphia newspaper, which read thus : " New China Works. Notwithstanding the various difficulties and disadvantages which usually attend the introduction of any important manufacture into a new country, the proprietors of the China Works now erecting in Southwark have the pleasure to acquaint the public that they have proved to a certainty that the clays of America are as productive of good Porcelain as any heretofore manufactured at the famous factory in Bow, near London." Later Messrs. Bonnin and Morris advertised for " broken flint-glass and whole flint-stone," and also for " shank-bones " to be delivered at the china factory in Southwark. In April, 1772, they advertised for " several apprentices to the painting branch," and encouragement was offered to " china painters either in blue or enamel," which latter notice shows that their china products were decorated. They also offered a reward for the production of *zaffre*, a compound of cobalt.

This china venture failed, the real estate of the company was sold, and the proprietors returned to England asking public attention and charity for their poor workmen. Thus forlornly ended the first porcelain factory in America ; and thus tamely subsided the rivalry between English and American china materials. When we consider the vast natural resources in America for the china-maker to draw from—the inexhaustible supply of raw materials—the unlimited beds of rich kaolin, the vast stores of pipe, potter's, ball, and fire clay—the endless mines of quartz and feldspar, the tinted earths of Alabama, the colored kaolin of Illinois, the mines of lithomarge in Tennessee—to say nothing of the boundless wealth of supplies in the far West—it seems to us that America was very slow—indeed is still very slow in taking advantage of the hints given by Cookworthy, by Champion, and by Wedgwood in the eighteenth century.

This quickly-ended china-factory of Bonnin and Morris is the one referred to in the *Edinburgh Weekly Magazine* of January, 1771, which says: "By a letter from Philadelphia we are informed that a large china manufactory is established there, and that better china cups and saucers are made there than at Bow or Stratford." Benjamin Franklin, writing to his wife from London in January, 1772, after thanking her for the cranberries and apples and various American home reminders that she had sent to him, adds, "I thank you for the sauce-boats, and am pleased to see so good a progress made in the china manufactory. I wish it success most heartily." But writing to an English potter in November, 1773, he says, "I understand the china-works in Philadelphia is declined by the first owners; whether any others will take it up and continue it, I know not."

Mr. Prime, in his book, gives the information that there were "some undoubted specimens of the work deposited in the Franklin Institute on exhibition." I do not know where those specimens now are. A pair of vases at the H. L. D. Lewis sale in Philadelphia, in December, 1890, were catalogued as having been made at this first porcelain manufactory. There is no existing record of the fact that they were produced there, and no stamp or mark to prove it, and I do not know why they were thus assigned. They were purchased by the Mount Vernon Association for eighteen dollars each, and can now be seen in Washington's old home. They stand ten inches in height, are flat in shape, about six inches in diameter, have gilded griffin handles and polished gilt faces, and are decorated with highly colored views of naval battles. They have an interest to all collectors as being specimens of the first china factory in America, as well as from the fact that they were early ornaments of Mount Vernon.

Philadelphia seems to have taken and kept the lead in the manufacture of porcelain in America, or else we are more fortunate in having the records of Philadelphia potworks preserved for us. The Pennsylvania Society for the Encouragement of Manufactures offered in 1787, a " plate of gold to the value of twenty dollars," as a prize for the "best specimen of Pennsylvania-made earthen ware approaching the nearest in quality to the delft white stone or queen's ware," and an equal prize for the best salt-glazed ware ; and in 1792 a prize of $50 for similar ware. In 1808 Alexander Trotter exhibited at Peale's Museum, in Philadelphia, some of the articles manufactured at his Columbian Pottery, which was situated on South Street, between Twelfth and Thirteenth Streets, in that city, while the warehouse was at No. 66 North Second Street. This business continued until 1813. The proprietor advertised " tea and coffee pots, pitchers, jugs, wine-coolers, basins, ewers, and baking dishes; " and it was also stated that an " elegant jug and goblets from the queen's ware manufactory" were used at the Republican dinner on July 4, 1808, at Philadelphia. This ware was similar to the Staffordshire stone wares. In the same year a firm named Binney & Ronaldson made in South Street, in Philadelphia, red and yellow tea-pots, coffee-pots, and sugar-boxes. At the beginning of the century D. Freytag advertised that, at 192 South 5th Street, Philadelphia, he would decorate piece china with gold and silver; hence he must have had a kiln for firing. In the year 1800 a pottery, called the "Washington Pottery," was established by John Mullawney on the north side of Market Street, near Schuylkill South, in the same city. The productions were called "Washington ware," and consisted of pitchers, coffee-pots, teapots, cream-pots, sugar-boxes, wash-basins, bowls, etc. It was carried on by the same proprietor until 1816, and was in operation for many years after. In 1813 the Northern Liberty Pottery was founded by Thomas Haig on the corner of Front and Market Streets, and the manufacture of earthen ware is still continued by one of his descendants. David G. Seixas had a similar manufactory at about the same time, from 1817 to 1822, at Market Street near Schuylkill 6th. In 1817 George Bruorton announced through the Philadelphia press, that he would enamel and gild arms, crests, ciphers, borders, or any device on china, or queen's ware as good as any imported. Also " china mended by burning in and warranted as sound for use as ever." In 1826 Joseph Keen also decorated china in

Market Street, near Eleventh Street. So we can plainly see how much the question of china decoration and
china-works was thought of in that town.

In the year 1828, William Ellis Tucker had a china
store at 86 Arcade, in Philadelphia. He thus advertised :
" American china of a quality equal in strength and
beauty to any that can be imported, and upon the most
reasonable terms. Initials or fancy work to suit the
taste of individuals will be executed agreeably to order
in the neatest style."

In the year 1868 Miss Peters presented to the Historical Society of Pennsylvania a porcelain pitcher
which had been made at the establishment of Messrs.
Tucker & Hemphill. At the request of the Society,
Mr. Thomas Tucker prepared the following paper on
the manufacture of porcelain in the United States.

PHILADELPHIA, May 13, 1868.

To the Historical Society of Pennsylvania :

GENTLEMEN : Herewith please find a small account of the
manufacture of porcelain in the United States.

William Ellis Tucker, my brother, was the first to make porcelain in the United States. My father, Benjamin Tucker, had a
china store in Market Street, in the city of Philadelphia, in the
year 1816. He built a kiln for William in the back-yard of the
store, where he painted in the white china and burned it on in
the kiln, which gave him a taste for that kind of work. After that
he commenced experimenting with the different kinds of clays, to
see if he could not make the ware. He succeeded in making a
very good kind of ware called queen's ware. He then commenced
experimenting with felspar and kaolin to make porcelain, and,
after much labor he succeeded in making a few small articles of

very good porcelain. He then obtained the old water-works at the northwest corner of Schuylkill, Front, and Chestnut, where he erected a large glazing kiln, enamelling kiln, mills, etc. He burned kiln after kiln with very poor success. The glazing would crack and the body would blister; and, besides, we discovered that we had a man who placed the ware in the kiln who was employed by some interested parties in England to impede our success.

Most of the handles were found in the seggars after the kiln was burned. We could not account for it until a deaf and dumb man in our employment detected him running his knife around each handle as he placed them in the kiln.

At another time every piece of china had to be broken before it could be taken out of the seggar. We always washed the round Os, the article in which the china was placed in the kiln, with silex; but this man had washed them with felspar, which of course melted, and fastened with every article to the bottom. But William discharged him, and we soon got over that difficulty.

In the year 1827 my brother received a silver medal from the Franklin Institute of Pennsylvania, and in 1831 received one from the Institute in New York. In 1828 I commenced to learn the different branches of the business. On August 22, 1832, my brother William died. Some time before he connected himself with the late Judge Hemphill. They purchased the property at the southwest corner of Schuylkill, Sixth, and Chestnut Streets, where they built a large store-house or factory, which they filled with porcelain. After the death of my brother, Judge Hemphill and myself continued the making of porcelain for some years, until he sold out his interest to a company of Eastern gentlemen; but being unfortunate in their other operations, they were not able to give the porcelain attention. In the year 1837 I undertook to carry it alone, and did so for about one year, making a large quantity of very fine porcelain, many pieces of which I still have. The gilding and painting is now as perfect as when first done.

I herewith present you with a pitcher which I made thirty-one years ago. You will notice the glazing and transparency of this specimen is equal to the best imported china ; but the gilding, having been in use so many years, is somewhat injured. I would like to give you a larger article, but I have but few pieces left.

Very respectfully yours, etc.,

THOMAS TUCKER.

I cannot understand why Thomas Tucker should have fancied that his brother was the first to make porcelain in the United States. Could he not have known of the ante-Revolutionary china-works of Bonnin & Morris ?

There are in the Trumbull-Prime Collection several specimens of Tucker's " natural porcelain." The paste and glaze are excellent, but the forms are commonplace, and the decorations indicate want of experience and taste, gold being profusely used.

At an early date, certainly in the eighteenth century, pot-works were established in Allentown, Pa., and in Pittsburg, where decorated pottery was made which resembled German manufactures, and which was often ornamented with mottoes and legends in slip decoration.

From 1793 to 1800 John and William Norton made red ware in Bennington, Vt.; since then stone-ware has been made in the same works. In 1847 Messrs. Lyman & Fenton started a pottery in Bennington, in which they made both pottery and soft-paste porcelain. These works continued for about twelve years. Specimens of their tortoise-shell wares are in the Trumbull-Prime Collection. One in the shape of a lion is here shown.

They also made figures of men and animals in Parian wares, the first, doubtless, produced in America. The impressed circular mark on some of the enamelled pottery was "Lyman Fenton & Co. Fenton's Enamel, patented 1849, Bennington, Vt."

Bennington Ware.

In the year 1837 by far the most important enterprise in the manufacture of pottery and porcelain that had ever been organized in America was started under the supervision of Mr. James Clews, who had been a potter in Cobridge, England, from the years 1819 to 1829, and who was the largest manufacturer of dark-blue Staffordshire wares at that date. An account of many pieces of his production in his English pottery, and of the stamps and marks used by him, is given in Chapter XVII.

He emigrated to America, and went to what was then the Far West—to Indiana; and with capitalists from Louisville, Ky.—Reuben Bates, Samuel Cassiday, William Bell, James Anderson, Jr., Edward Bainbridge, Perly Chamberlin, William Gerwin, John B. Bland, Willis Ranney, and James Lewis—incorporated a company, under the name of The Indiana Pottery Company, with a capital of $100,000 and power to increase to $200,000. A special act of January 7, 1837 (see Indiana Local Laws, Twenty-first Session, p. 7), states that these parties had "heretofore associated themselves together for the purpose of manufacturing earthen-ware and china in the State of Indiana, under the name and style of The Lewis Pottery Company."

The Indiana Pottery Company built its works in Troy, Perry County, thus having means of easy transportation by the Ohio River to New Orleans and other important points.

Mr. Clews had amassed much wealth in his Cobridge works, but he quickly lost it in this new enterprise in the new land, which proved far from successful. The chief difficulty lay in the hiring of proper workmen. The English potters proved wholly unreliable in this country, and the expense of importing fresh relays of workmen was too great to be endured. Nearly three hundred potters were brought over from England. The founders also found it impossible to make white ware with the clay in the vicinity of Troy, and of the

vast beds of fine kaolin which exist in Indiana they were
doubtless ignorant. The dark-blue ware which they
manufactured proved far from satisfactory, and though
so brilliantly started by practical and wealthy men, this
pottery was quickly closed, after making a considerable
quantity of yellow and Rockingham ware. In 1851 a
firm named Sanders & Wilson leased the buildings,
which were burned in 1854, but were rebuilt. There
are now two potteries in Troy.

In the early part of this century, probably in 1827, a
china factory was established in Jersey City, N. J., which
made hard-paste porcelain. Specimens of pure white
with gilded vines are in the Trumbull-Prime Collection.
In 1829 the works became known as the American Pottery Company, and pieces of their manufacture at that
date bear that mark. This pottery is still in existence,
though known by another name. They made from the
year 1830 the embossed brown pottery pitcher with
" hound handle," which was also such a favorite with
English potters from the time it was manufactured at Fulham. The design for these American hound-handled
pitchers was made by Daniel Greatbach, a prominent English modeller, who came to this country many years ago.
A specimen which I possess is of mottled tortoise-shell,
green, brown, and yellow, and bears the design of a hunt
around the body and grape-leaves on the top, but more
frequently the pitchers are simply colored brown. Some
have a mask of Bacchus on and under the nose, and one
I own has the nose formed by an American "spread
eagle." They were a favorite hot-water jug in the early

years of their manufacture, their size, strength, and shape making them particularly suitable for such a purpose.

Hound-handled Pitcher.

They were sometimes fitted with metal covers fastened to holes drilled through the pottery. I have seen them twenty inches in height, and at least three feet in circumference. In some parts of the country they are known as "tavern pitchers," perhaps from power of association. Such is the one herewith shown, now owned by Robert T. Van Deusen, esq., of Albany. Some were doubtless from English potteries, but many are American. Glazed brown "tobys" with the circular impressed mark "D. & J. Henderson, Jersey City," were also made, but the exact age of such pieces is unknown.

Of the later porcelain factories which have been established in America I will not speak—the factories of Trenton, Baltimore, East Liverpool, Long Island City—which now number over five hundred. Their story will doubtless be written ere long by some historian of the ceramic art in America, but hardly comes within the bounds of this work. Specimens of their manufacture, especially of the truly artistic productions of the Baltimore China Works, should, however, be secured by every china-collector, though they do not appeal so strongly to the china-hunter, to whom the pleasures of the chase often exceed the delight in the spoils, and to whom old china, like old wine, is better than new.

V

EARLIEST POTTERY WARES

THE first rare pieces of porcelain owned by the American colonists were India china; but Delft ware, salt-glazed ware, and the tortoise-shell or "combed" wares were the earliest forms of pottery that were imported to any great extent.

Many pieces of heavy blue and white Delft have been found in New England, some being Dutch, some English. The shapes, decorations, and pastes are so similar that it is impossible for even the most careful observer definitely to judge of the place of manufacture, and there are seldom guiding and aiding marks. In Connecticut much Delft is found, sometimes with Dutch words and inscriptions. Doubtless the Connecticut planters bargained and traded with the New York Dutch, who perhaps took onions and notions from the canny Connecticut men in exchange for Delft. In New York, along the Hudson River to Albany, much fine Delft is still preserved in old Dutch families, especially in the old Dutch farm-houses and manor-houses. At the Albany Bi-centennial Loan Collection, in 1886, a fine showing was made of old Delft by representatives of the families of the old patroons—of the Ten Eycks, Ten Broecks, Bleeckers, and Van Rensselaers.

A few stray Delft wanderers may be found in Massachusetts and New Hampshire—meat-dishes and plates, pale and ugly, as if the journey inland had faded them out. On Long Island, Delft is still kept and used in Dutch families—it is not the oldest Delft, however, nor is it much prized. The typical Delft vases, decorated in blue, yellow, and white, once graced the high mantel or beaufet of many a low, comfortable Dutch farm-house in Flatbush, New Utrecht, and Gravesend, and occasionally one can still be found. A fine set is in the old "pirates' house" at Flatlands. The Dutch made many teapots, we are told, but I have never found an old Delft one in America. I have seen a few dull blue and white Delft flower-pots — possibly one hundred years old — clumsy, ugly things, whether old or new. I wish I could drive through the old Dutch settlements on Long Island—New Utrecht, and Flatlands, and New Lots, and Gravesend—and ransack the great, spacious garret of every concave-roofed story-and-a-half farm-house I passed. I know I could bring many a piece of Delft to light—forgotten and unheeded by its stolid owners.

That Delft was not very highly prized by the Dutch settlers, nor by their descendants, may be proved by many inventories and lists, such as this, of the estate of John Lefferts, of Flatbush, made in 1792:

	£	s.
25 Pewter plates (1s. each)	1	5
37 Earthen plates.............................		10
9 Pewter dishes	1	15
8 Earthen dishes	1	
6 Sets china cups and saucers.................	3	
27 Delft plates		13

Pewter was plainly much more valued than Delft, and India china was still more highly prized.

Old Delft tea-caddies are both curious and pretty. Here is one shown, marked with the names " Aalta Evert and Gerrit Egben" and the date, 1793. It was

doubtless a wedding or betrothal gift. In this piece the dark-blue decoration is under the glaze, and the red and black quaint Dutch-dressed figures and the inscription are over the glaze, and were doubtless painted to order and

Delft Tea-caddy.

fired when the piece was purchased for a gift or token. This labor-saving device was brought to perfection by a Dutch potter named Zachary Dextra, though the cunning Chinese and Japanese had employed it when they held supremacy over the Dutch market. If a skilled painter painted under the glaze, an inferior workman could easily do the finishing touches over the glaze.

The Delft apothecary jars are the rarest and most curious pieces seen, and form a charming posy-holder. They are eight or ten inches in height, and are lettered with the abbreviated names of drugs. "Succ: E. Spin: C.," "U. Althae," and "C: Rosar: E." are on three of my jars. They frequently have a spout on one side, and are then usually globose in shape, with a spreading base. Some have handles. When the Dutch used these jars, a century or more ago, they covered the open top with tightly-tied oil-skin and poured the medicinal or chemical contents from the spout, which, at other times, was kept carefully corked. These jars are identical in shape with the old "sirroop-pots" of Dutch museums; for instance, the one made by Haarles, the eminent *plateelbakker*, in 1795, as a "proof of his skill," and now preserved in the archives at Delft.

The most familiar and universal decoration on Delft plates and meat dishes is the conventionalized "peacock" design. It sometimes takes rather a ludicrous appearance, often forming a comical caricature of a ballet-dancer. A coarsely-drawn basket of flowers is also common. I have also seen in America specimens of the "musical plates" of Delft. These bear designs of musical instruments, scores of song or dance music, or simply a staff with a few notes, a motif, accompanied usually by inscriptions, mottoes, or couplets, sometimes in Dutch, sometimes in French, the latter showing usually so decided a touch of extreme opera-bouffe *équivoque* that such "musical plates" would scarcely be in demand for family use, and make us turn to the Dutch-lettered pieces as being more desirable simply because the language of their decoration is less widely known and comprehended. Even these cannot be positively classed as Dutch, for the early English potters copied servilely the Dutch designs. The vases often have figures of men

Delft Vase.

and animals and Dutch landscapes. A fine collection of Delft plates and placques and vases may be seen in the Trumbull - Prime Collection.

"Fine Holland Tile" was advertised in the *Boston News Letter* of June 11, 1716—the first announcement of the sale of Delft in America, though not in the form of table-ware—and in the same paper, under date of August 10, 1719, we find a notice of "Dutch Tile for Chimney." From that date, all through the century, in the various newspapers, we find constantly recurring advertisements of Delft chimney tiles on the arrival of every foreign ship. They must have been imported in vast numbers, and were not expensive; "9 dozen Dutch tiles, £1 10s., 10 dozen Dutch tiles, £2 10s.," were the values assigned. In spite of these facts I have found them very rare in New England—they have wholly disappeared. In historical rooms, in museums, they may be seen, but seldom in old houses. The Robinson House in old Narraganset has a fine set; in a few old houses in the Connecticut valley I have seen sets of the coarsely painted " scripture tiles " so disparaged by Benjamin Franklin, but they are rare. Even on Long Island and on the banks of the Hudson they are now seldom found. Story-tellers of New England life usually place blue and white tiles around their Yankee fireplaces, but they are more plentiful in the imagination of such narrators than in reality. With the various changes in the manner of heating New England dwellings, the chimney tiles have all vanished, even when the houses still stand, and nearly all the old city houses have been entirely removed to make way for more modern business structures. English potters made tiles in such close imitation of the Dutch that it is impossible to distinguish between them. Doubtless many of the "blue and white chimney tile" so largely advertised were English manufactures imported under the name of Dutch tiles, while still others were not chimney, but roof tiles.

There have been found in New England, in numbers which seem rather surprising when we consider their age, ale-jugs of gray and blue stone-ware which are universally known as Fulham jugs. They resemble in quality and coloring the German stone-ware or our common crocks, being of the same gray ware with a lead glaze. They are decorated with rich blue like the German wares, and have an incised design of leaves and scrolls, circles or simple flowers. I have seen a number which bore in the front an oval medallion with the incised initials G. R., sometimes also a crown. These are said to refer to Georgius Rex, the first of the English Georges. I know of one G. R. mug which has an additional interest in the form of a bullet of the Revolution imbedded in its tough and uncracked side. Some of these Fulham jugs have apparently had silver or pewter lids attached to them. They are what are known as bottle-shaped,

round and protuberant, narrowing to a small neck and base; others are more slender, almost cylindrical. There are no marks to prove them to be Fulham jugs, but as such they are known.

Other Fulham jugs are found of brownish mottled stone-ware with hound handle and

Fulham G. R. Jug.

raised decoration in the body of figures of the chase, and with mask of Bacchus forming the nose. These have been frequently reproduced in American potteries and when unmarked, it is difficult to determine which are English.

Pieces of salt-glazed ware have been found in country homes by many china-hunters, and are among the most pleasing articles to be obtained. The date of their manufacture was from 1680 to 1780. An interesting story is told of the discovery of the process of glazing this ware. A servant maid having, in the year 1680, allowed a pot of brine to boil over, the dull earthen pot containing the brine became red hot, and when cold was covered with a bright glaze. A sharp potter perceiving it, at once utilized the hint. The story is pretty, but it can scarcely be true, for such a glaze could not be formed in an open place. But salt-glaze there is, and in America too, of the very earliest manufacture—Crouch-ware, or, as it is incorrectly and inappropriately called, Elizabethan-ware. Crouch is the name neither of a person nor of a place, but of the white Derbyshire clay. The paste made from this clay is very dense, and is of a greenish tint. The Elers-ware of buff ground with simple raised scrolls and rosettes of white are also of early date.

Some of the salt-glazed pieces were shaped by pressing the moist paste into metal moulds, other pieces were "cast" in moulds of plaster of Paris, the slip or liquid paste being introduced to line the mould, and allowed to set, and this operation being repeated until the piece was of required thickness. As the taste for light delicate wares increased, some were made as light and thin as paper. If the piece were "cast" the handles, nose, and feet (if it possessed any) were moulded and placed on separately. The moulds used were frequently the worn-out moulds that had been used for casting silver-ware; hence pieces of salt-glazed ware usually resemble in shape the pieces of silver of the same date.

The characteristic feature of salt-glazed ware—the quality from which it derives its name—is its glaze. This is easily recognized. It does not run and spread like other glazes, but seems to form into minute coagulated drops or granulations resembling somewhat the surface of orange-peel. The glaze is often unequal, being higher on some portions of the piece than others, the vapor of soda (through which the glaze was made) not penetrating with equal power to every point. Thus one side of a piece may be dull and the other highly glazed.

The largest and finest example of salt-glazed ware which I have seen in America is the exact duplicate of the best specimen in the Museum of Practical Geology, in Jermyn Street, London, numbered G. 111. It is thus described in the catalogue of that museum: "Large oval soup tureen, cover, and stand. Height, ten inches; greatest diameter, fourteen and one-half inches. Body decorated with pressed ornaments, including scrollwork and diaper and basket pattern; the tureen mounted on three lion's claws with masks." This tureen is dated 1763. The beautiful and delicate specimen found in America is absolutely perfect. It bore the difficult process of making and firing (specially difficult in so large a piece), crossed the water to the new land of Virginia, passed through generations of use and the devastations of the Revolutionary and civil wars, was gathered in by a travelling dealer, brought in safety by rail to New York, and ignominiously sold for a dollar and a half to its present proud possessor. It was doubtless cast in the same mould as the one in the museum. Another similar piece is in the well-known English collection of Lady Charlotte Schreiber.

A large number of smaller pieces of salt-glazed ware

have been found, including salt-boxes, creamers, and one beautiful teapot which is so graceful and unique in de-

Sportive Innocence Pitcher.

sign that it has been honored by being borrowed by a prominent china-manufacturer in England to reproduce in his modern ware. Thus this frail waif from the middle of the last century has thrice crossed the ocean in safety.

The pitchers shown are of salt-glazed ware and may be Crouch-ware, though they are apparently of rather

Farmer Pitcher.

later date. The first bears in a heart-shaped medallion a design of high-colored children at awkward play, and is labelled "Sportive Innocence." Similar ones are frequently found in America. I know of at least a dozen. Some bear on the reverse side a different design with the same children entitled "Mischievous Sport." In this the boy is frightening the little girl with an ugly mask. Other pitchers of precisely the same shape and border-decorations in orange, green, and blue have different designs in the medallion, a peacock being frequently seen. The farmer's pitcher has the motto "Success to Trade," and is surely older as well as gayer in color than the "Sportive Innocence" pitcher.

There were imported to America in great quantities, as is shown by many eighteenth-century advertisements, "tortoise shell" and "combed pattern" wares, also the pretty cauliflower, melon, and pineapple wares that have been reproduced in our own day. These were manufactured chiefly at Little Fenton by Thomas Whieldon, a man who influenced much the potters' art in England from the year 1740 to 1780, during five of which years he was a partner with Wedgwood. There are only two specimens of these wares in the Museum of Practical Geology, and Mr. Jewitt wrote in 1873: "These wares are now very scarce and are highly and deservedly prized by collectors." At the time he wrote he could have gathered in America scores, even hundreds, of pieces of the Whieldon wares for English collections. Dr. Irving Lyon, of Hartford, has a fine collection of them which he picked up in the cottages of the Connecticut Valley— a collection which any English china-lover would envy.

Whieldon was a man of great energy, with a practical knowledge of his art, and he spent much time in his works perfecting his patterns and processes. He compounded the bright green glaze so admirable in his ware, shown so beautifully in the cauliflower and melon patterns, through the contrast with the cream color. He also was a modeller, and from the imitation of leaves, and fruits, and vegetables derived his best-known and most successful patterns, and the novelty and ingenuity of many of them charm us even in the present day. The bird and animal shapes being grotesque rather than useful, seldom came to America. I have seen here, however, several tortoise-shell cows and one combed bird. The tail of the cow forms the handle of the pitcher, the liquid being poured from the nose. Reproductions of these are now made at Jeffords Pottery in Philadelphia. Little cradles and posy-holders, too, are found, sometimes with dates. Whieldon's two-handled "parting-cups," ornamented with raised grapes, leaves, and tendrils and a head of Bacchus, are much more scarce than the melon and cauliflower teapots, mugs, and dishes; and his perforated ware I have never seen in America. Some of the pieces of his manufacture are stamped and afterward shaped somewhat by hand, others are cast, others pressed in moulds. The "cast" pieces are considered to be of earlier date, and may be known by their being thinner and more delicate than the moulded ones. The mottled browns, greens, and yellows of the tortoise-shell and combed wares, like all of Whieldon's decorations, are under the glaze, and are very rich in tone, forming a delightful bit of color in cupboard or cabinet. Occasionally a purple mottle is seen. The colors were sponged, floured, or blown on, painting and printing on pottery being then unknown. These pieces of Whieldon's are all unmarked, and doubtless many specimens in America came from the Wedgwood factory, for similar wares were made there.

I hardly know how to account for the fact that I have found so few, comparatively few, pieces of undoubted Wedgwood ware in old houses in New England. That vast quantities came to America we cannot doubt. Wedgwood says so himself in his letter quoted on page 88. In other letters he refers again and again to consignments made to the American market, "the green and white wares," "the Queen's wares," "the cream wares," etc. That these consignments were sent largely to the various points supplied from the Charleston and Philadelphia markets is known, and in those regions the black basalts-ware, at least, is more plentiful than in New England. Much Wedgwood ware must have come also to the ports of Boston, Newport, and New Haven. These wares may have been plentiful in the Connecticut Valley, but I have seen little in other parts of New England. A good opportunity of studying the various productions of the Wedgwood factory is given through the specimens in the Trumbull-Prime Collection. There are at least one hundred "lots" of Wedgwood there shown, and the cameos and intaglios, the jasper-wares, the basalts, the queensware, the painted wares are all illustrated by choice and varied pieces.

The story of Wedgwood's life I will not even give briefly, though the beauty and lesson of it make one long to tell it till every American china-manufacturer learns to read between the lines the story of personal supervision, patient trial, unwearied labor, honest ambition, and liberal broadness that made his life a success and his productions a delight. Miss Meteyard and Mr.

Jewitt have given it in careful detail, and every word is of keenest interest and importance to the china-collector. From these books, and from the beautiful volumes of engravings and photographs of Wedgwood ware preserved in English collections, the American china-hunter can learn, if not from the specimens themselves.

A few of the Wedgwood cameo medallions are found in America. Wedgwood sent as a gift to Thomas Jefferson three exquisite medallions; two were oval and one oblong in shape. They were in blue and white jasper, with mythological designs. The largest was twelve inches long and six inches wide, and bore the lovely design of Cupid and Psyche with troops of attending loves. Jefferson had them set in the front of a mantel in a room at Monticello, and one of them dropped out and was destroyed before the family sold the house. The others were picked or cut out and stolen. Mrs. Ellen Harrison, the oldest living descendant of Jefferson, tells me that during a visit to Monticello, some years before the present owner took possession, she found on the floor a tiny bit of blue jasper showing the foot and leg of one of the loves. Thus did this English cherub cast from his feet the dust of an inartistic and relic-hunting nation of vandals. Oh, the pity that things so beautiful could be so wantonly destroyed! Would that everything that Wedgwood made had been endowed with qualities of immortality and indestructibility to live forever as lessons and examples for future generations of potters.

Occasionally a jasper medallion is found here with Wedgwood's famous anti-slavery design, a kneeling slave with fetters falling from his hands, and the motto, " Am I not a Man and a Brother?" Dr. Darwin says that "Wedgwood distributed many hundreds of these to excite the humane to attend to and assist in the abolition of the detestable traffic in human creatures."

> " Whether, O friend of art, the gem you mould
> Rich with new taste, with ancient virtue bold,
> Or the poor tortur'd slave on bended knee,
> From Britain's sons imploring to be free."

Many found their way to America and a few are still preserved.

Occasionally also a rich dessert-service of old Wedgwood ware is seen. Two superb ones were brought across the water by a sea-captain at the beginning of this century and landed at Hudson, N. Y. A fair young bride saw and coveted one of these china treasures, but stern and frugal parents were horrified at the thought of spending seventy dollars for such an unnecessary luxury. The bridegroom, Silas E. Burraws, at a later date the starter of the monument to the mother of Washington, more extravagant and more indulgent, bought it as a wedding gift. It is "queen's ware" of the rich blue, red, and gold design which is known among American dealers as "Queen Charlotte's pattern." The fruit dishes and comports are of the unique and perfect shapes often found in Wedgwood ware. I have seen a single plate of this pattern in a shop labelled with the price "thirty dollars." The price given for a similar one in the South Kensington Museum was four pounds. I know also of one or two dinner services of yellow Wedgwood ware, with the vine and grape border in white, early works of Wedgwood, clear and firm in outline and beautiful in quality.

The frail fluted bowl, the graceful pitcher with twisted handle, and the fragile creamer of queen's ware shown on page 1 are all Wedgwood of lovely shape and so thin and delicate a paste, that it is wonderful that they have been safely preserved for a hundred years outside a collector's cabinet, and stranger still, have been used upon the tea-table of a country home.

A pottery was founded at Castleford in 1770, and black basalt ware, much like Wedgwood's, was made,

Castleford Teapot.

and white stone ware which must have been imported to this country in vast quantity, for specimens are not rare. A teapot commonly seen is here shown. It is found both in black basalt, a curious brown ware, and salt-glazed cream ware. Special raised work designs of the figure of Liberty and the American eagle were used, and the sugar-bowls, creamers, and teapots bearing such designs were doubtless made entirely for this market. The white surface of Castleford ware was frequently divided into compartments by raised lines which were colored blue or green. Teapots were made with lids hinged on metal pins, or with sliding lids, and were exceedingly pretty and convenient. They are often called Wedgwood, as are also pieces of Castleford black ware.

VI.

ENGLISH PORCELAINS IN AMERICA

A S soon as porcelain was manufactured to any extent in England it was exported to America. The *Boston Evening Post* of November, 1754, advertised "a variety of Bow China Cups and Saucers and Bowls," and other sales of Bow china were made, and special pieces also brought across the ocean to wealthy Americans. Specimens of Plymouth and Bow china may still be occasionally found in America, but any such that have been preserved and gathered into private collections can be positively identified only by comparison with authenticated and marked pieces in public collections. It would be impossible to give any definite Bow marks. The stamp or design of the anchor and dagger is popularly considered proof that the piece thus marked is Bow. The triangle, formerly regarded as a positive Bow mark, now appears to have a rather shaky reputation, and is as frequently assigned to Chelsea. The character and shape of the ware, and the style of the decoration are better grounds to base identification upon than any marks. Excavations made upon the site of the old Bow china works revealed much débris of broken pieces of china, and these specimens afford the most positive means of identifying the paste and ornamentation. An account of these discoveries was given in the *Art Journal* of 1869. All the fragments found were of porcelain, milky-white in color, and relatively heavy for the thickness; some were ornamented in relief, with the May flower or hawthorn; with a little sprig of two roses and a leaf on a stalk; with the basket pattern; or with vertical bands overlaid with scrolls. Some were painted in blue under the glaze with Chinese landscapes, flowers, and figures. All were hand-painted, none were printed. These hints may serve as guides in the detection and identification of Bow china.

I have seen in America cups and saucers painted with the partridge pattern, which I believe are Bow, though the same pattern is found on Worcester and Plymouth china. The well-known and exceedingly valuable goat milk-jugs that, after forming for years the immovable standard from which streamed defiantly the flag of Bow, are now calmly turned over to Chelsea. These cream-jugs are ornamented with two white goats in relief at the base, and a bee is modelled on the front under the nose. The handle is rustic with raised flowers. These jugs often have the triangle mark. Some are painted with flowers, others are plain white porcelain. Mr. Jewitt says they were sometimes made without the raised bee, but I have never seen such an one. Two of these Bow jugs were in the Strawberry Hill collection.

A very excitable young woman came rushing home one cold winter day, in New York, with a demand for the "china books." She had seen in an antique shop, such a funny and pretty little pitcher, with a raised bee on it, and she was sure that there was a picture of it somewhere in the books—and she found it in Mr. Prime's book on pottery and porcelain—a Bow goat cream-jug. Well, it snowed, and was cold, and was late in the afternoon, and the confident young collector deferred a purchasing visit till the following morning. Alas! such a

Plymouth Salt-cellar. Bow "Goat Cream-Jug."

sickening disappointment—some miserable despoiler had chanced to "drop in" on his way up-town and had carried off the treasure. Worse still, the small boy who had sold it did not know the purchaser's name.

Deeply did she mourn her ignorance, her indecision, her indolence, her carelessness. The opportunity of a lifetime had thus been lost, to have a goat cream-jug such as was sold at the Cother sale in London, in 1876, for twenty-five pounds, to have such a jug offered for the paltry sum of one dollar, and to refuse it—not to know enough to grasp such a treasure. The bitterness of regret and of self-reproach nerved her to action, and with the friendly and actively interested aid of the antique-shop-boy, the jug-buyer was waylaid within a month's time and cajoled into reselling his purchase, which he did willingly enough. He had bought it to keep his shaving brush in, because his father used to keep his shaving brush in a similar one in England. With flecks of dried shaving soap clinging to the goat's horns, and mottling the bee's wings, she triumphantly brought her treasure home. It varies slightly in height and by the turn of a leaf and twig from my Bow goat cream-jug, which came from the Cavendish-Bentinck sale in London. The porcelain of the New York captive of the chase is not so pure and clear and it may be of Chelsea manufacture.

Another dainty piece of Bow found by a friend is a creamer or sauce-boat of the overlapping leaf pattern. The handle is formed by a leaf stem; raised flowers are at the base of the handle, and on the leaves flowers are delicately painted. This is like Number "H. 12" in the Museum of Practical Geology.

The beautiful tall coffee-pot here shown is Plymouth with embossed surface and Chinese style of decoration in blue. Its cover was destroyed, alas! by some careless Newburyport housewife. The salt-cellar of pure unpainted porcelain on page 121 is undoubtedly Plymouth also, being clearly marked. The design of vine leaves and grapes is very delicate and perfect. The piece came from an old home in Baltimore.

Though Bristol china was manufactured only from the

year 1768 to 1781, and though pieces are rare and high-priced in England, it is possible to obtain specimens in America. Perhaps some invoices of the ware of the short-lived factory were sent to the new land by Richard Champion, the founder of the Bristol Works, for he was

Plymouth Coffee-pot.

an enthusiastic lover and admirer of America. In the Trumbull-Prime Collection are a large number of pieces classed as Bristol because they have the Bristol cross, but not assigned definitely to that factory.

The few Bristol pieces I have seen in American homes are portions of tea-services, teapots being more plentiful than other forms. Some have an imperfect or blistered glaze, but occasionally fine specimens are found. It is impossible to state the value of Bristol china. In the

Governor Lyon sale there were two lovely Bristol cups and saucers decorated with a heavy gold rim and oriental landscape in dark blue, that sold for four dollars each. A plate with the same decoration brought only a dollar and a half.

The most beautiful and interesting piece of Bristol porcelain in existence is in America. It is owned by Mrs. James M. Davis, of Camden, South Carolina. She is a great-granddaughter of Richard Champion and inherited it from him. This lovely piece is a funerary design—a mourning female figure leaning against a pedestal bearing a funeral urn. In one hand she holds a wreath. The beauty of the figure, the grace of the attitude, and the elegance of the drapery combine to make this statue exceedingly exquisite. It was made by the English potter as a memorial for his daughter, Eliza Champion, who died in early youth—a memorial such as was tenderly though crudely suggested by the carefully-made burial urn of the Indian mother. The inscription is so simple and so touching, and is couched in such quaint old-time diction that I copy it in full.

ELIZA CHAMPION

Ob. XIII Octob. MDCCLXIX

AEtat XIV

Nat. XXI Mart. MDCCLXVI

On the cornice of the pedestal are the words:

" OSTENDENT TERRIS HANC TANTVM FATA NEC VLTRA ESSE SINENT."

Bristol Memorial Figure.

On the dado this inscription:

" We loved you, my dear Eliza, whilst you were with us. We lament you now you are departed. The Almighty God is just
and merciful, and we must submit to His will with the Resignation and Reverence becoming human frailty. He has removed you, Eliza, from the trouble which has been our Lot,
and does not suffer you to behold the Scenes of horror and
distress in which these devoted Kingdoms must be involved.
It is difficult to part with our beloved Child, though but for a
season. Yet our Interest shall not be put into competition with
her felicity, and we will even bear her Loss with Chearfulness.
Happy in each other, we were happy in you, Eliza, and will
with contented minds cherish your memory till the period
arrives, when we shall all again meet and Pain and Sorrow
shall be thought of no more. R.C.—I.C."

On the plinth lines altered from Book I., Ode XXIV.,
of Horace are printed thus:

QVIS DESIDERIO SIT PVDOR AVT MODVS
TAM CHARI CAPITIS?—
—CVI PVDOR, ET JVSTITIAE SOROR
INCORRVPTA FIDES, NVDAQVE VERITAS
QVANDO VLLAM INVENIENT PAREM?
DVRVM! SED LAEVIUS FIT PATIENTIA,
QVICQVID CORRIGERE EST NEFAS.

On the base:

"THIS TRIBUTE TO THE MEMORY OF AN AMIABLE GIRL WAS
INSCRIBED ON HER COFFIN THE 16TH OF OCTOBER, 1779,
BY A FATHER WHO LOVED HER."

Who could read, even after a century's time, this beautiful and tender tribute to the gentle young girl, who
died so many years ago, without feeling deep sympathy

with the bereaved father, "who loved her?" The unsuccessful worker and the patriot speak plainly also in the lines :

" He has removed you from the trouble which has been our Lot
and does not suffer you to behold the scenes of horror and
distress in which these devoted Kingdoms must be involved."

Mrs. Davis also possessed some of the beautiful Bristol figures of Spring, Summer, and Winter, and she patriotically sent them for exhibition at the Centennial Exposition in Philadelphia, in 1876. Like many another rare and beautiful article sent confidingly there at that time, they were never returned to their owner. This loss must have been hard to endure with patience, not only from the historical and hereditary value and interest of the pieces, but also because the previous year duplicate pieces of Bristol were sold in London for £54 each.

One of the most beautiful of Richard Champion's productions in England or America is the medallion plaque of Franklin, described in Chapter XIV.

Mr. Owen's description of Bristol china is very clear and concise. " The pieces are graceful in form and well moulded, the flowers brilliant in colour and skilfully painted ; and the gilding, bright though unburnished, is of that particularly rich and solid character that always distinguished the manufacture. Though it often bears Dresden marks, and is moulded in Dresden shapes, the quality of the paste is so different that it is easily distinguished from the Dresden. The glaze is rich and creamy white, while the Dresden has a cold, glassy surface."

Crown Derby is seldom picked up by the china-hunter — never I believe in country homes in New

Crown Derby Covered Dish.

England. Near New York a few rare pieces have been found. Miss Henrietta D. Lyon, of Staten Island, has part of an exceedingly rich and elegant Crown Derby dinner service painted in delicate colors and gold, one covered dish of which is here shown. The gilding and painting upon these pieces is in the highest style of artistic beauty and dexterity. They bear the mark used at the Derby factory from 1784 to 1796.

The most common piece offered to the china hunter in New England is what is known as the willow-pattern ware. It was made first by Thomas Turner, at Caughley, in 1780. He manufactured both pottery and porcelain. I often have wished that he had never invented that willow pattern. I have had it thrust in my face for purchase until I could scarcely bear to look at it. I have had visions of dainty Bow, Bristol, and Plymouth china brought before me through vivid but uncertain description, only to come face to face with more printed willow-pattern. I should imagine that a large proportion of all that ever was made was sent to America. And it has been made in vast quantities, too, for it has been certainly the most popular pattern ever printed anywhere on stoneware or porcelain. Mr. Jewitt says: "Early examples bearing the Caughley mark— the cups without handles and ribbed and finished precisely like the Oriental, are rare." Of course they are, in England, but not in America; as the prices prove at the Governor Lyon sale. Old willow-pattern plates sold there for one dollar each.

Pieces of willow-pattern ware are often of astounding age and fabulous value. Forty dollars is the favorite price that knowing country owners assert they can get in the city for their willow-pattern platters. I have a favorite formula which I always use in answer to these aspiring traders—my "willow-pattern answer." I reply, gravely, "Yes, that pattern is priceless." It does not mean anything and it pleases them, and if you told them that the platter was worth about two or three dollars they would look upon you as a swindler. Modern willow-pattern ware is also offered at fancy valuations. I have never been able to decide whether an old farmer who brought two willow-ware plates about a year old to sell to me, assuring me (though they bore the visible mark and stamp of modern production) that "this old crockery had been in his fam'ly more'n a hundred year"—I have never decided whether that ingenuous bucolic were a deep-dyed swindler or the innocent tool of some crafty sharper. I answered him soberly with my patent "willow-pattern answer"—"That pattern is priceless," and he went away hugging his antiques with delight. I have seen within a year at a well-known dealer's in New York, a modern willow-pattern platter upon which was pasted this printed inscription: "This platter belonged to Miles Standish, and was often used by him, and is therefore very rare and of great historical value." This was an auction label cut from the catalogue of a sale, and the dealer let it remain as a joke for the knowing ones, and possibly as a bait for the unsophisticated.

"The Broseley Blue Dragon" and the "Broseley Blue Canton" pieces and their imitations are frequently found. These patterns were also made at the Caughley or Salopian Works. The "cabbage leaf jugs" came from that manufactory.

I have never been able to understand why the willow pattern should have been so much more popular than the Blue Dragon. The latter is certainly very handsome and consistent, or rather congruous throughout, while the willow pattern is neither " fish nor fowl nor good red herring "—it is not English, and it is certainly not wholly Oriental. The color is good, as was all blue at that time.

At a later date than the reign of Lowestoft on " company " dinner-tables in New England, the fine " best tea china " of well-to-do people was English porcelain of copper lustre and pink and green decoration. Many of these pretty lustre sets are still preserved and can be bought of country owners. A terrible blow has been dealt, however, to the desire to purchase such wares by the fact that modern reproductions showing equal beauty of color and similar designs have appeared in large numbers within the past two years. Pitchers of pottery, " prankt in faded antique dress " of light brown or pinkish purple lustres are now manufactured. They bear no marks and cannot be distinguished from the old ones— and are just as good, perhaps, for every one but a china hunter. The solid lustre teapots, sugar-boxes, and pitchers—copper-colored, brownish lustre or silver on a pottery ground, have not, so far as I know, been reproduced. On many pieces the lustre is diversified by a pretty design in white, sometimes in relief or by painted flowers. The finest old pitcher of this ware that I have ever seen bore a graceful embossed design which was decorated upon the highest reliefs in pink, green, and

gold lustre. This was positively affirmed to be part
of the Mayflower cargo. Most of these lustre pieces
are unmarked, hence it is impossible to assign them
to any factory. A few of them, the clearest and purest
in paste, and most delicate in decoration are New Hall,
for I have plates so marked. The stamp is a cursive
New Hall not enclosed in a ring. This stamp is not
given in English books of stamps and marks. Mr. Jewitt says such pieces are rare in England. They certainly
have not been rare in New England. Some of the lustre
pieces may be assigned to Newcastle. The Woods also
manufactured them, while at Shelton were made pieces
with lustre borders and black printed designs signed
"Bentley, Weare and Bourne, Engravers and Printers,
Shelton, Staffordshire."

I have never seen a dinner set of lustre ware—only tea-
sets, comprising usually a teapot, sugar-box, creamer,
bowl, a dozen tea-plates (often of different design and
paste), two cake-plates, a dozen cups and saucers, and
sometimes a dozen little cup-plates. Salt-cellars, pepper-
boxes, and mustard-pots of similar lustre are seen, and
sometimes wine-glasses, or rather wine-cups—but never
any of the pieces of dinner-services. Pitchers appear in
various sizes. The china is usually clear and fine in
quality, but the design is often confused. A few punch-
bowls of copper lustre on coarse pottery have also been
found in New England, but are curious rather than
beautiful.

I have never been able to add to my collection,
through china hunting, but one piece of Worcester por-

celain, the one shown on page 29, nor have I ever seen in a country home a piece of Chelsea, Coalport, Pinxton, or Nantgawr porcelain, and but one set of Spode, which was seized from an English vessel by a Yankee privateersman in the war of 1812, and brought triumphantly into Salem Harbor. Nor, may I add, have I ever seen a piece of pottery or porcelain of Continental manufacture, save Delft. For any porcelain save that made in China and England, American collectors must turn to china dealers.

VII.

LIVERPOOL AND OTHER PRINTED WARE

AT the end of the past and beginning of the present century, great numbers of cream-colored pottery pitchers and mugs were printed in England with various designs and were sent to the United States for sale. These pieces were advertised in early Federal days, and are known as "yellow ware" and Liverpool ware, and are found in seaport towns on the Atlantic coast, especially in New England. Many bore mottoes, inscriptions, likenesses, and views relating to America and the celebrated Americans of the time, and thus form interesting mementos of the wars of the Revolution and of 1812. I have never seen a Liverpool pitcher in an inland country home, nor have I ever had one offered to me for sale in an inland town, either in a private home or an antique shop. The reasons for this are very simple : many of them were brought to America by Yankee sailors and sailing-masters who lived, as a rule, in seaport towns, and importations of these pitchers were not transported inland in ante-railroad days with the facility and safety that we find possible nowadays ; and, best reason of all, nine-tenths of them with their ornamentation of ships and brigs and ropes and anchors were made to tickle the fancy of a seafaring man, and did not appeal to the sentiment of a land-lubber of a farmer.

It is always a great delight to the inland-dwelling and novelty-seeking china hunter when she enters a low, single-storied seaside home, and spies on the mantelpiece a creamy Naval or Sailor pitcher flanked by a carved Indian idol and an elaborate model of the " Nimble Nine-pence," the " Belisarius," or the " Three Wives " (named by one stanch old widower after he was married to wife number four). Her joy is, as a rule, quickly turned to lamentation, for the housewife who values her Liverpool pitcher enough to place it on her parlor mantel, will never be " willing to part with it." And here let me render my thanks to the American merchant service. Blessings on those dead and gone old seafaring Yankees who risked their lives on the stormy seas and brought home " behind their wooden walls " the variety and wealth of china and crockery that have descended to us, a pathetic reminder of the weary watch on deck and the homesick hours in cabin or forecastle.

A few Liverpool plates with Masonic designs are found, and some teapots, but the majority of Liverpool ware that was imported to this country was in the form of mugs and what are known as " watermelon " pitchers. I know of one great yellow ware cheese-dish in Newport —a curious stand or frame in which a whole cheese two feet in diameter could be placed upright on its edge and thus served and cut on the table ; but such pieces are exceptional.

I am impressed when looking over the lists of sales and the catalogues of existing collections in England, that china collectors find in America more, cheaper, and more varied specimens of Liverpool wares, especially those bearing transfer prints, than can be found in England. They abound in American antique shops. Even the rarest and most interesting of all—prints on tiles, pitchers, and teapots bearing the mark of Sadler—are often discovered here. A whole set of Sadler's tiles was taken from an old colonial house in Newport.

Previous to the Revolutionary War no porcelain or pottery was made specially for America, or, at any rate, none with special designs; but after we became a separate nation the English potters made much china and crockery for the American market, and made patterns for individual purchasers as well. Washington and Franklin were the American names best known in England previous to the year 1800; and I have never seen Liverpool pieces that could be assigned to an earlier date of manufacture than 1800 that bore the names even of any other Revolutionary heroes or statesmen, except, possibly, two pitchers decorated with battle-scenes, which are entitled respectively, " Death of Warren " and " Death of Montgomery ; " a pitcher with a portrait of Adams, and one mug printed with the name and portrait of John Hancock. Englishmen had vague ideas of the names of our States as well, for Boston and "Tenasee" often appear on these wares in the list of the thirteen States.

The number of stars depicted upon the American

flag or shield on these and Staffordshire pieces is often held up as ample testimony to the date of the piece. Such reasoning is, of course, absurd. English engravers and potters were as ignorant about the number of States as they were about the names of the States, and might easily have given fifteen stars when there were only thirteen States, or clung to the number thirteen long after we had twenty States. I have seen several designs with the United States flag bearing twelve and even nine stars.

Many of these pitchers are decorated with designs relating to the character, life, and death of Washington, and such are known as Washington pitchers. A list of the prints upon these pitchers is given in Chapter XIII., devoted to the china commemorative of Washington. These pitchers bear portraits and sentiments, verses or inscriptions eulogizing the virtues and bravery of the "glorious American," or indicative of our national loss, and grief at his death. The lines, "Deafness to the ear that will patiently hear, and dumbness to the tongue that will utter a calumny against the immortal Washington," were much favored and printed by English potters, and were placed on pitchers and mugs of many sizes and shapes. The legend fails to tell, however, the awful fate which should fall on the hand which limned the senile, feeble, forlorn caricatures of the face of Washington which usually appear in company with the lines, and make us suspect intentional malice in the British artist. These absurd likenesses vary as much as did the canvas portraits of the Father of His Country at the recent

Centennial Loan Collection at the Metropolitan Opera House in New York, and in some cases bear no resemblance whatever to the well-known benign countenance,

An English Notion of Washington.

and are evidently a portrait of some English general falsely labelled Washington.

There is a print found on cream-colored teapots and plates and jugs that look like Liverpool ware, which is sometimes called "Washington and Martha Drinking Tea," by American dealers who assert that the two figures in the out-of-doors tea-party are intended for the

General and his "lady," as he called her. The man in this print certainly bears a marked though somewhat mincing likeness to our first President, while the fact that the servant who approaches with a teakettle is a negro, is offered as conclusive proof that the scene is laid in America; and indeed, I have seen one teapot upon which was pasted a paper label with the words, "Scene at Mount Vernon, George and Martha Washington Drinking Tea." Of course every china student, and indeed every person of art education, knows that the figures of negro servants appear in many English tea-party prints of that date, in such, for instance, as the watch-back of Battersea enamel engraved by Richard Hancock, of the Worcester China Works, and in the transfer prints by the same artist, shown on page 235, Vol. I., of Jewitt's "Ceramic Art in Great Britain." The pieces bearing this "George Washington" print that I have seen, bore no stamp to show the place of manufacture; but there is a tea-canister numbered G 252 in the Museum of Practical Geology, printed with this scene, which has the impressed mark "Wedgwood." It also has on the other side of the canister the same group of shepherds and sheep that I have seen on many pieces in America. I am afraid we cannot claim this as a Washington print. It was engraved when Washington was a struggling surveyor, when no Englishmen, and few Americans, even knew his name. Miss Meteyard says that this group is from one of Jenssen's printed enamels, and she gives an illustration of it on page 64, Vol. II., of her "Life of Wedgwood."

I only mention this among the Liverpool prints, and as possibly eligible to the Washington list, in order to prove (to make an Irish bull) that it is certainly not the one and probably not the other. It is quite as interesting, however, to the china collector (if not to the historical student or the relic hunter) as an example of Hancock's designs for transfer printing; and when one of these teapots is offered for $1.50 (as I have had one in a New York shop within a year), it is well for any collector to buy it.

I will say here that these cream-ware pitchers are not from Liverpool factories alone, they are from various Staffordshire potteries, but all cream-colored printed pitchers are generally known in America by the name of Liverpool ware. Some, of course, are unmistakably so, for they bear the various marks of the Herculaneum Pottery, or the figure of the bird which was the crest of the arms of Liverpool—the liver or lever. A special design or mark of the American eagle with the words " Herculaneum Pottery, Liverpool," seems to have been made for pieces intended for the American market, and often appears upon them.

The heroes and victories of the American navy form frequent decorations of the specimens of this printed pottery that are found in America. The first Naval pitchers bore the design of a ship or a frigate under full sail, with the American flag and the words, " Success to the Infant Navy of America." These were printed to commemorate Truxton's capture of the French frigates Insurgente and La Vengeance while he was commander of the Constellation during our little marine war with France in 1799. This capture was honored in a popular song called "Truxton's Victory," and was as great a source of delight to Englishmen as to Americans. Truxton received from England many tokens of esteem, including a service of silver plate worth over $3,000. Long and bitterly during the constant naval defeats of the English in the War of 1812 must those British merchants have regretted that silver token of encouragement to the American Navy. A gold medal was ordered by Congress to be struck in honor of this victory, as was also done in honor of each of the naval heroes of the war of 1812. And many pitchers and mugs were decorated with their portraits and names in order to commemorate their victories.

It seems odd that English potters should have made so many pitchers bearing testimony to the victories of their late enemies, unless they were ordered by American dealers specially for the American market; but I have never seen anything to prove that such orders were given.

Many pieces bear the portrait of Perry and the words of his famous dispatch, "We have met the enemy and they are ours." I never look at a Perry pitcher without thinking with interest and pleasure of this brave young captain, who was only twenty-seven years old when he achieved his famous victory. He fought the fierce naval battle clad in his sailor's suit, but changed at the last to his full-dress uniform in order to receive the surrendering English officer with full dignity. Nor do I ever see the jolly round face of Hull on pitcher or mug without thinking of his comical appearance during the naval battle between the Constitution and the Guerrière, in which he won such deserved honors. Hull was very fat, and being somewhat dandified wore very tight breeches. When, in that fierce contest, he gave his first roar of command to the gunners, " Now, boys, pour into them—Free Trade and Seamen's Rights ! " he bent over twice in his intense excitement and split his tight breeches from waistband to knee. He was more of a soldier than a dandy, however, for he finished the battle and captured the English ship in that " undress uniform."

Of course the pitchers decorated with American subjects are most interesting to Americans, but there are many other Liverpool pitchers found in New England, which bear, instead of American heroes and battles, such lines as these :

> " Dear Tom this brown jug
> Which now foams with new ale,
> Out of which I will drink
> To sweet Nan of the Vale."

Another has the jovial inscription, " One Pot more—and then—why then—Another Pot of course."

And this sharp warning is given to those who would wish to drink and not to pay :

> " Customers came and I did trust 'em,
> So I lost my money and my custom,
> And to lose both it grieves me sore,
> So I am resolved to trust no more."

A few pieces bear less decorous and elegant verses, such as the mug deriding the Established Church, labelled, " Tythe in Kind or the Sow's Revenge." A clergyman bent on collecting tithes is being attacked by a sow in a pigsty. The farmer's family are laughing while the parson is crying out :

> " The fattest pig it is my due ;
> Oh ! save me from the wicked sow."

Another pitcher has a fling at the Romish Church, for it bears a likeness of his Satanic Majesty and of a priest, with the words,

> " When Pope absolves
> The Devil smiles."

I have seen in America a number of drinking mugs of cream-colored ware, which may properly be spoken of here, though it is doubtful whether many of them were made in Liverpool. They have the raised figure of a toad or frog placed inside, with the pleasingly jocose intention of surprising and scaring the drinker, who would fancy as the ugly head rose out of the decreasing liquor that it was a real batrachian climbing up the side to jump down his throat. One of these mugs had the frog tinted a dull green and brown, entirely too natural and life-like in color to prove pleasant or appetizing. Another two-handled Frog mug was of coarse white ware, unpainted, and had an exceedingly modern look. This was probably Newcastle ware. The price asked for these in " antique shops " is usually three or four dollars apiece. I have seen none with mottoes as has the one numbered S 17, in the Museum of Practical Geology.

> " Though malt and venom
>   Seem united,
>   Don't break my pot
>   Nor be affrighted."

These Frog mugs are usually large in diameter, and are sometimes decorated externally with designs of ships or naval heroes. The frog's appearance in sight would then prove more effectually terrifying than if the drinker were warned by an instructive motto of the figured reptile within.

Another agreeable old English practical joke is in the shape of puzzle jugs, specimens of which exist in England, but have been rarely found in America. They were made in Liverpool and Staffordshire in the seventeenth and eighteenth century, and in salt-glazed stoneware at Nottingham in the eighteenth and nineteenth centuries. They were so constructed that when lifted to the lips they emptied by secret passages their liquid contents over the face and breast of the drinker. Sometimes there were three spouts from the rim. If the drinker covered two of the spouts with his fingers, he could drink from the third. This motto is on a puzzle jug of earthenware, of Liverpool make, in the collection of George M. Wales, Esq., of Boston :

> " Here, gentlemen, come try y^r skill ;
>   Ill hold a wager, if you will,
>   That you don't drink this liq^r all
>   Without you spill or let some fall."

Another rhyming inscription reads:

> " From mother earth I took my birth,
>   Then form'd a Jug by Man,
>   And now I stand here filled with good cheer—
>   Taste of me if you can."

Another short invitation reads:

> " This ale is good, taste."

And when you tasted, in good faith, you received a beery shower-bath, which was no doubt considered very funny by eighteenth-century Englishmen.

On another is written:

> " Mathew the V 16."

—not a very appropriate text-reference.

Still another rhyming challenge reads thus:

> "A Crown Ile bet
>   That None can get
>   The ale that's in this Jug,
>   Nor drink his fill
>   Without he spill
>   And shall not use a plug."

A puzzle jug in the possession of the Vintners' Company is in the shape of a milkmaid bearing a pail. The pail is set on a swivel, and when the drinker tries to swallow the liquor, the pail sends its contents over his chest.

Cream-ware pitchers bearing Masonic emblems are frequently found, usually having also the name of the person by whom they were ordered, or for whom they were

Masonic Pitcher.

made. These rather egotistical lines were prime favorites among these pitcher-buying Masons:

> "The world is in pain
>   Our Secret to gain,
>   But still let them wonder & gaze on,
> For they ne'er can divine
>   The word nor the sign
>   Of a Free and Accepted Mason."

Another much-used set of Masonic verses runs thus:

> "We help the poor in time of need
>   The naked cloath, the Hungry feed;

> 'Tis our Foundation stone.
> We build upon the noblest plan,
> Where Friendship rivets man to man
> And makes us all as one."

And a third:

> " To judge with candour and to speak no wrong,
> The feeble to support against the strong,
> To soothe the wretched and the poor to feed,
> Will cover many an idle, foolish deed."

Some of these Masonic pitchers are of enormous size, as if the buyers wished as much of a pitcher as possible for their money. Many of them were printed at the Worcester factory. I have also seen some fine designs that had been drawn with a pen by hand in mineral colors and then fired in. Pitchers and mugs of Chinese porcelain are also seen with decorations of Masonic emblems and mottoes.

Sailor pitchers are found in comparatively large numbers, with touching prints of a sailor bidding an affectionate farewell to his lass, under a flag and over an anchor, accompanied by such appropriate verses as the following:

> " When this you see
> Pray think of me
> And keep me in your mind;
> Let all the world
> Say what they will,
> Think of me as you find."

Or this legend, a misquotation from Charles Dibdin's song:

> " D'ye see a cherub sits smiling aloft
> To keep watch o'er the life of poor Jack."

This is often accompanied by the figure of a fat little cherub perched in the rigging of a ship. These Sailor pitchers were brought home frequently at the end of a voyage as gifts for a sweetheart or a wife, as is plainly seen by these verses printed with a picture called "The Sailor's Return":

> "I now the joys of Life renew
> From care and trouble free,
> And find a wife who's kind and true
> To drive life's cares away."

And also this tender sentiment:

> "The troubled main, the wind & rain,
> My ardent passion prove
> Lashed to the helm, should seas o'crwhelm
> I'll think on thee, my love."

Or these lines:

> "Kindly take this gift of mine,
> The gift and giver I hope is thine,
> And tho' the value is but small
> A loving heart is worth it all."

It is a curious fact that feminine owners are exceptionally unwilling "to part with" these Sailor pitchers. A halo of past romance, of sentimental fancy, surrounds the yellow-ware love token that "Uncle Eben brought from Injy to Aunt Hannah," or "my grandpa got painted in Chiny for my grandma when he was courtin' her" (for even these staidly sombre English pitchers are gloriously Oriental in country owners' eyes). This latent longing for sentiment, this tender sympathy with youthful love and affection, lies hidden deep in every woman's heart, no matter what her age; and, in the dull, repressed life of many New England homes, finds expression in a stolid clinging to the only visible token of a love and lovers long since dead. One stout old woman, with calm face but suspiciously shaky voice and hands, brought out for our admiring view, in company with a crimson silk crêpe shawl, a pair of small Liverpool pitchers printed with a spirited marine view of a full-rigged ship, the names John Daggett and Eliza Maxom, and this doggerel rhyme:

> " No more I'll roam,
> I'll stay at home,
> To sail no more
> From shore to shore,
> But with my wife
> Lead a happy, peaceful life."

"Who gave you them pretty picture pitchers, Grandma?" said the little child who was clinging to her skirts. " John Daggett ordered 'em painted for him an' me in Liverpool on the last trip he ever went on. He was the han'somest man ye ever see! He died on the v'yage home, an' yer Granpa, he was a-seafarin' then, he stopped an' got 'em on the way back, an' brought 'em home ter me." Alas! poor John Daggett! your thoughtful gifts of love furnished forth another wedding-feast with the considerate sailor-companion as groom and comforter. But though passed to " a happy, peaceful life " on a far-distant shore, you are not forgotten, but through the reminiscent power of your last gift, live a tender idealized memory, a dream of eternal unchanging youth and beauty, in your dear lass's thoughts. Your two Liverpool pitchers have never been thoughtlessly or carelessly used in your shipmate's, in "Grandpa's," home; they have lain for half a century unscratched, unnicked, unbroken, true cinerary urns of vanished hopes and promises, wrapped in the crimson crêpe shawl in the deep drawer of a high chest in your old sweetheart's "spareroom."

In this case we encountered a sentiment which we have met more than once—a willingness on the part of the owner, when she found we admired the piece, to let us have it, since we would cherish it safe and unharmed, rather than to give it or leave it to relatives who had openly derided it or called it a worthless old thing. As this New England sentimentalist expressed it, while she slowly folded the shawl around the beloved pitchers, " I'd almost ruther let ye have 'em, ye seem to set such store by 'em, than ter leave 'em ter Asa's wife, she aint brought up the children extry careful, an' I know they'd smash 'em in no time, or put 'em in hot water or knock the nose off. Come again next year an' I'll think it over, I hate ter part with 'em just yet after I've kep' 'em fer fifty-two year an' three months, but I'll see."

Various prints that are of more interest to Englishmen than to Americans are seen on these Liverpool pitchers; such is the view on the large mug owned by an old Newport resident, which bears the inscription, " An East View of Liverpool Lighthouse and Signals on Bilston Hill, 1788." In the centre of the design is a lighthouse with forty-four signals around it. Each signal is numbered, and below is a key with the names of the vessels and their owners. This print also occurs on plates. In the days before the telegraph Liverpool merchants were wont to go down to the riverside, about two or three hours before high tide, to see whether there were any flags hoisted on the lighthouse poles, as was always done when a vessel came in sight. Thus were owners notified a few hours in advance of the approach of their craft to port.

Another mug owned by the same gentleman has a map with a caricature of Napoleon Bonaparte standing with one foot on Germany. The other foot, having been placed on England, has been cut off by John Bull, who says, " I ax pardon, Master Boney, but, as we say, Pares of Pompey, we keep this spot to ourselves. You must not dance here, Master Boney." Napoleon is saying, " You tam John Bull, you have spoil my dance, you have ruin my projects." A second Bonaparte mug has a red print of John Bull sitting upon a pedestal, inscribed " The British Constitution." He looks across the Channel at Napoleon, who is weeping and crying out, " O ! my poor Crazy Gun Boats, why did I venture so far from home," while John Bull says, " I told you they would all be swamp'd, but you would be so Damned Obstinate." The inscription is " Patience on a Monument smiling at Grief," with this distich :

> " The Mighty Chief with fifty thousand Men
> Marched to the Coast and March'd back again.
> Ha ! Ha ! Ha ! "

A third Bonaparte mug is thus described in *Notes and Queries* :

" Under a trophy of arms are figures of John Bull and Napoleon. John Bull is in the act of striking his opponent with his right fist a severe blow on the nose ; the nether end of Napoleon is at the same time in collision with sturdy John Bull's left boot. Inscription, ' See here John Bull drubbing Bonaparte ! ' On either side of the picture we have,

' What ! to conquer all England how dares he pretend,
   This ambitious but vain undertaker,
When he knows to his cost that where Britons defend,
   He's unable to conquer one Acre ! '

' If your beggarly soldiers come among us, they'll soon have enough of it ; and, damn·me, if any ten of you shall have my person or property—so be off ! ' ' Damn ye ! you black-hearted, treacherous Corsican ! if you were not such a little bit of a fellow in spite of your large cocked hat, I'd crack your skull in an instant with my fist.' "

Another bears these short and pointed lines :

" May England's oak
Produce the bark
To tan the hide
Of Bonaparte,"

which, though shaky in rhyme, are certainly more effective than the illiterate, profane, and overlong inscriptions on other Bonaparte mugs.

A well-engraved and well-designed Liverpool print is that of " The Farmers' Arms," with armorial design ingeniously formed of hay-rakes, scythes, flails, ploughs, churns, sickles, etc., the mottoes being "In God we Trust," and "Industry produceth Wealth." On the other side are these verses :

> " May the mighty and great
> Roll in splendor and state,
> I envy them not, I declare it,
> I eat my own Lamb,
> My own chicken and ham,
> I shear my own sheep and I wear it.
> I have lawns, I have Bowers,
> I have Fruits, I have Flowers,
> The Lark is my morning Alarmer ;
> So you Jolly Dogs now,
> Here's God bless the plow—
> Long life and content to the Farmer."

One of these really artistic Farmer pitchers with this inscription and design sold at an auction in New York for only seven dollars and a half, in spite of the catalogue's alluring description of its "having once belonged to Robert Burns." A similar one, numbered S 32, is in the Museum of Practical Geology in London, and is also described in Mayer's " Art of Pottery and History of its Progress in Liverpool."

Besides the design of the " Farmers' Arms " is found that of the " Blacksmiths' Arms," with the motto " By Hammer and Hand all Arts do Stand ; " the " Bucks' Arms," with stag and huntsmen, and the motto " Freedom with Innocence ; " the " Bakers' Arms," and the motto, " Praise God for All ; " the " Hatters' Arms," with the motto, " We Assist Each Other in Time of Need."

Many of these Liverpool pitchers have an individual interest connected with their original manufacture. They were the favorite expression of respect of ships crews to their commanders, of workmen to their employers. Such is the beautiful pitcher owned by A. M. Prentiss, Esq., bearing the motto, "Success to Henry Prentiss and his Employ, 1789" Henry Prentiss was a Revolutionary hero, a member of the Tea Party, a wealthy Boston merchant, a large cotton manufacturer, a successful horticulturist, a man whose name brings to old residents of Boston and Cambridge the memory of many a story of his shrewdness and intelligence.

S. Yendell, great-grandfather of the present Governor of Massachusetts, was similarly honored by a mammoth presentation pitcher, which is owned by Mrs. Russel, of Cambridge. It bears a print of the Columbia, on which ship Mr. Yendell sailed on the famous voyage when the Columbia River was discovered, in 1791. That does not seem very long ago! Mr. Yendell lived till 1867. To be sure, he was then the oldest man in Boston, ninety-seven years of age.

The art of transfer-printing on pottery and porcelain, by which all these pieces are decorated, has completely revolutionized the business of china-decoration in England, and cheapened the price of decorated crockery, as did the invention of types and printing cheapen and multiply books. John Sadler, who invented the process of transfer-printing, was originally an engraver. He had his attention first called to the possibility and desirability of china-printing by a very trifling incident

—by seeing some children when playing "doll's house" paste on broken pieces of crockery, pictures cut from waste-paper prints which he had thrown away.

For years he and his partner, Guy Green, managed to keep his invention enough of a secret, so that he printed not only for Liverpool works, but for many others. Much of the Wedgwood Queens-ware was stamped by him, being made at the Wedgwood factory, carried in wagons over bad roads to Liverpool, and, after being printed, returned in the same manner to Burslem to be fired. In spite of all this manipulation and transportation it could be sold cheaply, for Sadler's tariff of prices for transfer-printing was very low. "For printing a table and tea service of two hundred and fifty pieces for David Garrick, £8 6s. 1½d. Twenty-five dozen half-tiles printing and colouring, £1 5s." These printed half-tiles were sold for 2s. 6d. a dozen, while the black printed whole tiles brought only 5s. a dozen.

Sadler's process was very simple. He printed on paper with an ordinary copper or steel plate, then laid the print while wet on the glazed piece of pottery. Then, upon pressing it, the ink was transferred to the pottery piece, and afterward burnt in. Nearly all these wares were printed in black, but some have the prints in blue, and some in vermilion. Others, printed in black outlines, are filled in by hand with various colors, sometimes with very good effect.

Hancock and Holdship followed quickly in Sadler's wake, in printing on pottery and porcelain in Worcester, and there bat-printing was introduced at a later date.

In this process linseed-oil was used instead of ink, and the oil design was printed on a "bat," or sheet of prepared glue and treacle, which, being pliable, adapted itself readily to the shape of the pottery article to be printed, and transferred to it the oil lines of the design. Powdered color was dusted on these oil lines, the superfluous color being removed by cotton wool, and then fired in. Engravings for bat-printing were usually in stipple work, and the prints can readily be recognized and distinguished from those of transfer-printing.

It is interesting to us to know that an American who seemed to have a hand in every invention of his day, had also his little share in the suggestion, if not in the discovery, of printing upon pottery and porcelain. Benjamin Franklin wrote thus from London, November 3, 1773, to some unknown person :

"I was much pleased with the specimens you so kindly sent me of your new art of engraving. That on the china is admirable. No one would suppose it anything but painting. I hope you meet with all the encouragement you merit, and that the invention will be what inventions seldom are, profitable to the inventor. Now, we are speaking of inventions, I know not who pretends to that of copper-plate engraving for earthen ware, and I am not disposed to contest the honor with anybody, as the improvement in taking impressions not directly from the plate, but from printed paper, applicable by that means to other than flat forms, is far beyond my first idea. But I have reason to apprehend that I might have given the hint on which that improvement was made ; for, more than twenty years since, I wrote to Dr. Mitchell from America proposing to him the printing of square tiles for ornamenting chimneys, from copper-plates, describing the manner in which I thought it might be done, and advising the borrowing from the booksellers the plates that had been used in a thin folio called 'Moral Virtue Delineated,' for that purpose. The Dutch Delft-ware tiles were much used in America, which are only or chiefly Scripture histories wretchedly scrawled. I wished to have those moral prints, which were originally taken from Horace's poetical figures, introduced in tiles, which, being about our chimneys are constantly in the eyes of the children when by the fireside, might give parents an opportunity in explaining them to express moral sentiments, and I gave expectations of great demands for them if executed. Dr. Mitchell wrote me in answer that he had communicated my scheme to several of the artists in the earthen way about London, who rejected it as impracticable ; and it was not till some years after that I first saw an enamelled snuff-box, which I was sure was from a copper-plate, though the curvature of the form made me wonder how the impression was taken."

Sadly and deprecatingly must " Poor Richard " have examined the printed tiles of John Sadler, for no "moral virtues delineated " thereon are depicted. He found, instead, the representation of such trivial and unmoral pastimes as dancing, beer-drinking, pipe-smoking, fortune-telling—the latter design being of an astrologer seated at a table telling the fortunes of two young women. One fair maid smiles with delighted anticipation as she receives a paper of prophecy inscribed " A brisk husband and son," while the other poor creature is departing, shedding bitter tears of disappointment, with a similar paper bearing the depressing words, " Never to be married." American children doubtless lost much desirable and laudable parental instruction when Franklin's worthy scheme failed in execution, but they were also spared many a fireside lecture and nagging. How they would have come to hate the sight of those moral lesson tiles !

And while I am speaking of transfer-printing, let me call attention to some pretty little ceramic relics of a quaint old-time fashion, that are sometimes overlooked by collectors—" mirror-knobs "—" Lookeing Glasse Nobs " I find them called in ante-Revolutionary advertisements. These knobs consisted usually of a painted or printed medallion, frequently enamelled on the metal, or on little oval porcelain placques or discs, which were then fastened in brass, gilt or silvered frames, and mounted on a long and strong screw or spike. Two of these knobs were screwed into the wall about a foot apart, so that the oval-framed medallions stood out two or three inches from the wall. The lower edge of a mirror or picture frame was allowed to rest on the iron screws behind these two ornamental heads. These mirror-knobs were also used to fasten back window curtains. The head of the mirror-knob was usually decorated by the process of transfer-printing ; sentimental views of shepherds and shepherdesses, mincing heads of powdered French dames,

and unintentionally funny likenesses of many of our
Revolutionary heroes and statesmen. The portrait of
Washington which was employed was fairly good ; of
Franklin in the fur-cap, quite well drawn; but the others
that I have seen vied with one another in comical ugliness, save that of John Jay, always too fine in feature to
be caricatured. In the Huntington collection in the
Metropolitan Museum of Art, in New York, may be
seen a few of these mirror-knobs with portraits of Franklin, John Jay, C. Thompson, W. H. Drayton, John Dickinson, S. Huntington, Major-General Gaines, and an exceptionally ugly one of H. Laurens, with a phenome-
nally attenuated neck, a mere bone of a neck. Often
these little printed miniatures are in black and white,
but more frequently they are printed in outline, and
faintly and delicately colored. I wish I knew where
they were made, and who ordered them and imported
and sold them, and who drew them. I think that they
were made in Worcester, not in Liverpool. Aged country people tantalizingly tell me of mirror-knobs made
of discs with white raised heads and figures on blue
grounds—Wedgwood medallions, were they not ? But
they have all vanished from my ken, even the printed
knobs are now seldom seen. I know one drawer of an
old dressing-case in quiet Hadley town that holds fifteen beautiful mirror-knobs, all whole, uncracked, unscratched ; but you will never see them nor buy them.
You might steal them, perhaps, if you only knew which
elm-shaded house contained them—you might steal the
whole dressing-case, indeed, if you were only quiet about

it, and you might walk the entire mile and a half of the beautiful main street with the stolen furniture on your back and meet not a soul to question or wonder.

Of the same class and decoration and of the same materials were many dainty snuff-boxes and patch-boxes that were made and used in England and imported to America. The latter pretty trinkets were tiny oval or round boxes about an inch and a half or two inches in diameter, frequently made of fine Battersea enamel, or of china medallions set in silver or gilt frames. Within the lid was always found a little mirror, usually of polished steel, in which the fair owner might peep to freshly set or rearrange her coquettish patches. One patch-box I have bears this motto on the top :

> " Have Communion with few,
>   Be familiar with one,
>   Deal Justly with all,
>   Speak evil of None."

Another has a more frivolous verse :

> " Within this Beauty views her face
>   And with the patch gives added grace."

Still another :

> " Love and Beauty conquer all,
>   Love to Beauty."

Sometimes, as with the mirror-knobs, a little painting of shepherds and shepherdesses is set in the lid, and, with the jewelled and enamelled border, form a trifle dainty enough to rival any modern bonbonnières. These patch-boxes and "Gum Patches," or "Patches for ladies," or "Face Patches," were advertised freely in American newspapers for many years previous to the Revolution—as early, surely, as 1750 in the *Boston Evening Post ;* and patches were universally worn by American beauties, as Whitefield and other pious travellers sadly deplored. "China Snuff Boxes" were offered for sale in the *Boston Evening Post* of April 16, 1773, were bought and filled with Kippen's snuff, were lost on Boston streets, were advertised for reward in Boston papers, and no doubt proudly and ostentatiously carried by Boston beaux, as well as by Charleston macaronis. A few snuff-boxes of Battersea enamel still remain to show us how lovely they were, but the frail china ones have nearly all been destroyed, and when still existing are usually sadly cracked and disfigured. China and Battersea enamel "tooth-pick cases" were also imported and carried by Boston beaux.

But we must leave these dainty quaint trinkets and go back to the far less beautiful Liverpool pitchers. Though they have no great charm of color, shape, or design, and are, in fact, the least graceful and beautiful of all the old English wares commonly found in America, all the historical pitchers must certainly be of great interest to students of American history, as records and relics of the early days of the United States. As new pieces bearing hitherto unknown designs are constantly being found, they will form, in fact do now form, with the old blue Staffordshire plates, a valuable and lasting ceramic record of the early days of our nation.

Let us hope that they will be carefully preserved by all who are fortunate enough to own them; and, if they are not placed in the safe keeping of museums or cabinet collections, at least be kept from the debasing uses and positions in which I have seen them in country homes. My patriotic heart has thrilled with wounded indignation to see mugs and pitchers bearing such honored and venerated names and faces, battered, nicked, and handle-less, despitefully used to hold herb-teas, soft-soap, horse-liniment, or tooth-brushes. I saw one Washington pitcher, noseless and fairly crenated with nicks, shame-fully degraded to use as a jug to carry to the hen-house the hot water with which to prepare the chicken-food; while another contained a villainous-looking purple-black liquid compound which the owner explained was "Pa's hair-restorer." In spite of careless use, however, many specimens still exist, for "antique" dealers find them for their shops. In one Newport bric-a-brac shop I saw, in the summer of 1891, at least fifteen Liverpool pitchers varying in price from five dollars for a small Sailor pitcher to thirty-five dollars for a fine perfect Apotheosis Pitcher.

Fortunate is the household, and happy and proud should be its members, that possesses one of these historic relics. I know of no better way to impress upon a child, or to recall to a grown person, the lesson of bravery, courage, and love of country, than by showing him the likenesses of Perry, Decatur, and Lawrence on mug or pitcher, and telling to him their story, and reading or reciting the old ballads and songs written about them.

Nor do I know of any more noble example of Christian piety than that of the brave Macdonough, whose name is so often seen on these pieces of old English ware. Before the battle of Lake Champlain, when the deck of the Saratoga was cleared for action, he knelt upon the deck with his officers and men around him, asked Almighty God for aid, and committed the issue of the contest into His hands. Let us echo the toast which was given to him at a large dinner in Plattsburg, shortly after his victory. "The pious and brave Macdonough, the professor of the religion of the Redeemer—preparing for action, he called on God, who forsook him not in the hour of danger. *May he not be forgotten by his country.*"

Let our respect and affection for our ancestors' adored heroes save to our descendants the Liverpool pitchers bearing such honored historical names.

VIII.

ORIENTAL CHINA

IN that delightful and much-quoted book, "The China Hunters' Club," the final chapter is devoted to a most humorous description of the disbandment and ignominious extinction of the club through a fierce quarrel over a disputed piece of china—whether it were Chinese or Lowestoft. Could I, as did Charlie Baker in that story, label both my china of like character and his chapter "Canton-Lowestoft," it would fitly express my feelings when I attempt to judge and write upon the old pieces of hard paste porcelain, so common in America, called Oriental, Canton, India, or Lowestoft, according to the belief or traditions of each individual owner. I cannot give any positive rules by which to classify this china, nor any by which to judge of independent specimens. If I followed my own convictions and my own researches on this puzzling subject, I should in ninety-nine cases out of a hundred firmly state the disputed piece of porcelain to be Chinese, and I could quote in support of my views such an authority as Franks, the great china collector, who says that,

"India china (that is, china made for the East India Company for European trade—what Jacquemart calls *porcelaine des Indes*) has on one hand been attributed to

Japan, and on the other, by a still more singular hallu-cination been ascribed to Lowestoft."

He also says, " There can be no doubt that there was a considerable manufactory of porcelain at Lowestoft, but this was of the usual English soft-paste. The evidence of hard-paste having been made there is of the most slender kind."

Mr. Owens, in his "Two Centuries of Ceramic Art in Bristol," says, with decision :

" There cannot be any doubt that hard porcelain, vitrified and translucent, was never manufactured from the raw materials, native kaolin and petunste, at any other locality in England than Plymouth and Bristol. The tradition that such ware was made at Lowestoft in 1775 rests upon evidence too slight to be worthy of argument. The East India Company imported into England large quantities of porcelain for sale; and in the provincial journals of the last century advertisements of sales by auction of East India china occur frequently. This particular ware, which is very plentiful, even at the present day, and which has of late acquired the reputation of having been made at Lowestoft, was simply, in form and ornamentation, only a reproduction by the Chinese of English earthenware models. The Chinese do not use saucers, butter-boats, and numbers of other articles after the European fashion, and the agents in China were compelled to furnish a model for every piece of ware ordered. These models the Asiatic workmen have copied only too faithfully. The ill-drawn roses, the coarsely-painted baskets of flowers, the rude borders of lines and dots are literally copied from the inartistic painting on the English earthenware of by-gone days."

He also says, " It is painful to see in public and private collections examples of Oriental ware · labelled Lowestoft, simply because, though hard porcelain, they bear English armorial coats and initials. Many porcelain punch-bowls are to be found in sea-port towns with names and portraits of ships and very early dates. Those bowls are often attributed to the works at Liverpool and Lowestoft. The officers of the East India Company's ships were accustomed to take out English Delft bowls and get them reproduced in common porcelain in China for their merchant friends, and many a relic now prized as of home manufacture was procured in this manner."

Mr. Prime writes more cautiously, after describing the pieces :

" These are supposed to have been made on special patterns furnished to the Oriental factories by the East India Company. They resemble European work in the decoration, and many of the Lowestoft paintings seem to be imitations of these. It is, therefore, necessary to be very cautious in classifying wares as of Lowestoft fabric."

And again he says, " The presence of a single decoration like a flower or sprig of flowers in European style on porcelain is not a sufficient reason for classing the porcelain as European. Many such pieces were printed in Japan and in China. And others are possibly the work of decorators in Holland."

Mr. Elliott says of Lowestoft in America:

"It seems certain that this kind of decoration was done at Lowestoft; it is equally certain that it was also done in China, from designs sent out there. I have myself seen pieces so decorated which were imported direct from China to New Haven about the end of the last century."

On the other hand, that standard authority, Mr. Chaffers, author of "Marks and Monograms," says that "the question about hard-paste porcelain having been made at Lowestoft is placed beyond dispute upon the best authority. It was introduced about 1773," and he offers a mass of testimony to prove his statements.

Mr. Owens fancies that sailing-masters took out English Delft bowls to be reproduced in China; Mr. Marryatt and Mr. Franks, that Chinese porcelain was imported to Holland and painted in Delft; another collector believes that Chinese kaolin and clay were brought to Lowestoft, and there mixed, shaped, fired and painted; and still another, that Lowestoft porcelain was taken out to China to be decorated. The Catalogue of the Museum of Practical Geology in London very shrewdly and non-responsibly says of its Lowestoft specimens: "It should be understood that several of the following pieces are exhibited as 'Lowestoft china' simply in deference to the opinions of certain collectors and not as authenticated specimens."

To show the doubtful eyes with which the Lowestoft aspirants are regarded by authorities in England, I will state that in this last-mentioned catalogue but twelve lots of Lowestoft porcelain and pottery are named—a small proportion—and a sharp lesson to American collectors with their reckless and sweeping Lowestoft classifications. None of the twelve bear any distinguishing Lowestoft marks or names. The descriptions of some of these are not at all like our American Lowestoft wares. One reads : "Two plates ornamented with borders in brown and gold, and with views of a Suffolk village and river painted in sepia in a circular panel in centre of each plate."

From these few extracts which I have taken from various authorities, it is plainly seen that no decision, no judgment can be given in this Lowestoft case, that each seeker after china and truth must judge for himself.

The history of the production of hard-paste china at Lowestoft is exceedingly curious as an example and proof of the suddenness with which recent facts and circumstances may be forgotten. It seems fairly incredible that the true particulars of the manufacture of this ware (which it is alleged was produced in such great quantities from the year 1775 to 1803) should be entirely lost and forgotten in half a century's time. The descriptions and history of Lowestoft china in Mr. Llewellyn Jewitt's article in the July number of the *London Art Journal* in 1863, were the first to call attention to Lowestoft china, and I still consider him the best and most trustworthy authority on the subject. Previous to that time, in the catalogues of English Loan Collections and Museums, the name even of Lowestoft does not appear, though the ware was seen everywhere labelled vaguely "Foreign," or "Oriental." At a later date Mr. Chaffers's book appeared with a warm endorsement and enthusiastic setting-forth of the Lowestoft factory and its wares, so warm and embracing in its description that Mr. Jewitt in his later book, "Ceramic Art in Great Britain," fairly has to protest against such broad sweeping into the Lowestoft net; and he must feel that he "builded better than he knew" when he "wrote up" the Lowestoft factory. He says : "Let me utter a word or two of caution to collectors against placing too implicit a reliance upon what has been written concerning Lowestoft china, and against taking for granted that all which is nowadays called Lowestoft china is really the production of that manufactory. If all that is ascribed to Lowestoft was ever made there the works must have been the most extensive, and—if all the varieties of wares that are now said to have been produced there were made it is asserted simultaneously—the most extraordinary on record. The great bulk of the specimens now unblushingly ascribed to Lowestoft I believe never were in that town, much less ever made there."

When Mr. Jewitt wrote thus he knew nothing about the vast additional stock of Lowestoft in America, enough additional weight to swamp forever the Lowestoft pretensions. Mr. Jewitt also resented with proper indignation some criticisms which Mr. Chaffers dared to make upon his *Art Journal* paper, saying, with truth, that he (Chaffers) was indebted to him for nearly every scrap of information about the Lowestoft factory that he has embodied in his work. He might say for every scrap of any importance. The three accounts form a typical example of the controversies in private life, of the minor disputes that always arise among china collectors, not only over the claims of the Lowestoft factory, but over even a single piece of Lowestoft hard-paste porcelain.

The specimens of what are called Lowestoft ware that are most frequently seen in America, are parts of tea-services, punch-bowls and pitchers, coffee-pots and mugs. The pieces often bear crests, coats of arms, or initials. Shields supported with birds, and escutcheons in dark blue are also frequent. The initials are usually very gracefully interlaced. Sometimes the tea-caddy will bear the crest or coat of arms with the initials, while the remainder of the tea-service will have the initials only.

On many of the pieces the border is of clear cobalt blue (often in rich enamel), varied with gold stars or a meander pattern in gold. Some unreasoning collectors take their stand upon this blue and gold-starred border as being the only positive indication and proof to their minds that the piece thus decorated is truly Lowestoft ; but I have seen many pieces that were positively imported directly from China to America that bore this Lowestoft border. A red trellis-border and a peculiar russet-brown or chocolate border also abound on these disputed pieces, and the scale pattern in purplish pink. A raised border of vine-leaves, grapes, flowers and squirrels is seen on the beakers ; I have found both this form and decoration rare in America.

When a flower pattern appears on Lowestoft china the rose predominates. Chaffers says that the reason for this use of the rose is twofold; the arms of the English borough in which the china is said to have been manufactured or painted, is the Tudor, or full-blown rose surmounted by an open crown; and the cleverest painter of Lowestoft ware was Thomas Rose, and he thus commemorated his name. He was a French refugee, and it is to his French taste we owe the delicate style of whatever flower ornamentation appears on this china. It is sad to read that he became blind and spent the last days of his life as a water-vender, plying his trade with two donkeys that had been given him by the town. The pieces alleged to have been painted by him, and indeed all the Lowestoft pieces, were seldom profuse in decoration. Roses without foliage or stems, little bouquets, or narrow festoons of tiny roses with green leaves, were his favorite designs. Often a piece bore only a single rose.

The mugs and tea and coffee pots usually have twisted or double handles crossed and fastened to the main body of the piece with raised leaves or flowers. The large pieces, such as punch-bowls and pitchers and the helmet creamers, sometimes have an irregular surface, as if, when in the paste, they had been patted into shape by the hands. I have often seen this appearance also on blue and white undoubted Chinese ware. The mugs are both cylindrical and barrel-shaped; the cups are handleless, as are usually the cups of all Oriental china manufactured at that date.

Mr. Chaffers says that occasionally the smaller pieces of Lowestoft will be seen embossed with the rice pattern or basket work. I have never seen a piece thus embossed but was as plainly and unmistakably Oriental as a Chinaman's pigtail and his almond eyes.

The oval teapot shown on page 208 is a typical Lowestoft piece, though not a choice one; and by many ignorant collectors all teapots of that particular shape, with twisted handles held to the body with embossed leaves, no matter with what other decoration, are firmly assigned to the Lowestoft factory. Many unmistakably Chinese pieces, however, are seen in this exact shape; for instance, a beautiful rice-pattern teapot in the Avery Collection, in the Metropolitan Museum of Art. This piece is rich in gold and blue, but has the knobs, twisted handles, and embossed leaves of the Lowestoft pattern. Perhaps, in spite of its Chinese rice-pattern, and the quality of the paste, Chaffers would class it as Lowestoft.

There are found in America certain Oriental vases of typical Lowestoft decoration which are usually in one or the other of two shapes, cylindrical with suddenly flaring top (or rarely an ovoid cylinder with similar top), or a vase with small base, sharply bulging out at half its height, and as suddenly contracting to a small neck. These vases, in sets or garnitures of three or five pieces, the two end vases always alike, graced the mantel of many a "parlour" a century ago, and were frequently decorated with initials or coats of arms. Such are the beautifully-shaped vases with exquisite blue, brown, and gold decoration, given by Lafayette to Cadwallader Jones of Petersburg, Va., one of which is here shown. These vases exhibit the impressed basket-work design;

Lowestoft Vase.

they are in perfect preservation, and have recently come by gift into the possession of the Washington Association of New Jersey.

There are in English collections a few specimens of the early soft-paste Lowestoft manufactures, which were always decorated in blue, which bear Lowestoft names or distinguishing dates. Indeed, these blue and white pieces are the only ones that do have designating Lowestoft marks, or bear dates, which seems to me a very significant fact. I have never found any of these blue and white Lowestoft pieces in America, either marked or unmarked, nor do I know of any marked Lowestoft pieces in any American collection. There are none in the Trumbull-Prime Collection. I have seen a few rather coarse blue and white Delft-ware pieces which I suspect might be classed as Lowestoft.

I fear that in this attempt to throw light, or rather borrow light, on the Lowestoft question, I have not succeeded very well, and have perhaps cast a deeper shadow. There is one other condition which has influenced and helped me to form my condition of mind about Low-estoft china, and that is the situation of the town. It is the absolute " Land's end," the extreme eastern point of England; the sand and some of the clay necessary to make all this porcelain would have had to be trans-ported from the extreme western " Land's end" of Corn-wall, and the great supply of coal to burn in the kilns, from the extreme northern coast of Northumberland and Durham—two most inconvenient and expensive contingencies. It was, however, near to Holland, that great producer of Delft-ware, and had an extensive trade with that country, and Dutch vessels constantly entered the Lowestoft port. And the first productions —the only marked and dated ones—are all blue and white and resemble Delft-ware : none are of porcelain. The Dutch also were great importers of Oriental china. Of course we must believe that some china also came out of Lowestoft, but these are some of the very be-wildering accompanying conditions that we cannot crowd out of our minds.

It is difficult to assign prices or values to pieces of Lowestoft china, for, as in other wares, the quality of the decoration, of course, influences the price. Tea-pots similar to the one shown on page 208 are often offered for from four to eight dollars—one sold in the Governor Lyon sale in 1876 for $5. At that same sale Lowestoft plates of ordinary design, with single rose decoration, brought $1.50 each; cups and saucers of similar design, the same price. A pretty dish of gold and buff, with brownish bird in the centre, brought $3.

A helmet creamer, with decoration of grapes and vines in gold and brown, brought $4 ; this is a decoration and shape frequently seen in America. One bearing the Morse coat of arms is here shown. One very curious piece, a custard - cup belonging to a "marriage set," sold for $6.50. This cup was decorated with festoons and bunches of roses, and on one side was a hand holding two medallions, with initials, t i e d together with a lovers' knot

Helmet Creamer.

of ribbon, with the motto "Unit." On the other side were two coats of arms held and supported in the same manner. It is said that this idea of a marriage set was in high fashion a hundred years ago. At the S. L. M. Barlow sale in New York, in February, 1890, the prices of Lowestoft pieces were higher—partly because the specimens were better. A sugar box with blue and gold ribbon decoration sold for $5, teapots for $8 and $10.

A device found on Lowestoft pieces is very common in America—or at any rate, in New England—and is frequently and erroneously supposed to be an armorial bearing. It is a monogram or cipher written within an oval or an escutcheon, backed by an ermine mantle, surmounted by a wreath on which are perched a pair of doves. This device was doubtless sent to China to be painted on a service as a wedding gift, and proving popular was often repeated. I have seen it on many pieces in many families, in gold and various colors, the monogram or initial only being different. A letter is in existence, written by a gentleman in China in 1810, to a fair bride in Hartford, saying that he sends to her as a wedding gift a set of porcelain with this decoration. Portions of the set are still owned by the bride's descendants. This of course proves the device to have been painted in China. Perhaps it was painted in England also, but I doubt it.

There is a very pretty Lowestoft design which I have seen upon dinner- and tea-sets belonging to several families in New England, which may have been made specially for the American market, or at any rate must have been sent here in large quantities. It consists of the American shield and eagle in shades of brown touched with gold, with a pretty delicate border of the same colors, and tiny dots of vermilion. I speak specially of this design because it is often offered for sale as " George Washington's China," on the slight foundation, I suppose, of having upon it an American shield and eagle; and not only offered but sold, and no doubt exhibited with pride by collectors of Washingtoniana. One lucky dog of a relic-hunter recently secured in New York a "Washington" teapot with this design for the sum of $75 — a paltry amount, as he considered it. There are a number of pieces bearing this decoration in the Trumbull - Prime Collection, a portion of a set belonging to a member of Mr. Prime's family. A coffeepot of the set is here shown. This service was purchased in England in 1804. The gilt lettering on it, as on others that I have seen, is much worn, while the decoration is in perfect condition.

"Washington" Coffee-pot.

As an indication of the vast amount of Lowestoft wares to be found in America, let me state that in the Governor Lyon sale there were forty-nine lots labelled Lowestoft, and many more among the historical pieces, while there were only six of Delft, three of Bristol, five of Chelsea, etc. As Governor Lyon collected nearly all his pieces of English porcelain in America this might be thought to be a fair means of judging of the proportionate prevalence of china called Lowestoft, but I think the number is hardly high enough. In the Trumbull-Prime Collection are at least a hundred and fifty pieces of Lowestoft, to which, however, Mr. Prime does not definitely assign that title, but explains the doubts and questions as to the ware. There are no rice-pattern or basket-work pieces among them.

In New England seaport towns, where there has been during past years a large direct trade with China, vast quantities of Lowestoft ware are found. It would, of course, be argued from this fact that such porcelain is Chinese, and in truth it is Chinese in nine cases out of ten. And I presume the reason that I am so incredulous about Lowestoft china, is that I have really seen so little, my Lowestoft studies having probably all been in Chinese porcelain. Then, too, the Lowestoft factory, had it sent all its wares direct to America, could never have furnished our vast supply, from which we still have plenty of specimens to dispute and quarrel over.

And is it not strange that we have no record of this vast trade in English porcelain? Who ever knew of a vessel arriving in an American port from Lowestoft? Who ever saw an advertisement of Lowestoft china in an old American newspaper? On the other hand, we know well how Chinese porcelain could have been brought —nay, was brought—in vast quantities to New England; for though New York took the lead in sending a single ship direct to Canton in 1784, the question of the China trade had been agitating Salem for a year previously, and in Connecticut, state aid had been asked to further direct commerce with the Orient. This aid had been at once refused by the prudent home-staying farmers in the Legislature. Providence, Newport, and Boston quickly awakened to the rich possibilities of the new commercial opening with the Orient, but Elias Haskett Derby, of Salem, known as the "Father of the East India Trade" crowded his great vessels across the ocean to Canton and brought home rich stores of Oriental products. His fine Grand Turk sailed from Salem in 1785, and the return cargo doubled the money invested; and in the rooms of the East India Marine Company at Salem is a great Lowestoft bowl bearing paintings of the Grand Turk and the date, Canton, 1786, which proves that that piece positively was neither made at Lowestoft, painted at Lowestoft, brought to Lowestoft, nor exported from Lowestoft. From that year to 1799, of the hundred and seventy-five voyages made by Derby's stanch ships, forty-five were to India and China. He had four ships at one time at Canton. In 1793 three Indiamen brought into New England ports $14,600 worth of "China-ware;" one of these ships, the Rising Sun, landed at Providence. And Billy Gray, of Salem, the largest ship-owner in the world at that date, sold many a hogshead of china-ware from the cargoes of his great ships, the Light Horse, the Three Friends, the Lotus, the Black Warrior.

Though Connecticut farmers and law-givers looked with timid and unfavoring eyes on the possibilities and dangers of Oriental commerce, Connecticut merchants were not to be left behind in the race for the golden prizes of India. A great ship was fitted out in New Haven, and the story of her first voyage in 1799 and of its rich results reads like the wonder-tales of the East. The ship was manned by thirty-five Connecticut men, sons of respectable and well-to-do families; many of them were graduates of Yale. In its provisioning and furnishing merchants of New Haven, Hartford, Weathersfield,

Farmington, Stamford, and other neighboring towns joined or "ventured." The ship took no cargo. She sailed to the Falkland Islands. The crew killed 80,000 seals, packed away the skins in the ship's hold, and then sailed to Canton. The Neptune was the first New Haven ship that furrowed the waves of the Pacific. The sealskins were sold to Canton merchants for $3.75 each. With $280,000 of the profits the Connecticut boys laid in a rich store of Oriental goods, tea, silks, and 467 boxes of fine china. These goods were sold in New Haven at enormous profits. The ship paid to the Government, on the results of that single voyage, import duties which amounted to $20,000 more than the entire State tax for the year. Mr. Townsend, the builder of the ship, cleared $100,000 as his share of the profits; the super-cargo, that useful and obsolete officer, took $50,000, and the thirty-five Yankee sailors and the Yankee merchants all tasted the sweets of this phenomenal venture. Thirty-six other Connecticut merchants joined at once in a venture in another ship, and the Cowles Brothers, of Farmington, fitted out three vessels for Canton, and vast amounts of Lowestoft porcelain were brought back by them to New Haven.

It is only recently, and even now only among china-collectors and what a Newburyport dame called "city-folks and Yorkers" (that is Bostonians and New Yorkers—or city people in general), that the pieces spoken of in the last few pages would be called Lowestoft. In country homes all are still Chinese or India porcelain. It is the favorite tradition told of nearly every piece, even of undisputed English wares of the last century, that "my grandfather brought that bowl to us from Hong Kong," and even when you point out the Caughley or Staffordshire marks, the owners are unconvinced and openly indignant. Chinese porcelain evidently denoted much higher aristocracy than English ware in early Federal days, and the sentiment lingers still among simple folk. Crests, arms, and initials are very common, "put on for us in China," and the "China" or "India" tradition, must in such cases never be openly doubted.

Much specially decorated porcelain did come to us from China; there is plenty of proof in old letters, bills, diaries, and shipping receipts, that persons in both America and England ordered services of porcelain such as we now call Lowestoft, to be made and decorated for them in China. These orders were sometimes filled in a manner which was vastly disappointing. Miss Leslie, the sister of the eminent painter, related that she ordered a dinner-service to be made and painted for her in China. She directed that a coat of arms should be placed in the centre of each plate, and made a careful drawing of the desired coat of arms and pasted it in the centre of a specimen plate, and wrote under it, "Put this in the middle." What was her dismay when, on the arrival of the china, she found on every piece not only the coat of arms, but the words, indelibly burnt in, "Put this in the middle"

Another person ordering porcelain in China sent out a book-plate as a guide for outline in decoration, and was much disgusted when the service arrived to find it painted by the literal-minded Chinese artist in lines of funereal black like the book-plate, instead of the gay colors the china-buyer had desired, and which were then so fashionable.

But I feel that in all this about the questionable Lowestoft I am neither quite fair nor quite liberal to the claims of the far Orient. We do not regard with doubt or with question of English co-operation all the contributions of China to our early table-furnishings. About the pieces just described, many collectors are reckless in judging and naming, and too often unjust to our Asiatic ceramic purveyors; but much porcelain came to America which is known and acknowledged to be Chinese, and which has never for a moment had the shadow of suspicion of Occidental manipulation cast over it—I mean "blue Canton china." A hand whose clear and perfect touch made beautiful, yet rendered truthfully everything she described, wrote thus of such porcelain:

"The china here, as in all genuine Salem cupboards, was chiefly of the honest old blue Canton ware. There were shining piles of these plates, which while they are rather heavy to handle, always surprise one by being so thin at the edges. There were generous teacups like small bowls, squat pitchers with big noses, and a tureen whose cover had the head of a boar for a handle. And in all this the blue was dull and deep in tint, with a certain ill-defined vaporous quality at the edges of the lines, and the white of the cool greenish tinge of a duck's egg. You can buy blue Canton to-day, but it is not old blue Canton."

The stanch ships of Elias Haskett Derby, of William Gray, of Joseph Peabody, brought to Salem hogsheads and boxes and crates of this old blue Canton china; it still lingers close-hidden and high-shelved in Salem cupboards; it has been crushed grievously under foot in Salem attics; has been sold ignominiously to Salem junkmen, and also proudly and eagerly bought by Salem collectors.

Many a "venture" was sent out by New England dames to "far Cathay" in these East India trading-ships, and many a pretty blue Canton teapot and cups and saucers, or great ringing punch-bowl came home from China in return for the hoarded egg-money, the inherited Spanish dollars, or the proceeds of the year's spinning and weaving. Do you know what a "venture" was a hundred years ago? It was a gentle commercial speculation in which all Puritan womankind longed to join, just as all New England ministers legally and soberly gambled and revelled in the hopes and disappointments of lottery tickets. An adventurer in those days was as different from an adventurer of to-day as was an undertaker of 1792 from an undertaker of 1892. When a ship sailed out to China in the years following the Revolutionary War, the ship's owner did not own all the cargo (if cargo of ginseng it bore), nor send out all the contents of the bags of solid specie that were to be invested in the rich and luxurious products of the far land. There were no giant monoplies in those days. All his friends and neighbors were kindly and sociably allowed to join with the wealthy shipmaster in his risks

and profits, to put in a little money on speculation—in
short, to send out a sum large or small on a "venture."
Sometimes orders were given that this "venture" should
be invested in special forms of merchandise; sometimes
it was only placed in the supercargo's hands to share in
its proportion the general profit. Complicated books
must Elias Haskett Derby have had to keep through all
these petty "ventures," but good profits did that honest
man render, though he left at his death the largest fortune of any American in that century. Women, fired
by these alluring profits and assailed by a gambling ob-
session, sold their strings of gold beads, their spring
lambs, their knitted stockings, and eagerly sent out the
accumulated sum by the ship's purser, and received in
return tea, spices, rock-candy, crapes, china, anything
they coveted for their own use or fancied they could sell
at a profit. Men, too, sent out a "venture" as a gift to
their new-born children, or to fill their own pockets; fair
maids bought through a "venture" their bridal finery.
From Bristol one young miss sent in to a ship-owner
her gold earrings to "venture" for "a sprigged and bordered India muslin gown of best make," and she got it
too, thin and sheer, close-sprigged and deep bordered,
just as well selected and carefully conveyed as if she had
"ventured a hundred pound."

The newspapers of the times abounded in advertisements of blue Canton china, such as this from the *Columbia Centinel* of December 19, 1792:

"Superfine Nankin blue enamelled landscape and
fancy pattern China-ware direct from China: among

other articles are complete dinner setts, tea coffee & breakfast do; Teacups & saucers & Teapots separately do; dinner breakfast & dessert flat & Deep Plates; Punchbowles Mugs & Pitchers."

Frequently the china was sold direct from the vessel, or from the wharf alongside. How truly Oriental that old Canton china must have been to Boston and Providence and Salem dames when they had tiptoed down on the rough old wharf in wooden clogs or velvet-tipped golo-shoes, their fair faces covered with black velvet masks if the weather waxed cold or the wind blew east; when they had seen the great weather-beaten ship, with its stained sails and blackened ropes and cables—the ship that had brought the fragile porcelain cargo to port—the Lively Prudence, the Lively Peggy, the Lively Sally, the Lively Molly, or any of the dozen great ships named by Yankee shipmasters and ship-owners for the lively young women of their acquaint-ance. They had been on board the Indiaman, perhaps, and smelt its bilge-water and its travelled stale ship-smells; had watched the strange picturesque foreign sailors, barefooted and earringed, as they brought the packages and spread out the boxes on deck, or carried in their brawny arms the great crates on Scarlett's or Rowe's Wharf, and with their bronzed tattooed hands took out the precious porcelain from its rice-straw pack-ing and rice-paper wrapping. How that old blue Can-ton must have savored forever to the fair buyers of the "bloom raisins," the cinnamon, the ginger, palm-oil, gum-copal, and ivory, the tea, the otto-of-roses, that had been fellow-travellers for months in the good ship's hold; and have spoken, too, of far-away lands and foreign sights, and of "the magic and mystery of the sea." Truly, we of to-day have lost all the romance, the sentiment, that brightened and idealized colonial shopping, when we know not the ship, nor scarcely the country from whence come our stores.

In Newport, in Bristol, in Providence, in Boston— wherever ships could sail from port, and wherever favoring winds wafted them back again, vast stores of this old blue Canton ware have been and can now be found; "tall coffee-pots, with straight spouts, looking like lighthouses with bowsprits; short, clumsy teapots with twisted handles and lids that always fall off;" jugs, tureens, helmet-pitchers, and sauce-boats. At the recent disbandment of the family and selling of the home of one of the old presidents of Brown University, a score of old Canton platters were found behind trunks and old furniture under the eaves in the garret. Too heavy, too cumbersome to be used on our modern tables, they were banished to the garret rafters, and there prisoned, were forgotten. In past years when roast-pig and giant turkeys were served on that hospitable board, these great platters proudly held their steaming trophies; but now we have changed all that—the turkey is cut up surreptitiously in some unseen corner, and the blue Canton platters, dusty and cobwebbed, lie forgotten in the garret.

These vast stores of blue Canton were doubtless part of the cargo of the Ann and Hope, the beautiful and stanch ship that in 1799 bore into Providence " one hundred and thirty boxes of chinaware in tea- and dinner-sets." In 1800 she again brought into port three hundred and sixty-two boxes and one hundred and twenty-four rolls of chinaware, together with such other delightful Oriental importations as two bales of gauze ribbons, seven boxes of lacquered ware, five hundred Chinese umbrellas, sixty bundles of cassia and five boxes of sweetmeats, forty jars of rock-candy, and twenty tubs of sugar-candy. In 1802 came on the Ann and Hope one thousand and forty-eight boxes of chinaware, but, alas! no sugar-candy, or sweetmeats for Providence lads and lasses, but instead forty disappointing boxes of rhubarb.

Hot-water plates of Canton china did every well-regulated and substantial New England family own, deep hollow vessels, with their strong heavy bottoms and little open ears. Not very practical nor convenient of use were they — or, at least, so it seems to us nowadays. And another and common form of coarse blue and white Chinese ware which our grandmothers had by the score need not be despised by china collectors—the old, highshouldered ginger-jars that fifty and seventy-five years ago were so good in color. Some are mammoth jars holding nearly a gallon, that are decorated with a chrysanthemum pattern in clear dark blue, and when set on the top of a corner cupboard need not fear even the proximity of a cabinet specimen of costly old hawthorn. A few members of the aristocracy of ginger-jars exist, not in common plebeian blue and white, but with a greenish ground covered with red and yellow enamelled flowers. These were never sold in China, but were used as presentation jars, being usually given by some Chinese grandee or trader to some Yankee sea-captain, or sent to America as a token of respect to some American merchant or ship-owner. They sell readily for $5 each in an out-of-the-way antique shop, for thirty in a fashionable one. Six shockingly dirty specimens were found in a hen-house on an inland farm on Long Island, and after being pumped upon for a long season at the horse-pump, and swept off vigorously with a birch-broom, they revealed their original glories of color, and after a thorough cleansing and disinfecting now grace teak-wood cabinets in New York homes.

A very dainty form of Oriental china was seen in many hospitable homes in the beginning of this century, a form now obsolete. I mean a "toddy-strainer." It was a shallow, circular saucer or disk of fine Oriental ware, blue Canton or Nankin, or white and gold Oriental porcelain, and was pierced with tiny holes. It was about four or five inches in diameter and bore two little projecting ears or handles, which were fastened to the body of the strainer by embossed leaves. On the edge of a flip mug or a toddy glass the ears of the toddy strainer rested when used, and when the toddy was poured from the great punch pitcher into the glass, the strainer prevented the lemon- and orange-seeds from entering the glass below. These toddy strainers are no longer imported in our temperance-ruled and invention-filled days, and being of frail china, have seldom outlived the years when they were in such constant, jovial, and hospitable use. Nor have I seen them elsewhere than in the seaport towns of Narraganset Bay. I fancy some luxury-loving, toddy-drinking, money-spending old Newport merchant invented, explained to the Chinese, and im-

Chinese Ewer.

ported to America these pretty porcelain toddy strainers.

Sometimes a single odd or beautiful piece of Oriental china was brought to America in the olden times by those far-roving and home - bringing old sea-captains, and the single specimen still exists—a stranger in a strange land. Such is the graceful little ewer here shown, a piece of Persian shape, but of pure Chinese paste, and " with antick shapes in China's azure dyed." This design, with its " little lawless azure-tinted grotesques," forms a piece curious enough to be worthy a place in any cabinet. Such also is a dull-green enamelled and crackled bowl which I own, and a Chinese dish of antique earthenware, which has been mended and riveted by some Oriental china-mender with gold wire. A great blue

and white tall jar with red lacquered cover is unique
in size as it is in its contents — long strings of sugar-
coated Chinese sweetmeats, sweetmeats so unpleasant
and outlandish in flavor and so mysterious in appearance that they were regarded with keen disfavor by
simple stay - at - home New Englanders, who invested
the innocent sweets with alarming attributes, and laid
them under suspicion of concealing within their sugary
surfaces bits of all the heathenish edibles—sharks' fins,
birds' nests, puppies' tails, and other unchristian foods
that had been seen and even tasted in foreign lands by
bold travelled mariners. Hence there still lie at the
bottom of the great jar a few silken strings of shrivelled,
unwholesome-looking black knobs like some strange
Oriental beads; despised by generations of sweet-toothed
children of the Puritans, and now too adamantine in
consistency to be tasted or nibbled even by the boldest
gourmand or curiosity-seeker of to-day.

" Posy holders " are found of India china with a rich
decoration of red, blue, and gold, with little flecks of
green, the cover pierced with holes to keep the stems of
the flowers in place; "bowpots" also of similar porcelain
and ornamentation.

I have not found in my china hunting any old blue
hawthorn jars, nor any fragile pieces of " grains-of-rice "
porcelain, nor sets of covered saki-cups in scarlet and
gold, nor dainty translucent cups that seem naught but
glaze, though I have been shown them in other collections as country treasure-trove. I have seen a few tall
green crackle vases and jars, of age and dignity enough

to chill unspoken within our lips any inquiry regarding or suggesting purchase.

A few stray polychrome Chinese bowls of the description known as " real Indian " I have found, and I hear

Persian Vase.

that whole dinner - services of such wares were imported. General Gage had one in Boston, and a few of its beautiful plates escaped destruction at the " looting " of the Province House. But the old services of Oriental china that I have seen have all been blue Canton or Lowestoft. The graceful blue and white vase here shown I at first sight fancied to be Chinese, but now believe to be Persian. As the country owner of this oddly-shaped and rather curiously-decorated vase knew nothing of how it had been acquired by the members of her family, nor how long it had been possessed by them, nor whence it came, nor indeed anything, save that it had stood for many years on her grandmother's best room mantel-shelf, it may be a comparatively modern piece of ware. I have woven about it and haloed around it an Arabian Nights romance of astonishing plot and fancy, in which a gallant Yankee sailor, a hideous Arabian merchant, and a black-eyed, gauze-robed houri fill the leading parts ; and perhaps my imaginative story of the presence of the Persian outcast in a staid New England farm-house is just as satisfactory as many of the wondrous china tales we hear.

An everlasting interest rests in all Oriental china in attempting to translate the meaning of the Oriental stamps and marks. I have never deciphered any save a few of the hundred forms of *Show*—the Chinese greeting, " May you live forever," and the marks on one old Chinese bowl, which signified *wan*, a symbol used only on articles made for talented literary persons ; *Pŏ koo chin wan* " for the learned in antiquities and old curiosities," and the mark of the instruments used by authors —the stone for grinding ink, the brushes for writing, and the roll of paper. I was highly delighted, and indeed very proud, when I discovered the meaning of these Chinese letters. I tried to fancy that it was a significant coincidence—a friendly message from the old world to the new—that pointed out that I too belonged to what is in China the ruling class, the literati. But the more closely I examined my literary tickets, the more depressed I became. I found, alas, that these flattering marks were never placed on my bowl by the Orientals ;

they were skilfully painted over the glaze in oil colors by the base, jesting Occidental who gave the piece of old porcelain to me.

The china called Lowestoft was, without doubt, the kind most desired and most fashionable in early Federal times throughout both North and South. Such was the dinner-service of the Carrolls of Carrollton, with bands of rich brown and gold and a pretty letter C. Such was the family china of William Morris; of John Rutledge, with the initials J. R. and the shield and eagle; and the tea-service of John Dickinson, with blue and gold bands and his initials. Of Lowestoft china was one of the beautiful services of General Knox—his "best china" that was used on state occasions. It was banded with delicate lines of pale gray, black, and gold, and the rich coloring of red, blue, and gold was confined to the decoration in the centre of the plate. This was an eagle with extended wings, bearing on his breast the seal of the Society of the Cincinnati, a round shield with a group of appropriate figures surrounded by the motto, "Omnia relinquit servare rempublicam," a motto certainly very significant of General Knox's patriotism. The eagle was surmounted by a wreath of palm or laurel leaves tied with a knot of blue ribbon. Beneath the eagle were delicately formed initials about half an inch in height—L. F. and H. K.—the H. and K. intertwined just as General Knox always wrote them. This beautiful service was a gift to Mrs. Knox from her rich grandfather, General Waldo; a wedding gift, it is often asserted, though I had hardly supposed that her relatives, being so bitterly opposed to the *mésalliance* of the "belle of Massachusetts" with the young clerk in a book-shop, had given her any such rich tokens of approval. Then, too, the runaway match was made at the beginning of the Revolutionary War, and Mrs. Knox, following her husband from battle-field to battle-field, would hardly have needed or thought of such fine china. The fact that it bears the decoration of the seal of the Cincinnati, points to a date after the establishment of that society.

Lowestoft, too, was the china table-ware of John Hancock, the table-ware that he ordered to be thrust one side and replaced by old-fashioned pewter. And when he lay in his bedroom groaning with the gout and heard the rattle of a china plate on the table in the dining-room below, he ordered his servant to throw the precious but noise-making dish out of the window, and the thrifty black man saved the dainty Lowestoft by throwing it on the grass.

But the every-day china, the common table-ware, of all these good American citizens and patriots—Knox, Hancock, Paul Revere, the Otises, Quincys, and a score that might be named—the plates and dishes of china from which they ate their daily bread, were not of Lowestoft, but of honest old blue Canton.

IX.

THE COSEY TEAPOT

IT is small wonder that the craze for the gathering together and hoarding of teapots has assailed many a feminine china-hunter in many a land, and that many a noble collection has been made. Teapots are so friendly and appealing, one cannot resist them. No china-loving woman can pass them by, they are so domestic as well as beautiful ; a steam of simple cheer and homeliness ascends forever (though invisible) from their upturned spouts, and a gentle genie of cosiness and welcome dwells therein.

And then their forms are so varied ! Plates, from their nature, necessarily show a prosaic flatness and similarity of outline ; cups and saucers are limited in their capabilities of diversification ; but teapots ! you may find a new shape for every day in the year.

In America we have an extra incentive and provoker of interest in the extraordinary great age assigned to teapots. You can hardly find one of any pretension to antiquity in America that is asserted to be less than two hundred years old ; and two centuries and a half are as naught to teapot-owners. Sophisticated possessors are a little shy about assigning their old teapots to the Mayflower invoice, since we have heard so many incredulous

and bantering jibes about the size and tonnage of that
capacious ship; but country owners are troubled by no
such fears of ridicule, and boldly assert the familiar tradition; while the pages of our catalogues of loan collections containing entry after entry of " teapots brought
over in 1620," " teapots three hundred years old," show
the secret faith and belief of even more travelled and
studied teapot-owners.

1630—1640—1650! It would seem, could we trust tradition, that teapots just swarmed in America in those
years. There were none then in England or Holland or
China, and no tea even in England; but it is proudly
boasted that we had teapots and, of course, tea also in
America. I wonder we do not claim the teapot as a
Yankee invention! The Chinese knew naught of any
such " conveniencys " at that time; they stupidly
steeped their tea in a cup or dish or bowl; indeed, they
do so still in the great shops, and tea-gardens, and yaa-
mens of China, and would doubtless have conservatively
clung to the same simple and primitive fashion in all
their houses to this day, had not the opened traffic with
the western world shown them the restless craze for
change common to nearly all Europeans and awakened
in them a desire for novelty and improvement.

The first mention of English teapots which I have
chanced to see is in the private memorandum book of
John Dwight, of Fulham, potter. The date of the entry is previous to 1695. It is a receipt for " the fine
white clay for Dishes or Teapots to endure boiling water."
Under date of November, 1695, he says: " The little fur-

nace where the last Red Teapots was burnt I take to be a convenient one for this vse." An entry dated 1691 tells of a "strong Hardy Clay fit for Teapots;" and again of a "dark colour'd Cley for marbled Dishes and teapots to endure boiling water." In Houghton's Collections of 1695 we read: "Of teapots in 1694 there came but ten, and those from Holland, but to our credit be it spoken, we have about Fauxhall made a great many, and I cannot gainsay but they are as good as any came from abroad." The first successful experiment of Bottcher in the manufacture of porcelain took the form of a teapot; and potters of succeeding years have spent much time and thought in inventing new shapes and decorations for tea-drawing vessels. Would it not be interesting to have a cabinet with a chronological and also a cubical succession of teapots, from the tiny ones of Elersware used in the time of Queen Anne, when tea was sold in ounce packages at the apothecaries, down to the great three-quart teapot used by Dr. Johnson and sold at the sale of Mrs. Piozzi's effects? There would I stop and never admit as a teapot the ugly great spouted earthen casks made in Japan, to satisfy abnormal-minded and craving collectors. Into one of these hideous monstrosities in the possession of a well-known collector, two men were able to crawl, seat themselves, and have the cover placed over them—a sight to make the judicious china-lover grieve.

In still another china-succession might we write the history of the teapot in America, from the simple plebeian undecorated earthenware pot in which was sparingly placed the precious pinch, through the gayly-colored and larger teapot, earthen still, through Wedgwood's varied wares in which our patriotic grandmothers drank their wretched "Liberty Tea," to the fine porcelain treasures of Worcester, Minton, Derby, Sèvres, and Dresden of to-day—a story of the growth of our nation in luxury and elegance.

The earliest known mention of the use of tea by Englishmen is in a letter written in 1615 by one wanderer in China to another fellow-soldier, asking for a "pot of the best sort of chaw" and also for "three silver porringers to drink chaw in." By 1664 it appears to have been sold in England in some considerable quantity, in spite of Pepys's oft-quoted entry in his diary in the year 1665 about tasting "thea a China drink" that he never had drunk before. Pepys was far from rich at that time, and tea may have been in frequent use for some years among persons of wealth and quality without his ever having tasted it. It quickly grew in favor in the court, the first importations all coming from the Continent, from Holland, and soon was plentiful and comparatively cheap. Among the common people and conservative country folk, however, beer still held its own at breakfast and supper until Swift's time.

New England dames followed the fashions, fancies, and tastes of their sisters in Old England as soon as their growing prosperity allowed. When in 1666 the fragrant herb cost sixty shillings a pound in England, I hardly think our frugal Pilgrim Fathers imported much tea. The first mention of tea which I have found shows that in

1690 Benjamin Harris and Daniel Vernon were licensed to sell " in publique," in Boston, " Coffee Tee & Chucaletto." The following year two other tea-houses were licensed. Dr. Benjamin Orman had a "Tinn Teapott" in Boston previous to his death in 1695, an article of novelty and luxury that probably few of his neighbors possessed. Though Felt, in his "New England Customs," and Weeden, in his " Social and Economic History of New England," both say that green tea was first advertised for sale in Boston in 1714, I find in the *Boston News Letter* of March, 1712, "green and ordinary teas," advertised for sale at " Zabdiel Boyltons (or Boylstons) Apothecary Shop," and in the same year teapots and tea-tables were sold at the Swing Bridge by " Publick Outcry." In 1713 Zabdiel Boylston had Bohea tea ; in 1714 " very fine green tea, the best for color and taste," was advertised ; and in 1715 tea was sold at the Coffee House, thus showing that it was being imported in larger quantities. The taste quickly spread, and wherever there was tea there was also a teapot. Weeden says that it is strange that Judge Sewall, with all his fussing about wine, and "chokolet," and "cyder," and "pyes," and cakes, and "almonds and reasons," and oranges and figs, says naught of tea. He does speak of it ; he drank at a "great and Thursday" lecture, at Madam Winthrop's house in the year 1709, "Ale Tea & Beer," and he does not especially note it as a rarity. I do not believe, however, though he lived until 1730, when it was sold in every Boston dry-goods, grocers', hardware, millinery, and apothecary shop, and advertised in every Boston newspaper, that he often drank the " cup that cheers but not inebriates." He may have regarded it as did Henry Saville, who wrote deploringly of tea-drinking in 1678 as a " base and unworthy Indian practice," saying sadly, " the truth is, all nations are growing so wicked."

In 1719 Bohea tea was worth twenty-four shillings a pound in Philadelphia. In 1721 it had risen six shillings higher in price, while by 1757 it cost only seven shillings a pound. In 1725 they had both green and Bohea tea in Virginia and the Carolinas, as is shown by the writings of the times ; while, though I have not found it advertised till 1728 in New York, the "tea-water pump" showed its large use in that town. When tea was first introduced into Salem it was boiled in an iron kettle, and after the liquor was strained off, it was then drank without milk or sugar, while the leaves of the herb were placed in a dish, buttered and salted and eaten.

A letter printed in " Holmes's Annals," and written in 1740, thus complains : " Almost every little tradesman's wife must sit sipping tea for an hour or more in the morning, and maybe again in the afternoon, if they can get it, and nothing will please them to sip it out of but chinaware. They talk of bestowing of thirty or forty shillings on a tea equipage, as they call it. There is the silver spoons, the silver tongs, and many other trinkets that I cannot name." Bennett, in his Travels, told the same tale of Boston women. Each woman then carried her own tiny teapot when she made one of those much-deprecated tea-drinking visits, and often her own teacup also, else she might have to drink from a pewter cup. And she frequently brought her own precious thimbleful of tea, especially if she chanced to have a decided fancy in the variety of the herb that she used.

In the latter half of the eighteenth century tea and teapots were common enough in America, and the "China herb" played a part in our national history that would have immortalized it had it no other claims to our love and consideration. In December, 1773, Boston Harbor was made one great "tea-drawing," and after that memorable event many American dames gave up from a sense of duty their favorite beverage, but they did not destroy their tea-sets. Here is the lament of one matron over her empty urn :

> " Farewell the tea-board with its gaudy equipage
>   Of cups and saucers, Cream-bucket, Sugar-tongs,
>   The pretty tea-chest, also lately stored
>   With Hyson, Congo and best Double Fine.
>   Full many a joyous moment have I sat by ye
>   Hearing the girls tattle, the old maids talk scandal
>   Though now detestable.
>   Because I am taught and I believe it true
>   Its use will fasten Slavish chains upon my Country
>   To reign triumphant in America."

There is in New Bedford one very interesting old teapot which lays a very definite, decided, and special claim to having been brought over in the Mayflower. It is said to have been the property of Elder Brewster, and is known as the "Elder Brewster Teapot." It is a pretty little cylindrical vessel with fluted bands, and is

decorated with gilt lines and dark red flowers and border.
Scoffers, of course, will bring up to you all the oft-
enumerated points—that the Pilgrims had no china, that
tea was not known in England, and probably not known
in Holland in 1620; that teapots are a comparatively
modern invention—but still we feel an interest in this
" Elder Brewster Teapot." It brought at the sale of
Governor Lyon's effects only $45, which low price was,
I fear, an indication that the belief of the scoffers pre-
vailed among the buyers there assembled. The firm of
Richard Briggs & Co., of Boston, caused to be manufactured in 1874 a number of reproductions of this teapot. Before taking the original to Messrs. Wedgwood,
at Etruria, they were careful to obtain the opinion of a
china expert, Mr. Townsend, of the South Kensington
Museum, who pronounced the " Elder Brewster Teapot "
old Delft, and showed to Mr. Briggs several specimens
similarly decorated. Whatever it may be—old Delft,
old Meissen, old Staffordshire, or even comparatively
modern ware—the reproduction is certainly a pretty little
teapot, even if the Mayflower episode in the career of
the original be said to be fabulous. The story of the ac-
quisition of this teapot by Governor Lyon is very interesting. He bought it from an old lady in Vermont, but
only after repeated visits, much cajolery, many rebuffs,
and a very stiff purchase sum.

There is in Morristown, in the beautiful old colonial
mansion known as Washington's Headquarters, a tall
teapot which is dissimilar in shape to the Elder Brewster
teapot, but which is exactly like it in paste, in decoration

of dull vermilion and maroon, and as a further resemblance, it has the same rather curiously modelled flower as a knob on the cover. This teapot is labelled " Old English ware," and old English Delft it apparently is. It certainly looks like a sister of the Elder Brewster teapot.

At this home of the Washington Association may be seen many other curious and interesting teapots—old Spode, Staffordshire, and Wedgwood. Black basalts and cream-ware specimens of good design are found in the well-kept and well-arranged cases. All have a story or a history of past owners to make them interesting, aside from the longing we feel for them as "specimens." I would we could pour out from their spouts in old-time words the stream of Continental tattle that has been poured into them ; we could write therefrom a social and economic history of our country that would excel in point of detail Boswell's Johnson, Pepys's Diary, and Horace Walpole's Letters all rolled into one.

A famous and curious teapot was the shape known as the Cadogan. They were also used for coffee, and were formed from a model of Indian green-ware brought from abroad by the Marchioness of Rockingham, or the Hon. Mrs. Cadogan, and from her received the name. They were made at the Rockingham works ; and George IV., then Prince Regent, a connoisseur in tea, chancing to see one and to praise the tea that came from it, the Cadogan teapots sprang at once into high fashion. Mortlock, the dealer, ordered for one season's supply £900 worth. This teapot was all in one piece ; it had no cover. It was filled through a hole in the bottom. A slightly spiral tube ran up from this hole nearly to the top of the teapot. It can plainly be seen that when it was filled with an infusion of tea and inverted, that the liquid could only escape through the spout. The teapots were decorated on the outside with raised leaves and flowers. Some of these Cadogan teapots of course came to America, and are now found in collections. I have also seen Japanese " puzzle teapots " fashioned in the same manner, to be filled at the bottom. Another Japanese " puzzle-teapot " looks like a gray earthen doughnut with a handle and spout, the tea being poured into it through the hollow handle.

George IV. was a connoisseur in teapots not only from a gastronomic point of view, but he was a collector of them as well, and had at the Pavilion at Brighton great pyramids formed of a vast variety of teapots. Many collections of them have been made in England. Mrs. Hawes left to her daughter three hundred choice teapots which were arranged in a room built specially for them. A number that had belonged to Queen Charlotte were in this gathering. Such a collection is interesting and instructive, the pieces being from various factories and lands. Even more instructive still, because gathered with a definite purpose and forming a serial guide to the perfect knowledge of the ceramic productions of a single country, is such a collection of teapots as that in the unrivalled Morse Collection in the Boston Museum of Art. But collections of modern Japanese teapots, gathered simply for the sake of seeing how many different kinds and what grotesque shapes one can get, do not appeal to me. Such is said to be the modern "assorted lot" of Madame de Struve, the wife of the minister to Japan, who gathered together nine hundred and seventy-five Japanese teapots. Such a collection can be formed in a week by any person having money enough to pay for them and interest enough to order the cratefuls sent home; while a collection of good old teapots of Oriental, English, French, and German wares is a matter of a life-time, especially if historical interest is a desideratum, and good taste as well.

I have not seen in America, as may be found in boudoirs and dining-rooms in France and England, any friezes "three row deep" of teapots round the top of the room; but one fair New York china-maniac, who says with the vehement exaggeration so typical of American women, "I love my teapots and my tea as I love my life," has a narrow shelf quite round the wall-top, about a foot below the ceiling, filled closely with a gay procession of vari-colored, vari-formed teapots. It is a unique and striking decoration—in good taste, since the frieze teapots are none of them gems, but simply gay and effective bits of Oriental color and grotesque shape. In a cabinet, glass-covered and screened, are all the old teapots which she owns, a rare and dainty company of ancients and honorables.

At Stockbridge, in the possession of Mrs. Plumb, may be seen, arranged on shallow shelves, a large and good collection of teapots, gathered chiefly from farmhouses in the country around. Over one hundred old English pieces are among the number, some of them being very beautiful and rare.

Mottoes, names, and inscriptions are often found on ancient teapots found in America. One of Leeds-ware bears on one side the words:

> " May all loving friends
> Be happy and free
> In drinking a Cup
> Of Harmless Tea."

Another bears these verses:

> " My Lad is far upon the Sea
> His absence makes me mourn
> The bark that bears him off from me
> I hope will safe return
> And from his earnings I'll save up
> If lucky he should be
> And then when old with me he'll stop
> And go no more to sea "

Another friendly teapot has the lines:

> " Kindly take this gift of mine
> Full of love for thee & thine.   1769."

A fourth this good advice:

> " Drink only tea
> & Sober keep."

Many of the sailor mottoes found on Liverpool pitchers are also seen on teapots of Liverpool ware, as if made to some sailor's order for a gift.

Lowestoft Teapot.

Perhaps the teapots most commonly used by our grandmothers are the types here shown; one a cylindrical Canton china teapot known now as Lowestoft, and one a gayly painted Bristol pottery teapot. Specimens of the latter and Staffordshire pottery teapots differed much in shape, an hexagonal form being frequent, and the swan or dolphin knob being seen on many of the varied shapes. The black Jackfield teapots with raised designs, looking like black glass, are sometimes found, silver mounted and quaint.

For the perfection, the idealization of

Bristol Pottery Teapot.

the teapot we must turn to the productions of Josiah
Wedgwood. Appropriate and convenient in shape, elegant in decoration, perfect in manufacture, they have
handles adjusted in precisely the best possible balancing
place, spouts shaped to empty the contents in the most
perfect and thorough manner, covers that slide or fit with
ease and yet with exactitude, bases that are perfectly
proportioned and levelled—in a Wedgwood teapot we
find elegance and fitness equally combined, it obeys and
satisfies every artistic, economic, and mathematical rule ;
" built by that only law — that use be suggestive of
beauty." Our modern tastes do not run now to the
black basalts, the blue jasper, the cream-ware of Wedgwood ; we fancy a glazed, painted porcelain for every-day
use, but the fact remains the same—the Wedgwood teapots are the best, the most perfect ever made ; even in
China and Japan, the acknowledged home of teapots,
where the little vessels are not only used to hold tea,
but as an omniparient cistern of every other liquid, even
in those countries can be found no more perfect teapots
than those of Wedgwood. They deserve the appellation
of De Quincey. " an eternal teapot."

X

PUNCH-BOWLS AND PUNCHES

THERE is no individual piece of china around which shines such a glowing halo of warm hospitality, of good-fellowship, of good cheer, as around the jolly punch-bowl. A plate, a mug, a pitcher, is absolutely devoid of any interest or sentiment save what may come from knowledge of past ownership, or from beauty or quaintness of decoration ; a teapot conveys a sense of cosiness and homeliness ; but a punch-bowl, even a common, ugly, cracked crockery punch-bowl—visions of good company and good companions rise at the very sight, even at the very name.

What tales of colonial and continental times an old American punch-bowl could tell if it only could and would repeat half that it has heard ; what gay drinking-songs, what stirring patriotic speeches, what sharp legal wit, what sober and circumspect clerical jokes, what kindly eleemosynary plans would echo cheerfully out of its great sounding bell could it, like the phonograph, give forth what has rung into it in the past ! What scenes of rollicking mirth, of dancing feet and dicing-games have been photographed on its insensitive and unchanging glaze ! In what scene of cheerfulness and of seriousness alike did not the colonial punch-bowl take

its part ? It encouraged the soldier on eve of battle, it
bade the sailor God-speed.   The heavy Delft bowl stood
filled and refilled to the brim at the husking-party, the
apple-bee, the wood-spell, the timber-rolling, the muster, the house-raising, the lottery-drawing, the election ;
while the big India china bowl stood even on the church
steps at an ordination or a church dedication. It held
the water to christen the baby; it made cheerful the
wedding-feast ; and even in times of sadness it was not
banished, but side by side with the funeral baked meats
the omnipresent punch-bowl stood to greet and cheer
every sad comer.

Indeed, at a funeral the punch-bowl specially shone.
Great pains were taken and no expense spared to properly
concoct and serve the sombre funeral-punches. " Rum,
lemons, a loaf of sugar, and spices," sometimes also
" Malligo raisins and rose-water," were items on every
reputable and *à la mode*, as they called it, undertakers'
bills. A sober, responsible, and above all, an *experi-
enced* committee was appointed to carefully mix and
flavor the last libation that could ever be offered to the
dead friend. Small wonder with such good cheer that
even sober Judge Sewall openly called a funeral a "treat."
And we can understand why a very worthy old gentleman, a lover of the olden times, complained with much
bitterness in the early part of this century that " temperance had done for funerals." The gayly-flowered and
gilded punch-bowl was not sadly draped in trappings of
woe, nor set one side in seclusion, but standing cheerfully in a prominent position with its spicy welcome,

made even sad mourners feel that life was still worth living.

The punch-bowl certainly flourished proudly in America through the eighteenth century, just as it reigned in honor in England at the same time. Previous to that date the English prototype of the punch-bowl had been the posset-pot, and that primitive form still exists, and indeed is made and used in Derbyshire and the neighboring English counties to the present day. A few posset-pots have made their way to America with Derbyshire emigrants and have been gathered in by rapacious collectors. On Christmas eve in olden times the great vessel, which sometimes held two gallons, was filled with the "good drink," and a silver coin and a wedding-ring were dropped in when the guests assembled; each partaker in turn dipped out a great spoonful or ladleful of the drink, and whoever was lucky enough to fish up the coin was certain of good luck during the ensuing year, while the ring-finder would be happily and speedily married. Posset was a very good mixture—a "very pretty drink"—not so good as punch, of course, but to us invested with a reflected glory. Hath not Shakespeare oft spoke to us of posset? In my little "Queen's Closet Opened," a book of culinary, medical, and potatory recipes collected by and for Queen Henrietta Maria, I find half a dozen rules for the brewing of "sack-posset." "To make a Sack Posset without Milk or Cream: Take eighteen Egs, whites and all, taking out the Treads, let them be beaten very well, take a pint of Sack, and a quart of Ale boyl'd, and scum it, then put in three quarters of a pound of suger and a little Nutmeg, let it boyl a few wames together, then take it off the fire stirring the Egs still, put into them two or three Ladlefuls of drink, then mingle all together, and set it on the fire, and keep it stirring til you find it thick then serve it up "—and not drink it, but cut it up and eat it, one might fancy.   There is no recipe for punch in my " Queen's Closet."   I fear Queen Henrietta did not know about that new drink, punch, in 1676, when this quaint old book was published.   Had she done so, she had not needed so many nostrums for insomnia.   Englishmen in India knew of it ; " spiced punch in bowls the Indians quaff," wrote one in 1665, and in 1697 Tryer spoke of it and basely libelled it as " an enervating liquor."   The punchless Queen knew, however, how to make hypocras, metheglin, mead, caudle, cordial-water, aqua-cœlestis, aqua-mirabilis, clary-water, gilly-flower-wine, usquebarb, and, best and delectablest of all, she knew how to make a Damnable Hum, and I doubt not she served it in a punch-bowl as was befitting so noble a drink.

The posset-pot had some cousins in England—the goddard, the wassail-bowl, the gossip-bowl, the caudle-cup—poor relations, however, and feeble ancestors of the glorious punch-bowl.   To the Orientals, not to the English, we owe our punch-bowls and our punches. Punch or " pauch " was an Indian drink, and the word meant five, and was named from the five ingredients used in its composition—arrack, tea, sugar, water, and lemon-juice.   A " pauch " was also a conclave of five men, a "pauch-pillav" a medicine of five ingredients, and so on.

The English people took very readily to the new Oriental drink and the new vessel to hold it, as it did to everything else in India. We read in the old ballad of "Jock-o'-the-Side," "They hae gard fill up a punch-bowl," and when a ballad adopts a word, then it is the people's. As the potter's art advanced in England, great bowls were made to hold punch at taverns and halls, often for the special use of the potters themselves. Cheerful mottoes did these potters' punch-bowls some-times bear. For simplicity and terseness this excels, "One Bowle more, and then"—does it not speak a never-ending welcome? A blue and white potter's bowl ten inches in diameter has this descriptive motto:

> "John Udy of Luxillion
>   his tin was so fine
>   it glidered this punch-bowl
>   and made it to shine.
>   pray fill it with punch
>   let the tinners sitt round
>   they never will budge
>   till the bottom they sound."

Glider meant to glaze, not to gild, and the verses refer to the stanniferous opaque white glaze formed by the use of Cornish tin.

Another bowl has these sententious lines:

> "What art can with the potter's art compare?
>   For of what we are ourselves of such we make our wares."

More serious rhymes still are found. At North Hylton, in England, were made many punch-bowls of lustre ware, and the proprietor, Mr. Phillips, must have been a very serious-minded and inconsequential man, or he never would have put these lines on so worldly a vessel :

> " The loss of gold is great,
>   The loss of health is more,
>   But losing Christ is such a loss
>   As no man can restore."

This bowl may, however, have been for a parson. On another specimen of the Hylton pottery gayly decorated with a print of a ship, a public house, and a hat-and-feathered young woman with an umbrella and small dog, are these sober and comically incongruous verses :

> " There is a land of peaceful rest
>   To mourning wanderers given,
>   There's a tear for souls distrest,
>   A balm for every wounded breast,
>   'Tis found above in Heaven ! "

Were it not for the public house, and the hat and feathers, we should know that this punch-bowl was surely made purposely to use at funerals.

One of the finest punch-bowls ever figulated is twenty inches and a half in diameter. It is of Liverpool Delft, painted in blue with ships and a landscape, and the inscription, " Success to the Africa Trade, George Dickinson." When we remember of what the " Africa Trade " consisted—the slave-traffic—we wonder the punch did not poison the drinkers. I have often seen this bowl referred to by authors as of extraordinary and unique size. It is not as large as the grand blue and white punch-bowl used by the first Continental Congress, a bowl which is now at Morristown, at Washington's Headquarters. I do not know whether this mammoth Congressional bowl is Canton china or English delft, for, since it stands in a cupboard, one cannot examine it closely. The color and design are good, and the size impressive, and altogether it is a noble relic, for this courage-giver of those troubled and anxious Federal days may have played no unimportant part in the affairs and history of our nation; I regard it with grateful awe and veneration, and also with a rather unworthy pride and satisfaction in its great size.

There were hosts of punch-bowls at that date in America. Watson wrote in 1830, of old colonial Philadelphia: "A corner was occupied by a bcaufet, which was a corner closet with a glass door, in which all the china and plate were intended to be displayed for ornament as well as for use. A conspicuous article was always a great china punch-bowl." And they needed a punch-bowl, and a large one too, if we can trust the local annals of the time. William Black recorded in his diary in 1744, that he was given in Philadelphia cider and punch for lunch, rum and brandy before dinner, punch, Madeira, port, and sherry at dinner, bounce and liqueurs with the ladies, and wine and spirits and punch until bedtime. Well might he say that in Philadelphia "they were as liberal with wine as an apple-tree with its fruit on a windy day."

A clergyman named Acrelius gives us the most abundant proof why Philadelphians and their neighbors always should need a punch-bowl. In 1759 there was printed in Stockholm a detailed account of Pennsylvania or New Sweden, written by this Parson Acrelius. He fairly revels in his descriptions of the appetizing drinks to be had in the new land, and he unctuously explains how to concoct the "mixed drinks" in the most approved fashion. Here is the list of American drinks that he sent back to Sweden to encourage emigration. French Wine, Frontenac, Pontac, Port-a-port, Lisbon Wine, Phial Wine, Sherry, Madeira Wine, Sangaree, Mulled Wine, Currant Wine, Cherry Wine, Raspberry Wine, Apple Wine or Cider, Cider Royal, Mulled Cider, Rum "which is like French Brandy, only with no unpleasant odor," Raw-dram, Egg-dram, Egg-nogg, Cherry-dram, Cherry Bounce, Billberry Bounce, Punch, Mamm, Manathann (made of small beer, rum and sugar), Hotchpot (also of beer, curd and rum), Sampson (of warm cider and rum). More familiar and modern names appear also : Tiff, Flip, Hot Rum, Mulled Rum, Grog, Sling ; then come Long-sup, Mint-water, Egg-punch, Milk-punch, Sillabub, Still Liquor (which was peach brandy), Anise Cordial, Cinnamon Cordial—in all a list of fifty drinks with an added finish of liqueurs, "drops almost without end," meads, metheglins, and beers. Now, do you wonder that they had great and many punch-bowls in Philadelphia ? What a list to make a toper wish that he had lived in Pennsylvania in colonial days.

Sober Boston was not one whit behind its Quaker

neighbor.   As early as 1686 John Dunton had more
than one " noble bowl of punch " in that Puritan town.
Bennett, a visitor in Boston, in 1740, wrote, " As to
drink they have no good beer.   Madeira wines and rum-
punch are the liquors they drink in common."   Boston
people of fashion served a great punch-bowl of flip or
punch before dinner.   If the bowl were not too large
it was passed from hand to hand, and all drank from
it without the ceremony of intervening glasses.   I doubt
not it was a test of high fashion to handle well and
gracefully the punch-bowl.

Various and strange were the names of the contents of
these punch-bowls—names not on Parson Acrelius's list.
Madam Knights wrote in 1704, that " the Bare-legged
Punch had so awfull or rather awkerd a name that we
would not drink."   Berkeley wrote that the strong drink
of Virginia in 1710 was " Mobby Punch, made either of
rum from the Caribbee Islands, or Brandy distill'd from
their Apples and Peaches."   Another Virginian traveller
wrote in 1744, " Our liquor was sorry rum mixed with
water and sugar, which bore the heathenish name of
Gumbo punch."   " Pupello punch " was made from cider
brandy.   " Sangry punch " was probably an accented
sangaree.   " Rack punch " was made from arrack ; while
" Jincy punch " I leave to the philologists, antiquaries, or
expert bartenders to define or analyze.

Where are all those great punch-bowls now that we
read of in history ?   I wish I could see the punch-bowl
used by the Newburyport ministers in their frequent
social meetings, the punch-bowl in the picture painted

over Parson Lowell's mantel, the picture with its great
bowl, the parsons all smoking, and the cheerful motto,
" In Essentials, Unity ; in Non-essentials, Liberty ; in
All Things, Charity."

I should like to see the bowl which played such an important part in the transfer of the four hundred acres of
land which formed the birthplace of Thomas Jefferson.
Old Peter Jefferson made a very canny trade when he
acquired the deed of that large tract in exchange for
" Henry Weatherbourne's biggest punch-bowl full of
arrack punch." Golden should have been that bowl,
and vast its size, to justify its purchase-power.

I would I could see the great punch-bowls used by
the rollicking, hunting, drunken clergy of Virginia in
ante-Revolutionary times, at their " Monthly Meetings,"
the tale of whose disgraceful revelry has been told us by
Mr. Parton in his " Life of Jefferson." Where is the
punch-bowl used at the Wolfes Head Tavern in Newburyport, on September 26, 1765, "at the greate uneasyness and Tumult on acasion of the Stamp Act ; " the
bowl from which the alarmed citizens of Newburytown
drank fifty-seven pounds worth of " double and thribble
bowles " of punch, and in company with which they had
two pounds worth of supper and coffee. Well might
we say, " O monstrous ! But one penny worth of bread
to this intolerable deal of Sack ! " " Greate uneasyness,"
no doubt, they felt.

One of the oldest punch-bowls—indeed, one of the
oldest pieces of china in the country—is the beautiful
India or Chinese bowl now owned by Edmund Ran-

dolph Robinson, Esq., of New York. It is eighteen inches in diameter, of rich red and gold decoration, and is mounted upon a black wood stand upon which is a silver plate bearing the noble historical names of its past owners, so far back as known. It is supposed to have been brought to America by William Randolph, as his son, Sir John Randolph, is known to have long possessed it. This gentleman was one of the early Governors of Virginia, and Attorney-General in the first part of the eighteenth century. His son Peyton was president of the first Continental Congress in 1774, and Attorney-General of Virginia. From him it passed to Edmund Randolph—also Governor and Attorney-General of Virginia—aide-de-camp to Washington, and first Attorney-General and second Secretary of State of the United States. He was the great-grandfather of the present owner. This beautiful relic has passed through good service as a christening-bowl for many generations of Governors and Attorney-Generals, as well as enduring a vast amount of use on less solemn occasions.

How many punch-bowls did George Washington own? The great India china bowl with a picture of a frigate; the "rose china" bowl now at Mount Vernon; the fine great bowl now in the National Museum; the china bowl given by him to William Fitzhugh. He gave a beautiful punch-bowl to his friend and aide-de-camp, Colonel Benjamin Eyre; another to Tobias Lear, and another to Mrs. Allen Jones, of Newberne, N. C. And still less can we number the punch-bowls out of which he once drank. We all have one in the possession of some member of our family—I wonder, with all his punch-drinking, that the father of his country was ever sober.

This beautiful great bowl, eighteen inches in diameter, was given by Washington to Mrs. Allen Jones, and has had sad usage. It was buried in the ground to hide it

Bowl Given to Mrs. Allen Jones.

from Tarleton's men, and is grievously cracked and broken. It is of richest decoration of red, blue, and gold on an India china ground. It is now owned by the Washington Association of New Jersey.

Washington's India china punch-bowl, which was at Arlington House in 1840, is thus described by Mr. Lossing. "The great porcelain punch-bowl has a deep-blue border on the rim spangled with gilt dots. It was made expressly for Washington, but when, where, and by whom is not known. In the bottom is the picture of a frigate and on the side are the initials 'G. W.' in gold upon a shield, with ornamental surroundings. It is supposed to have been presented to Washington by the French naval officers."

And the "rose china" bowl at Mount Vernon! That was purchased by the Mount Vernon Association in 1891 from the Lewis estate, for $250 — and it is broken too. It is sixteen inches across and five and a half in depth. On the rim, both inside and outside the bowl, is an odd pink and yellow band. Scattered over it are flowers of various colors, in which pink predominates.

The beautiful Chinese bowl given to Colonel Benjamin Eyre, the Revolutionary patriot, by Washington, is now in the possession of Colonel Eyre's great-grandson, Benjamin Eyre Valentine, Esq., of Brooklyn. It is about fifteen inches in diameter and five and a half inches high, of fine Canton china, and bears around the outside of the bowl a scene in a Chinese town, and at regular intervals flaunting flags of all the known nations which were then engaged in maritime pursuits, our new flag — the stars and stripes — being conspicuous among them. This bowl thus possesses an additional historical interest, in that it is the oldest known piece of Chinese porcelain bearing the decoration of the American flag. It is a counterpart in size and shape to the Washington bowl now in the Smithsonian Institution, but the latter is decorated with Chinese landscapes and figures. It came into the possession of the Government through the sale of Washington relics by the Lewis family.

The most curious Continental punch-bowl that I have ever seen is the great bowl which is here shown. It is now owned by the Washington Association of New Jersey, and once belonged to Colonel Richard Varick, aide to Washington. It is a beautifully-proportioned vessel of Lowestoft or Canton china, about eighteen

Cincinnati Bowl.

inches in diameter. It has a dark-blue border with festoons of gilt, and bears on the side, in well-chosen colors, all the words and design of the full certificate of membership of the Society of the Cincinnati. The winged figure of Fame, and the other symbolical figures are carefully painted, and all the lettering, including the fine text of the Latin mottoes on seal and crest, is clear and exact. Doubtless a certificate of membership was sent to be copied when the bowl was ordered by Colonel Varick. It is in perfect condition, and is one

of the finest historical relics of early Federal times that
I have ever seen. It plainly shows the pride and delight of Revolutionary heroes in their new country and
new associations. There are in the same building—
Washington's Headquarters—half a dozen other punch-
bowls, all of historical interest, and all large enough to
show the vastly hospitable intent of the new-made citizens of the new Republic.

How pleased good, plain American Republicans were
with that Society of the Cincinnati, and how it tickled
their pride to wear the Order! Adams and Franklin
were seriously alarmed at the powerful hold and influence the decoration seemed to have, and used argument
and ridicule against it. One patriotic and vain citizen
had his portrait painted in the bottom of his punch-bowl,
with the Order proudly displayed around his neck.
Around him encircled that favorite emblem, the thirteen-
linked chain; great black links these were, with the
name of a State in each. On the side of the bowl the
Order was again displayed in larger size.

There is a gallant ten-gallon bowl in Upper Faneuil
Hall, which belongs to the Ancient and Honorable Ar-
tillery of Boston. Captain Ephraim Prescott, when in
China in 1795, procured this great bowl as a suitable
present for his companions at arms. The generous captain died during the voyage home, and on its arrival in
port the punch-bowl fell into strange hands. Thirty
years later Hon. Jonathan Hunnewell heard of its existence, bought it for $15, and gave it to the military
company for whom it was originally purchased. Curi-

ous old orders and entries exist about the purchase of wine, rum, sugar, and "sourings" for the manufacture of the ancient and honorable punches. "But if sowrings be scarce & dear, wine & rum only." You might make a punch without lemons, on a squeeze, but not without wine and rum.

"Sourings" ought to have been cheap enough. Even as early as 1741 lemons were plentiful and not at all dear. In the *Salem Gazette* in 1741, is this notice: "Extraordinary good and very fresh Orange Juice, which some of the very best Punch Tasters prefer to Lemmons, at one dollar per gallon. Also very good Lime Juice and Shrub to put into Punch, at the Basket of Lemmons. J. Crosby." So there was with all the punch-bowls, a regular profession of punch-tasting; just fancy it.

Occasionally there is some definite means of tracing the age of one of these pieces. Thus the fine, perfect punch-bowl owned by William C. Townsend, of Newport, is said to have been brought out by Captain Jacob Smith, of the Semiramis, a ship that, returning home in 1804 after an absence of three years, was lost on Nantucket Shoals. Of her cargo, valued at three hundred thousand dollars, but little was saved; but, strange to say, this great punch-bowl, twenty-two inches in diameter, holding eight gallons, was brought off in safety. It has the typical Lowestoft border of blue enamel with gold stars, and on the sides are large medallions so European in appearance that at first they seem to stamp the bowl as English. Examination, however, shows that the figures have the almond eyes of the Chinese, as well as other Oriental characteristics, and were undoubtedly copied from French or English prints sent to Canton.

A modern writer thus sadly deplores the "good old times:"

"Fifty years ago the punch-bowl was no mere ornament for the side-board and the china-cabinet; it was a thing to be brought forth and filled with a fragrant mixture of rum, brandy and curacoa, lemon, hot water, sugar, grated nutmeg, cloves, and cinnamon. The preparation of the bowl was as much a labor of love as that of a claret-cup, its degenerate successor. The ladles were beautiful works of art in silver—where are those ladles now, and what purpose do they serve?" Yes, it is true, the days of universal use for the punch-bowl are over—ornamental and curious they now are, and nothing more. Lucky it is for us china collectors, that dinners and everything else *à la russe* did not obtain with our hospitable ancestors. No great tureens, no generous pitchers, no vast platters, and no noble punch-bowls should we now have to admire and gloat over, and place in our cabinets as monuments of ceramic art. Had they lived as we do, not a single punch-bowl should we have to glory in and grow sentimental over. An ignorant butler would have carelessly and prosaically mixed the drink in his pantry in any kind of a pot or a pan, and then ignominiously bottled it, and brought it in when required in driblets, in stingy little glasses that say plainly: "Drink this, and no more."

Indeed, I doubt we ever would have had punch, for in the gustatory and potatory laws of cause and effect,

I know the punch-bowl evoked or generated punch instead of being made to hold punch. I would not go back to the rollicking, roaring, drunken ways of the olden time, but on the whole I am glad our grandfathers had those ways and bequeathed to us the glorious, great, ringing punch-bowls, in which they brewed and mixed and concocted, and from which they drank that "most insinuating drink" with which so often they got sadly, hopelessly "lusky, bosky, buffy, boozy, cocky, fuddled, balmy, pickled, screwed, funny, foggy, hazy, groggy, slewed, ruddled, dagged, jagged, comed, elevated, muddled, tight, primed, mainbrace well spliced, gilded"—or whatever elegant, chaste, colonial appellation our synonym-lacking language afforded to express being drunk.

One worthy tribute to an old punch-bowl has been written by one of our best-loved poets. I would his bowl had been like my theme, china instead of silver— ah, no! I do not, for had it been of "tenderest porce-lane" it might have been broken a century ago, and we should have known neither his punch-bowl nor his perfect poem. How true the opening verses!

"This ancient silver bowl of mine, it tells of good old times,
Of joyous days, and jolly nights, and merry Christmas chimes ;
They were a free and jovial race, but honest, brave, and true,
That dipped their ladle in the punch when this old bowl was
    new."

And can I end better than with the concluding verses ?

"I tell you there was generous warmth in good old English cheer,
I tell you 'twas a pleasant thought to bring its symbol here ;

'Tis but the fool that loves excess—hast thou a drunken soul?
Thy bane is in thy shallow skull, not in my silver bowl!

" I love the memory of the past, its pressed yet fragrant flowers,
The moss that clothes its broken walls, the ivy on its towers—
Nay, this poor bauble it bequeathed—my eyes grow moist and
    dim,
To think of all the vanished joys that danced around its brim.

" Then fill a fair and honest cup and bear it straight to me,
The goblet hallows all it holds whate'er the liquid be,
And may the cherubs on its face protect me from the sin,
That dooms one to those dreadful words, ' My dear, where have
    you been ? ' "

XI.

GEORGE AND MARTHA WASHINGTON'S
CHINA

IN the long and apparently extravagant orders which George Washington sent to England previous to the Revolutionary War, for the purchase and exportation to him of dress goods and house and table furnishings of various descriptions, I find no mention of table china. In 1759 he wrote for " four Fashionable China Branches or Stands for Candles," and for " Busts of Alexander the Great, Charles XII. of Sweden, Julius Cæsar, and King of Prussia, fifteen inches high and ten wide. Others smaller of Prince Eugene & Duke of Marlborough. Two wild Beasts twelve inches high and eighteen inches long, and Sundry Small Ornaments for the chimney piece." As these were to be "finished neat and bronzed with copper," or to be gilt, they were doubtless all of plaster or some similar composition. A portion of the items in the order were sent to him, the wild beasts being "Two Lyons." These two plaster "lyons," shorn of their golden lustre and painted ignominiously black, stood for years over a doorway at Mount Vernon, were inherited by Lawrence Washington, and sold in Philadelphia on April 22, 1891, for thirty dollars.

I can find no hint of any china possessions of Washington until the War of the Revolution was gloriously ended. He had plenty of pewter—dinner dishes of that humble metal with his initials and crest are still preserved. His camp-service of forty pieces was entirely of pewter, and I doubt not the greater part also of his home table-furnishings in his early married life.

In his directions for remodelling and refurnishing his house at Mount Vernon, after the expiration of his terms as President, he ordered that a small room be appropriated for "the Sèvres china and other things of that sort which are not in common use." Mr. Lossing says :

"He undoubtedly referred to the sets of china which had been presented, one to himself, and the other to Mrs. Washington, by the officers of the French Army. The former was dull white in color, with heavy and confused scroll and leaf ornaments in bandeaux of deep blue, and having upon the sides of the cups and tureens, and in the bottoms of the plates, saucers, and meat dishes, the Order of the Cincinnati held by Fame personated by a winged woman with a trumpet. These designs were skilfully painted in delicate colors."

While this description of Mr. Lossing's is accurate as to the decoration of the china, if not as to the quality of the decoration, a china collector would at once discover that the "Cincinnati set" was not Sèvres, but was plainly Chinese. It is the well-known dull white, hard paste of Canton manufacture, with a border of commonplace Oriental design in deep blue under the glaze. Some of the pieces have (all, perhaps, had originally) a narrow

rim of gilt on the
outer edge, and a
narrow line of gilt
within the border.
The rather insig-
nificant and un-
dersized figure of
Fame has bright
brown wings and
trumpet, a robè of

light green, a scarf of bright pink, while the bow-knot
sustaining the colored Order of the Cincinnati is light
blue. This design is not painted at all skilfully but quite
crudely over the glaze. Some of the covered dishes

Cincinnati China.

bear upon the
cover the order
without the fig-
ure of Fame.
In a note made
by Governor
Lyon he states
that this service
was " made in
Canton in 1784,
the design being
furnished by
General Miran-
da." Though
the design be in-
significant and

the execution crude, much interest is added to the Cincinnati china to know that the "most gentlemanlike of fillibusters" made the drawing for the decoration. That plausible and brilliant man who "talked so like an angel" that Americans, Russians, and Englishmen vied in endeavors to assist him in his visionary schemes; who helped to establish independence in America, to give freedom to France, to liberate his native land, Venezuela; who aided in freeing thousands of others, died himself in a Spanish dungeon a slave, a most miserable captive, in chains, with an iron collar around his neck.

No one was apparently better fitted to give information on the subject of the Cincinnati china than Governor Lyon, for he was a frequent visitor at Mount Vernon and Arlington House in the middle of this century; he was also collecting facts and details with a view to writing a "History of the Ceramic Relics of the Revolution." Unfortunately he relied much on his memory, and hence left few notes.

Much ignorance about this Cincinnati china is displayed, even by writers upon pottery and porcelain. The author of "The Ceramic Art" calls it Sèvres, and places the most Chinese-looking illustration of it alongside the print of equally Frenchy Sèvres vases. That careful observer and exact recorder, the author of "The China Hunters' Club," falls into no such error, and though unable to examine specimens closely, says "they looked like so-called Lowestoft, and may have been Chinese, English, or of some French factory." Another well-known writer says that this set was given to Washington in 1780. As neither the Society of the Cincinnati, nor its badge, existed until 1783, this statement is palpably false.

The authorities at the National Museum, and all the owners of pieces of the set, consider that it was presented to General Washington by the entire Society of the Cincinnati, and not by the French officers alone, as Mr. Lossing states. It would seem probable that had the French officers made the gift, it would have been of French china of some elegance, instead of such commonplace Chinese porcelain. Hon. Hamilton Fish, the President of the Society of the Cincinnati, tells me that the general society, and, as far as known, the individual State societies, have no records of the gift of this china to Washington; nor have I seen any letters, any entries, any notes of the time, to prove, or even hint, that this china was the gift of the Society of the Cincinnati. Though Martha Washington mentions the set in her will, she does not specify it as a gift, as she does the "set given me by Mr. Van Braam."

While I have never seen any statements to prove that this set of china was the gift of the Society of the Cincinnati, there is in the possession of Ferdinand J. Dreer, Esq., of Philadelphia, a letter which would seem to indicate that Washington may have bought the china himself, or, at any rate, it proves that china with the decoration of the badge of the Cincinnati was ordered for the general American market. The letter, which is very characteristic of Washington's thrift and prudence, is addressed to Colonel Tench Tilghman and runs thus :

MT VERNON 17th Augst 1785.

DEAR SIR : The *Baltimore Advertiser* of the 12th inst announces the arrival of the ship at that Port immediately from China, and by an advertisement in the same paper I perceive that the Cargo is to be sold by public Vendue on the first of Octo. next.

At what prices the enumerated articles will sell on the terms proposed can only be known from the experiment, but if the quantity at market is great, and they should sell as goods have sold at vendue bargains may be expected.—I therefore take the liberty of requesting the favor of you, in that case, to purchase the several things contained in the enclosed list.

You will readily perceive my dear sir, my purchasing or not depends entirely upon the prices—If *great bargains* are to be had, I would supply myself agreeably to the list. If the prices do not fall *below* a cheap *retail* sale, I would decline them altogether or take such articles only (if cheaper than common) as are marked in the margin of the Invoice.

Before October, if none of these goods are previously sold, and if they are, the matter will be ascertained thereby, you will be able to form a judgment of the prices they will command by Vendue—upon information of which, I will deposit the money in your hands to comply with the terms of the Sale.

Since I began this letter I have been informed that good India Nankeens are selling at Dumfries (not far from me) at 7/6 a pc this Curr F—— But if my memory has not failed me, I used to import them before the war for about 5S sterl. If so, though 50 per cent is a small advance upon India Goods through a British channel (and the duties and accumulated charges thereon) yet quaere ? would not 7/6 be a high price for Nankeens brought immediately from India, exempted from *such* duties and charges ? If this is a conjecture founded in fairness, it will give my ideas of the prices of the articles from that country and be a government for your conduct therein, at or before the day appointed for the public Vendue.

With the highest esteem and regard

I am Dr Sir,

Yr affect friend and Obedt Serv't

G. WASHINGTON.

Invoice of Goods to be purchased by Tench Tilghman Esqr on account of Geo Washington agreeable to the letter accompanying this of equal date.

A sett of the best Nankin Table China

Ditto—best Evening Cups & Saucers

* A sett of *large* blue & white China

Dishes say half a dozen more or less

* 1 Doz. *small* bowls blue & white

* 6 Wash hand Guglets & Basons

6 Large Mugs or 3 mugs & 3 jugs

A Quart^r Chest best Hyson Tea

A League of Battavia Arrack if a League is not large.

About 13 yards of good blu : Paduasoy

A ps of fine muslin plain

* 1 ps of Silk Handkerchiefs

12 ps of the Best Nankeens

18 ps of the second quality or coursest kind for servants.

G. WASHINGTON.

17th Augst 1785.

* With the badge of the society of the Cincinnati if to be had.

The sentimental and high-flown announcement in the *Baltimore Advertiser* of the arrival of the vessel referred to by Washington reads thus :

" On Tuesday evening last arrived here, directly from China, the ship Pallas commanded by its owner Capt. O'Donnell. She has on board a most valuable Cargo consisting of an extensive Variety of Teas, China, Silks, Satins, Nankeens, &c., &c. We are extremely happy to find the Commercial Reputation of this Town so far increased as to attract the attention of Gentlemen who are engaged in carrying on this distant but beneficial Trade. It is no unpleasing Sight to see the Crew of this Ship, Chinese, Malays, Japanese and Moors with a few Europeans, all habited according to the different Countries to which they belong, and employed together as Brethren; it is thus Commerce binds and unites all the Nations of the Globe with a golden Chain."

The advertisement of the auction sale is also given:

" To be sold at Public Vendue at Baltimore on the 1st of October next in Lots The Following Goods Just Imported in the Ship Pallas, direct from China: Hyson Teas, of the first Quality in Quarter-Chests and Canisters of about 2¼ lb each; Hyson Tea of the second sort in Chests; Singlo, Confee, Hyson-Skin, and Gunpowder Teas of the first Quality in Chests; and a large Quantity of excellent Bohea Tea; Table-Sets of the best Nankin blue and white Stone China; white stone and painted China of the second Quality in Sets; Dishes of blue and white Stone China 5 and 3 in a Set; Stone China flat and Soup Plates; Breakfast Cups and Saucers of the best blue and white Stone China in Sets; Evening blue and white Stone China Cups and Saucers; Ditto painted; *Ditto with the Arms of the Order of Cincinnati;* Bowls—best blue and white Stone China in Sets; blue and white Stone China Pint Sneakers; Mugs— best Stone China in Sets; small Tureens with Covers;

Wash-Hand Guglets and Basons; brown Nankeen of the first and second Quality; plain, flowered and spotted Lustrings of all Colours; Satins, the Greatest Part Black; Peelongs of different Colours, in whole and half Pieces; Sarsnet of different Colours; embroidered Waistcoat Pieces of Silks and Satins; Silk Handkerchiefs, very fine, and 20 in a piece; spotted and flowered Velvets; painted Gauzes; Bengal Piece-Goods and Muslins, plain flowered and corded; Silk Umbrellas of all Sizes; elegant Paper-Hangings; japanned Tea-Chests; Ditto Fish and Counter Boxes; Sago; Cinnamon and Cinnamon Flowers; Rhubarb; Opium; Gamboge; Borax; very old Battavia Arrack in Leagures; with Sundry other Articles; the enumeration of which would take up too much Room in a Public Paper."

Then follow the terms and methods of the sale.

Though this inventory is of special interest to us on account of the specification of the china with the Arms of the Order of Cincinnati, the other items also merit attention as showing the goods and merchandise imported at that date to America. And the strange, obsolete names of the china articles excite our curiosity. A "guglet" is a juglet or little jug; and the word "sneaker" is not a low Baltimorean Americanism, but good old Addisonian English; for we read in *The Freeholder*, No. 22, these lines: "After supper he asked me if I was an admirer of punch, and immediately called for a sneaker." A sneaker was originally a smaller drinking mug or beaker than was ordinarily used, and was drunk from by a "sneak-cup," that contemptible creature who wished to shrink from his convivial duties by "balking his drink," or, to speak plainly, who wished to drink less than his companions fancied he ought to. It came gradually to be used as the name of a small mug, and as such frequently appears in the inventories of china made and sold at Worcester. Washington was no "sneak-cup," he boldly and liberally ordered large mugs instead of pint sneakers.

We can well imagine the pride of Washington as he read this announcement of the arrival of the ship direct from China with its load of rich goods, his pride in the prosperity and increasing commerce of the new Federal nation. The Pallas was the second ship only to arrive in the United States direct from Canton—for Canton was at that date the only Chinese port open to European and American vessels.

Watson, the author of the "Annals of Philadelphia," states that the first ship to bring porcelain direct to America from China was commanded by Captain John Green, and sailed patriotically from New York on February 22d, Washington's birthday, 1784, and landed in return on May 11, 1785. He says : " I have now a plate of the china brought by him—the last remaining of a whole set." This ship was the Empress of China, and one of her officers was Captain Samuel Shaw, a brave Revolutionary officer who had been one of the original and active founders of the Society of the Cincinnati ; in fact, one of the framers of the constitution of the society. Thus it is easy to see the means and manner by which the pattern of the figure Fame bearing the Cincinnati badge, which had been drawn by General Miranda, was conveyed to China. It is possible, of course, that Captain Shaw brought home with him in the Empress of China the " Cincinnati set," as a gift for General Washington ; but General Knox had a similar set. It remained in his great china-closet at his beautiful home in Thomaston, Me., until the year 1840. A two-handled cup of this set, bearing General Knox's initials as well as the Order of the Cincinnati, sold for twenty-one dollars at the Governor Lyon sale in 1876. Two of the plates that had belonged to General Washington's set sold at the same time for one hundred dollars each. Though I have had two of these Cincinnati plates offered to me by dealers, within a year, for a smaller sum, one with an authentic history cannot now be purchased for less than three hundred dollars. A plate and bowl were sold by Sypher in 1890 for six hundred dollars. At the Loan Collection held at the Metropolitan Opera House in New York, in 1889, on the occasion of the centennial celebration of the inauguration of George Washington as President of the United States, there were shown several pieces of the Cincinnati china that had belonged to Washington, one plate belonging to Luther Kountze, Esq., of New York; a plate and saucer belonging to Edmund Law Rogers, Esq., of Baltimore, who is a grandson of Eliza Parke Custis, the granddaughter of Martha Washington. Mrs. Caleb Lyon also exhibited two plates, a tray, and teapot. These pieces, with a pickle leaf and " small terreen," are now in the possession of Miss Lyon, of Staten Island, and from them the illustrations on page 231 were taken. There are no fewer than forty pieces of this set in the National Museum in Washington; most of these were purchased by the Government from the Lewis family in 1878.

There are also in the National Museum several pieces of the china known as the Martha Washington set. The smaller of the plates shown on page 9 is one of this set. Of this china Lossing writes:

"The set of china presented at the same time by the French officers to Mrs. Washington was of similar material, but more delicate in color than the General's. The ornamentation was also far more delicate, excepting the delineation of the figure and Cincinnati Order on the former. Around the outside of each tureen and the inside of each plate and saucer is painted in delicate colors a chain of thirteen large and thirteen small elliptical links. Within each large link is the name of one of the original thirteen States. On the sides of the cups and tureens, and in the bottom of each plate and saucer, is the interlaced monogram of Martha Washington—M. W.—enclosed in a beautiful green wreath composed of the leaves of the laurel and olive. Beneath this is a ribbon upon which is inscribed, in delicately-traced letters, '*Decus et tutam enabillo.*' From the wreath are rays of gold which give a brilliant appearance to the pieces. There is also a delicately colored stripe around the edges of the cups and saucers and plates."

This description conveys an excellent idea of the set to a careless observer, but is not wholly correct. The "delicately colored stripe" is a blue and gold snake with his tail in his mouth—a significant emblem. There are fifteen long and fifteen short links instead of thirteen, Kentucky and Vermont having at that time been added to the thirteen original States. And the motto upon the pink ribbon scroll to me appears to be, "*Decus et tutamen ab illo.*" Mr. Lossing also says : "At that time the china like that presented by the French officers was only made at the Sèvres manufactory, the art of decorating porcelain or china ware with enamel colors and gold being then not generally known." This, of course, is an incorrect statement, since it was at the time of the greatest splendor in the English factories. The decoration of china with gold was forbidden for some time in France except in the Sèvres factory, but this Martha Washington set is not Sèvres. It is apparently Chinese. Mr. Lossing wrote me a long letter on this subject. In it he says that the French officers would not have sent as a gift to Washington china from any factory save Sèvres ; but it seems now to be very doubtful whether this set was the gift of the French officers. In the National Museum at the Smithsonian Institution are pieces labelled, "Presented to Martha Washington by LaFayette." There is no authority for the ascription to Lafayette of the gift of this china. The only reason given at the National Museum for thus labelling it is a good one—that the ticket was on the china when it was in the Patent Office in 1871, and so it will still be kept on it until some good evidence is brought that such a label is incorrect. The pieces exhibited at the Loan Collection in 1889, by individual owners—Edmund Law

Rogers being one—were marked as the gift of Mr. Van Braam.   Mrs. Beverly Kennon, of Washington, D. C., is the niece of George Washington Parke Custis, and owns a cup and saucer of this set.   She tells me that the " Martha Washington china was presented (so said my mother and uncle—both grandchildren of Mrs. Washington—who certainly ought to have known) by General Washington's early friend, a Hollander named Van Braam.   It was made in China and painted in England." Mr. Custis thought that Mr. Van Braam was a merchant in China ; the Dutch at that time had the closest business connections with that country.   Miss Lyon also says that Mr. Custis told her that the set in question was the gift of Mr. Van Braam.   In addition to all this testimony in favor of Mr. Van Braam, may be given the clause from Martha Washington's will, referring to the "sett of china given me by Mr. Van Braam."   Captain Van Braam was a friend of Washington's youth and taught the future President the art of fencing.   The gay fencing-master cut but a sorry figure at a later date, being more than suspected of treason and unsoldierly behavior.

Though neither of these sets were of Sèvres porcelain, Washington is said to have owned two sets of Sèvres. In the National Museum are twenty pieces of a service called Sèvres that belonged to him, and which he used both while he was President and at Mount Vernon.   At the Governor Lyon sale a white Sèvres plate, catalogued as having belonged to Washington, brought twelve dollars.   Miss Lyon still owns a custard cup of the set.   It has a pretty gold "dontil" rim and a gilt cherry as a knob on the cover. It bears the Sèvres mark.

Another white and gold breakfast service, marked "Nast"—a well-known French china-maker—also belonged to Washington. Miss Mary E. M. Powel, of Newport, has a coffee-cup and saucer of the set. It was presented to Colonel John Hare Powel, of Powelton, by Mrs. Custis, in 1812. The butter-dish of this service is illustrated in "Mount Vernon and its Associations."

Another white and gold set of Canton china still has existing pieces to show its character. This was probably a dessert service. A berry-dish and two dessert-plates were sold in Philadelphia, in 1890, for H. L. D. Lewis (one of the Washington heirs), for fifty dollars. They were purchased by the Washington Association of New Jersey (and can be seen at their building in Morristown), with a cup of white porcelain with maroon ribbon and wreath decoration, which also came from Mount Vernon. Still other pieces of Washington china were sold in Philadelphia in 1891, among them portions of a set of Crown Derby with tiny sprigs and flowered border. Pieces of this set were owned by the late William Henry Harrison, Esq., of New York.

A very interesting plate is in the possession of Doctor Allan McLane Hamilton, of New York. It was given as a keepsake to Mrs. Alexander Hamilton by Mrs. George Washington. It descended from Mrs. Hamilton to Philip Hamilton, the father of the present owner. It is of French porcelain, twelve and a half inches in diameter, with slightly crenated edges. On the left rim it is decorated with a festoon of oak leaves with gold acorns; on the right with a border of laurel or myrtle. Above is a lyre with a garland—both in gold. In the centre of the plate is an eagle, perched upon a bundle of thunder-bolts, while on his head are the thirteen stars, all in gold; beneath, in script, are the letters G. & M. W., surrounded by a wreath of roses and forget-me-nots. This plate is unique, the remainder of the service being either lost or destroyed.

In the diary of Baron Von Closen, under the date of July 19, 1792, this entry is found: "On my arrival Mrs. Washington requested me to invite Count de Custine—who was then at Colchester—with all the officers of his regiment, to dinner for the next day. The Count accepted the invitation with ten officers of the regiment, and sent Mr. Bellegarde before him with a very valuable present, a set of china coming from his own manufactory at Niederweiler, near Pfalzburg, in Lorraine. It was ornamented with a coat of arms and initials of General Washington, surmounted by a laurel wreath, and was received by Mrs. Washington with most hearty thanks." I can well believe the latter statement, for this Niederweiler china was by far the most beautiful in quality, decoration, and shape that Washington ever possessed. The pieces were all slightly different, the only universal decoration being a beautiful cipher of Washington's initials surrounded by a golden-brown cloud background, and surmounted by a tiny rose-wreath. The other decorations were of festoons or interlaced wreaths. A saucer of this set, owned by J. Chester Lyman, Esq., is now at the Metropolitan Museum of Art. It was given to Timothy Dwight, Mr. Lyman's ancestor, by Mrs. Custis. The design on this piece consists of festoons of very delicate leaves in various shades of gold.

Another piece has wreaths of tiny roses around the edge. A sugar-box and bowl, owned by Mrs. Beverley Kennon, of Washington, bear still different designs. A covered jug of the set is here shown. The mark on this china was the interlaced Cs, the stamp used by Count Custine, and it also is numbered "No. 29." Martha Wash

Washington's Niederweiler China.

ington divided this set among her three granddaughters during her lifetime, which is the reason it is not mentioned in her will.

At Mount Vernon are two beautiful dishes which were presented to the Association by Mr. Corcoran, and are said to have been George Washington's. One is a salad or berry-dish, seven and a half inches square and an inch and a half deep; the edges are irregularly and gracefully scalloped. There is a narrow rim of gold around the edge; within, a wide band of blue broken by a chain of circular rings in gold, each enclosing a gold dot; within this a narrow band of gold; and a delicate gold beading forms the inside edge of the border. Little bunches and sprigs of flowers are scattered over the centre, having gold stems and leaves and blue blossoms. The plate has the same decoration. Both have the small blue S of the Salopian or Caughley works on the base. Mrs. Russel, of Cambridge, Mass., has a plate of this set, which was given to her by Mr. Corcoran. These three pieces are evidently part of a dessert-service—but where are the other pieces?

The "blue and white china in common use," referred to in Martha Washington's will, was of a kind familiar to us all, "old blue Canton." Several pieces of it are now in the National Museum. Miss Lyon has two dishes of rather better quality that came from Mount Vernon, Nankin china apparently. Others have recently been sold at auction in Philadelphia in 1891. Washington used this cheerful, substantial Canton china "for common use" on his everyday table, just as did every other good and wealthy American citizen of his day and time. Besides the pieces of blue and white Canton china which he ordered of Colonel Tilghman in 1785, Washington also wrote to General Robert Ridgway, on September 12, 1783, a long and carefully expressed letter ordering wine and beer glasses, and decanters and china. "If a neat and complete set of Blue & white Table China could be had upon easy terms, be pleased to inform me of it, and the price—not less than six or eight doz., however, and proportionable number of deep and other Plates, Butter-Boats, Dishes & Tureens will suffice. These things sometimes come in complete Setts ready packed; should this be the case and the number of Pieces greater than what is here mentioned, I should have no objection to a case on that acc't."

Washington had very decided opinions and tastes about table-furnishings, as he had about dress. When wine was served to him and his visitors in some very ugly cups at Princeton, and he was told that the cups were made by a man who had since turned Quaker, he replied, with his cumbersome and rare humor, that it was a pity the man had not turned Quaker before he made the cups.

The china of Mary Washington did not go to her illustrious son. By her will, made in 1788, she left to her grandson, Fielding Lewis, "half my crockery ware, half my pewter, and my blue and white tea china," and to her granddaughter, Betty Carter, the other half of the crockery and pewter, and "my red and white china." Perhaps she fancied the General had enough china, as he apparently did.

Washington progressed in mantel decoration somewhat beyond the plaster "Lyons" and busts that decorated the home of his early married life. The mantel vases described by Mr. Lossing, and shown in an illustration in his book, were sold in Philadelphia, in February, 1891, for four hundred and fifty dollars each. They stood about eighteen inches high, were decorated with butterflies and flowers on a dark-blue ground, and had covers surmounted by the Dog Fo. Other vases which once graced the chimney-pieces of Mount Vernon are still owned by members of the Custis family. The profuse mantel decoration of to-day was, however, undreamt of by him.

There are many other pieces of table china now in existence, and proudly shown, that are said to have belonged to Washington. Doubtless their owners consider that they have sufficient proof of the authenticity of their relics, but as I know not the value of their proofs I will not mention their china. I think, with the great number of punch-bowls that once belonged to Washington, and that are mentioned in another chapter, with the vast assortment of rich glass-ware that once was owned by Washington, and that is now in the National Museum, in other public and in many private collections, that the amount of china already named will quite swell up a value far beyond the item in the sworn inventory of the executors of George Washington's will—" Glass & China in the China Closet, & that up-stairs, & that in the cellar, $800." What would be a relic-lover's estimate of the value of that glass and china to-day?

XII.

PRESIDENTIAL CHINA

THE sets of china used by other Presidents than Washington, while their various owners were living in the Executive Mansion, deserve to be mentioned and described on account of historic interest, though not always for their value as ceramics, and because specimens of them are within the possibility of possession by a china collector. I think the true china lover will, however, care little to own any piece of porcelain simply because it is said to have belonged to or was eaten from by some great man—if that be its only virtue ; and I am sure will care little for much of the china that has graced the table at the White House.

Jefferson was, without doubt, as profusely hospitable a President as ever dwelt in the Executive Mansion of the United States. For this lavish hospitality he may have had a double reason—not only to gratify his well-known liberal disposition and his love of good company as well, but to prove his shrewd suspicion, or rather his firm conviction, that a well-cooked dinner was often a potent factor in accomplishing his desired end when his smooth and persuasive argument or his apparent candor would have failed. A good illustration of his crafty, worldly wisdom is shown in the result of the historically renowned dinner given by him, when Secretary of State, in 1789, at Philadelphia, to President Washington and the prominent leaders of both parties of the House and Senate. A fierce dispute between the Northern and Southern members of Congress had risen over the location of the national capital. The Southerners insisted that the banks of either the Delaware or Potomac should be chosen as a site; the Northerners were equally determined upon the borders of the Susquehanna. An amicable and peaceful settlement followed this famous dinner, and shrewd Jefferson had his own way—the seat of government was placed at Washington, on the Potomac. This lavish hospitality, both in the Executive Mansion and in private life, doubtless had much to do with Jefferson's subsequent financial embarrassments. Very few of the pieces of table-ware used and owned by Jefferson, either in public or private life, are now to be found. His married life was short, and his housekeeping, both when Secretary of State and President, was entirely in the hands of servants, a condition never favorable to the preservation of china. The dispersion of his household effects caused the disappearance from sight and knowledge of what few pieces remained. Though his silver is carefully preserved by his descendants, they own no china.

An octagonal plate of Rockingham ware, used by Jefferson when President, is now in Washington. It bears the stamp "BRAMELD." It is of the dark blue shade frequently used in the Chinese designs on that ware, a blue so rich and deep that it gives a character and tone rarely found on pottery, and makes the plate as glorious in tint as a block of choicest lapis lazuli. The glaze is "crazed" on the entire surface of this particular plate, both glaze and color being splintered in places from the brownish pottery body. The plate has evidently been frequently and severely heated in an oven. I have seen other pieces of the same shape, bearing the same design, which had not, however, the honorable distinction of having been owned by Jefferson.

An exceedingly beautiful plate was sold at auction in New York, about fifteen years ago, that was catalogued as having been the property of Jefferson and used on his dinner-table. It was apparently of Chinese manufacture of the type known as Lowestoft. The rim and inner border were diapered in dark blue, relieved by dainty lines of gold. In the centre was the letter "J," in gold, enclosed in a shield outlined in blue enamel adorned with thirteen stars. Above the shield was a blue and gold helmet with closed visor. This plate brought $40, being of ceramic value as well as of historic interest. There was sold at the same time, for $2.50, a custard-cup of French porcelain painted with detached bachelor's-buttons, which was also said to have been Jefferson's.

Of the china used by either President Adams I have no definite knowledge, though I have seen several pieces of Oriental china that bore the reputation of having been used by these Presidents during their terms of office.

The china used by Madison was a set of finely painted

Lowestoft. Portions of it are owned by descendants in Virginia. He also owned a set of fine French china with his initials.

The next White House china-service of which I have seen authentic pieces is the one known as the Monroe set—Madison's official china having been destroyed at the burning of the Executive Mansion by the British in 1814. This Monroe set is of French china of good quality. It has around the edge a half-inch band of pale coffee color or brownish buff, edged with a burnished gilt line on either side. It has a small and pretty coffee-cup with extraordinarily flat saucer.

The Andrew Jackson set was of heavy and rather coarse bluish porcelain, apparently of Chinese manufacture, with bands of ugly dull blue and coarsely applied gold, and a conventional and clumsy shield in the centre. It was not very tasteful nor beautiful, any more than was its Presidential owner, and very fitly furnished forth his dining-table.

In Franklin Pierce's time what is now known as "the red-edged set" was bought, the border being of dark red and gilt, with an inner circle of gilt. It was of French china of fair quality. The cups of this set were very large, while the saucers were exceedingly diminutive; though people of fashion, even at that date, had not wholly given up drinking tea from their saucers. A lady at whose home Judge Story and Daniel Webster were frequent visitors, tells me that those two representative men of their day always drank their cooled tea from their saucers.

The Buchanan set was of very commonplace ware, with a stiff, meagre, and ill-painted spray of flowers in the centre of each plate and on the side of each dish. Ugly as they are, the plates are now valued at forty dollars each. The saucers of this set were disproportionately large, holding much more than the cups. A few pieces

Lincoln China.

of this Buchanan set still remain in Washington, though none are preserved at the White House.

A very full set of Presidential china was bought in Abraham Lincoln's time. It is of finest French porcelain, with a border of crimson purple or plum color, with delicate lines and dots of gold, and the plates, platters, and saucers have slightly scalloped edges. In the centre of the plates and on the sides of the dishes and small pieces is a very spirited version of the coat-of-arms of the United States, with the motto "E Pluribus Unum" upon a clouded background of gold. A plate and cup of this set, now in the possession of Miss Henrietta D. Lyon, of Staten Island, is here shown. This design is very dignified and appropriate, and, with the substitution of a blue border with gilt ears of Indian corn, has been reproduced for the present mistress of the White House. Plates of this Abraham Lincoln set sold at the Gover-

Grant China.

nor Lyon sale for $4.25 each, and little covered custard- or egg-cups for $1.50 each. I have recently had some of these plates offered to me for $25 apiece. Portions of this set still remain and are used at the White House.

The General Grant set is well known, and is very handsome. The border is of buff and gold, broken once by a small United States shield in high colors. In the centre is a well-painted spray or bunch of flowers, many being the wild flowers of the United States. The coffee-cups of this set were ordered to use at the wedding of the President's daughter, and were known as the "Nellie Grant cups." A plate said to have been ordered for the White House in General Grant's time is here shown.

Of the beautiful and costly set ordered by Mrs. Hayes
too much is known, and too many cheaper copies have
been sold, and may be seen in any large china-shop, to
make it worth while to give any detailed description
here. It was made at Limoges by the Havilands, as
was also the " Grant set." It makes a fine room decoration when the various pieces are arranged in the beautiful buffet that President Arthur had made for it, and is
more satisfactory in that position than when in use on
the table.

It may be asked how all these pieces of Presidential
china come to be found in private collections, and
offered for sale, and so generally distributed over the
country. A very reprehensible custom existed until recent years (and indeed may still be possible) of selling
at auction at the end of each Presidential term, or in
the middle if thought necessary, whatever household
effects the house steward and house occupants chose
to consider of no further use. These Presidential sales
were, of course, eagerly attended by relic-hunters. At
such a sale in President Grant's day a lot of " old truck,"
as it was irreverently called, valued at $500, brought
$2,760. As there must be, of course, much breakage
of china in the pantry and dining-room of the White
House, and as it was considered for many years necessary to have full "sets" of china table-ware, enough
to serve an entire dinner, the odd plates, cups and
saucers, and dishes were ruthlessly " cleared out " whenever an appropriation was made by the Government, or
the President desired to buy a new set. It seems a pity

that a few pieces of each of these "state sets" should not have been preserved in a cabinet at the White House to show us the kind of china from which our early rulers ate their daily meals and served their state dinners, as well as to show our varying and halting progress in luxury, refinement, and taste.

XIII.

DESIGNS RELATING TO WASHINGTON

ONE scarcely knows where to begin or end this list when one considers the vast number of pieces of pottery and porcelain that bear the name and ostensibly bear the portrait of Washington—more and more varied even than the Lord Nelson prints in England. Often Washington's portrait is found with that of Franklin or Lafayette; in such cases I have given the subject of the most prominent or the named design the honor of determining the place on the list. The largest number of these Washington designs occur upon Liverpool mugs and pitchers in black prints. Some few are in blue upon Staffordshire earthenware. In the Huntington Collection at the Metropolitan Museum of Art, in New York, may be seen a vast number of ceramic likenesses of the great American. Many of these are single specimens painted by hand—both by artists and amateurs, apparently. One set of four plaques has copies of the Savage, Trumbull, Peale, and Stuart portraits of Washington. Such I have not attempted to describe or classify. One specially comical portrait-plaque, painted in China, shows an almond-eyed Washington with his hair *à la chinoise*, with feminine hair ornaments, while on his republican shoulders rests the dark blue sack garment familiar to us as the festival garb of our Chinese washermen. There are in the Trumbull-Prime Collection a large number of Washington pitchers, from which some of the entries on this list are described.

One Liverpool print deserves special mention, for a very interesting story is attached to it, and is told in detail by Benson J. Lossing in his "Mount Vernon and Its Associations." A dealer in Philadelphia imported a number of pitchers of various sizes, each bearing a portrait of Washington, the design for which had been taken from Gilbert Stuart's picture painted for the Marquis of Lansdowne. Nutter had engraved this portrait for Hunter's edition of Lavater, and a copy of the engraving was printed upon the pitchers. Mr. Dorsey, a sugar-dealer of Philadelphia, purchased several of these pitchers, and after a number of unsuccessful attempts to separate the part bearing the portrait from the rest of the pitcher, managed at last, by using the broad-faced hammer of a shoemaker, to break out the picture unharmed with a single sharp blow. The pottery fragment bearing the portrait was handsomely framed by Mr. James R. Smith, of Philadelphia, and sent to Judge Washington at Mount Vernon, where it was hung and was known as the pitcher portrait. A copy of it is here shown.

Mr. Smith owned a crayon portrait of Washington, a copy made by Sharpless himself of his original picture of Washington. On the back of this Sharpless portrait was a long eulogy of Washington, written by an English gentleman. Mr. Smith copied a portion of this eulogy

on the back of the pitcher portrait—as much of the inscription, in fact, as there was room to write. It ran thus,
as given in "Alden's Collections of American Epitaphs

. Pitcher Portrait.

and Inscriptions:" "Washington the Defender of his
Country, the Founder of Liberty and the Friend of Man.
History and Tradition are explored in vain for a paral-
lel to his character. In the annals of modern greatness
he stands alone, and the noblest names of antiquity lose
their lustre in his presence. Born the Benefactor of

Mankind he united all the qualities necessary to an illustrious career. Nature made him great, he made himself virtuous. Called by his country to the defense of her liberties, he triumphantly vindicated the rights of humanity and, on the pillars of National Independence, laid the foundations of a Great Republick. Twice invested with supreme magistracy, by the unanimous vote of a free people, he surpassed in the cabinet the glories of the field; and voluntarily resigning the sword and the sceptre, retired to the shades of private life. A spectacle so new and so sublime was contemplated with the profoundest admiration, and the name of Washington, adding new lustre to humanity, resounded to the remotest regions of the earth. Magnanimous in youth, glorious through life, great in death, his highest ambition the happiness of mankind, his noblest victory the conquest of himself. Bequeathing to posterity the inheritance of his fame, and building his monument in the hearts of his countrymen he lived—the ornament of the eighteenth century, he died—regretted by the mourning world."

The centre portion of this inscription has been within a few years cut out of the back of the frame by some vandal hands. The entire eulogy, as written on the back of the Sharpless portrait, can be seen in Lossing's "Mount Vernon and Its Associations," and in Sparks' "Writings of Washington," and as a masterpiece of flattery—and honest flattery, too—it knows no equal.

This pitcher portrait descended to Lawrence Washington, Esq. It was exhibited at the Philadelphia Stat

House in 1876, and was sold at auction April 22, 1891, at Philadelphia, for $75.

Liverpool pitchers bearing the design like that of the pitcher portrait are rare in America, but are found in a few private collections; and oval plaques are also found bearing the same portrait. These latter have a swelling surface, as if cut from the side of a pitcher. There are specimens with this print in the Trumbull-Prime Collection. Some years ago a framed pitcher portrait was found in the attic of an old house in Washington Street, Newport, and is now in the possession of Benjamin Smith, Esq., of Philadelphia.

Some very interesting ceramic portraits of Washington were made in China, early in this century, on four porcelain toddy-jugs, by order of Mr. B. C. Willcocks, of Philadelphia. It is said that the portraits were copied from one of these pitcher portraits, but the head on the toddy-jugs is longer and narrower, and the neck is much longer. This elongating may have been done by the Chinese artist, but it looks more like the other Stuart portrait, the one with lawn ruffles; the pitcher portrait has a lace ruffle. One of this quartette of covered toddy-jugs was kept by Mr. Willcocks, and the other three he presented to three life-long friends who met frequently and regularly to play whist with him. One of these Washington toddy-jugs is now in a Washington collection in Newport. It is a foot in height and seven inches in diameter, of white Chinese hard porcelain. It has foliated handles, heavy rim, and "chimera" knob on the cover, all of gilt. On one side is the portrait of Washington, but by reason of the bluish shade of the hard porcelain it lacks the softness of the print on the Liverpool ware. The portrait is banded with a heavy gold edge, and in a similar gilt oval on the opposite side of the pitcher is a pretty cipher, B. C. W.

To this pitcher-portrait design, since so much honor has been paid to it, I will assign the first place on my Washington list.

Washington Monument Pitcher.

1. Washington. Head from Stuart's Portrait. Liverpool.

On oval plaques and pitchers. Described on pages 258 *et seq.*, and shown on page 259.

2. Washington. Head from Stuart's portrait. Canton.
   On Chinese toddy-jug. Described on preceding page.

3. Washington. Medallion head on monument. Liverpool.

   This oval design is printed on pitchers of three sizes. In the centre is a monument bearing a poor medallion portrait of Washington, surmounted by a laurel wreath and urn, and bearing the words "George Washington Born Feb 22, 1732

Died Decr. 17, 1799." Below the coat-of-arms of the Washington family, a shield bearing five bars in chief three mullets. A weeping female figure leans against the monument, and a very sad eagle droops in the foreground, with two equally drooping willows on either side. Above the design are the words, "Washington in Glory," below, "America in Tears." A pitcher bearing this design is here shown.

4. Washington. Medallion head. Liverpool.

Similar design to No. 3, but more coarsely engraved, while the inscriptions are within the oval line of the print.

5. Washington. Medallion. Liverpool.

This is printed in black on mugs and pitchers of various sizes. One is shown on page 139. The portrait is mean and poor to the last degree. On the right stands America with the words, "Deafness to the ear that will patiently hear, and dumbness to the tongue that will utter a calumny against the immortal Washington." On the left Liberty says, "My favorite Son." Below, the inscription, "Long Live the President of the United States." This, of course, was made previous to 1799, the date of Washington's death.

6. Washington. Portrait. Staffordshire.

Printed in black. Marked F. Morris, Shelton. Liberty holds a wreath over the head of Washington. The inscription reads, "Washington Crowned with Laurels by Liberty." This is surrounded by a chain with fifteen large links inclosing the names of fifteen States.

7. Washington. Monument.

A plate of cream-colored ware printed in dull reddish brown. Within a ring dotted with fifteen stars is the figure of the Goddess of Liberty, with a shield and olive branch. Behind her stands a pyramidal monument bearing a portrait of Washington and inscribed, "Sacred to the Memory of

Washington." On one side is seen the ocean with a ship, and at the foot of Liberty is an eagle and a scroll with the words, " E Pluribus Unum." Around the edge of the plate are long oval medallions of stripes and stars.

8. Washington. Portrait. Liverpool.

Printed in black or red. A poor portrait of Washington, over which a cherub holds a wreath inclosing the word "Washington." Justice and Liberty on either side of portrait, and Victory at base. A ribbon scroll has the names of fifteen States and incloses fifteen stars.

9. Washington. Apotheosis. Liverpool.

Oval print, with a label at the base, the word Apotheosis. A tomb with seated figures of Liberty and an Indian in the foreground. Time is lifting Washington, clothed in a shroud, from the tomb, while an angel holds the patriot's hand and points up to rays of glory. On the tomb the words, " Sacred to the memory of Washington ob 17 Dec. A.D. 1799. Ae 68." Outside the oval are winged cherub heads. Often under the nose of the pitcher is seen the motto, " A Man without Example, A Patriot without Reproach." Pitchers bearing this specially hideous print seem to be eagerly sought after by all china collectors. It is a reduced copy of a large engraving three feet long and two wide, which was issued by Simon Chandron and John J. Barradet, in Philadelphia, in January, 1802. This engraving is still frequently seen in old Philadelphia homes, and was common enough in the middle of the century. In the large engraving many funny details can be seen which are lost or blurred in the pitcher print. For instance, the various decorations owned by Washington, including the Order of the Cincinnati, are proudly displayed, hanging over the stone of the open tomb. Sometimes the print is seen without the word Apotheosis. One of these pitchers is here shown.

Apotheosis Pitcher.

10. Washington. Monument. Liverpool.

This design is printed in a scalloped oval. In a landscape with water, ships, and a church, is a monument with a medallion portrait of Washington and the words: "First in War, First in Peace, First in Fame, First in Victory." Fame stands on the right, and a naval officer on the left. In front is an American flag, cannon, swords, etc. Around the edge of the oval are the names of thirteen States. I have several times had a pitcher with this design offered to me for purchase for $8, $10, or $15, according to the size and condition; but I saw one in a jeweller's shop in New York during the Centennial celebration in 1889, marked $150, and it was asserted that it was sold at that price. The revival of interest at that time in anything and everything that related to Washington, of course afforded the explanation of this enormous and absurd price.

11. Washington. Medallion Portrait. Staffordshire.

A poor full-face portrait, not resembling Washington, with same legend as No. 5. It is marked F. Morris, Shelton.

12. Washington. Profile Portrait. Liverpool.

This is printed in black on small pitchers. Over the portrait the legend, " He is in Glory, America in Tears."

13. Washington. On Horseback. Liverpool.

This design appears upon a gallon bowl in the collection of the Connecticut Historical Society, and also upon one in a collection in Newport. Pitchers also have been seen with it. Washington appears mounted, on a battle-field, with the accompanying inscription : " His Excellency General George Washington, Marshal of France, and Commander in Chief of the North American Continental Forces."

Though this inscription dubs Washington a marshal of France, it seems uncertain whether the title was correctly applied. It is said that when Colonel Laurens was special ambassador to France, a discussion arose as to the command of the united armies in America. Of course Laurens insisted firmly that Washington must have absolute control ; but Count de Rochambeau, an old lieutenant-general, could be commanded only by the king or a maréchal de France. Laurens with ready wit solved the difficulty by suggesting that Washington be made a maréchal. This suggestion was carried out, and the French at Yorktown addressed Washington as Monsieur le Maréchal. On the other hand, when Lamont, in his volume of poems, addressed Washington by his French title of maréchal, Washington wrote to him in 1785, saying : " I am not a marshal of France, nor do I hold any commission or fill any office whatever under that government." This letter would appear to be conclusive evidence.

The bowl also bears a fur-cap portrait of Franklin, the print of the soldier and the British lion described in No. 106, with the legend, "By virtue and valor we have freed our country," and also the "spatch-cock" American eagle and shield.

14. **Washington. On Horseback. Liverpool.**

This print is similar to No. 13, but is apparently of earlier manufacture.

The mounted figure has the right arm raised. One is upon an octagonal Liverpool plate in the Huntington Collection, and has the inscription, "His Excellency George Washington."

15. **Washington. Portrait. Liverpool.**

Small portrait of Washington in black print on Liverpool pitcher, with a design of Liberty cap and flags, and the verses :

> "As he tills your rich glebe your old peasant shall tell,
>   While his bosom with Liberty glows,
>   How your Warren expired, how Montgomery fell,
>   And how Washington humbled your foes."

16. **Washington. Medallion. Liverpool.**

A background of weeping willows. In the foreground a monument surmounted by an urn and bearing a medallion portrait of Washington. Beneath this the arms of the Washington family, and crossed swords with palm or laurel branches. Above the entire design the words, "Washington in Glory." This design resembles No. 3, but is smaller. On the reverse of the pitcher, a design of Ceres and Pomona at either side of a cannon, and a spread eagle with the words, "Peace, Plenty, and Independence."

17. **Washington. Map of United States. Staffordshire.**

Printed in black on bowls, plates, and pitchers. It is thus wittily described by George Champlin Mason in his book on old Newport : "Washington and Franklin are inspecting a map of the United States, which shows thirteen States. Liberty and History look smilingly upon the pair, while

Fame blows a trumpet and flourishes her heels in dangerous proximity to Washington's head, who is the more prominent of the two, Franklin being screened in part by the

"Map" Pitcher.

pine-tree flag." On
this map Louisiana
is called the Coun-
try of Mines, and
stretches up to Lake
S u p e r i o r.   The
pitcher is marked
F. Morris, Shelton.
There are t h r e e
s l i g h t l y varying
prints of this de-
sign, one h a v i n g
reference numbers
and a key with the
names of the fig-
ures. A bowl twelve
inches in diameter
bearing this print
can be seen in the

Huntington Collection at the Metropolitan Museum of Art.
There is also one in the Trumbull-Prime Collection. One in
Newport bears the date 1796. A pitcher from the Trumbull-
Prime Collection with this print is here shown.

18. Washington. Portrait. Liverpool.

A full-face portrait of Washington, with inscription " His Excellency Gen¹ Washington," and the fur-cap portrait of
Franklin, on the outside of a bowl which has on the inside a
design of a full-rigged frigate, the Insurgente, and the same
legend as No. 101. It also has the motto :

> " My love is fixed,
>   I cannot range ;

I like my choice
Too well to change."

19. Washington.   Cameo.   Wedgwood.

Made in white on colored grounds and in pure white. Mentioned in Wedgwood's Catalogue of 1787.

20. Washington.   Intaglio.   Wedgwood.

In highly polished black ware for use as a seal. Though so small a head, the likeness is good. In Wedgwood's Catalogue of 1787. A specimen may be seen in Huntington Collection.

21. Washington.   Medallion.   Wedgwood.

Made both in black basalt and blue and white jasper. This head is very fine, and an excellent copy may be seen in the Huntington Collection.

22. Washington.   Bust.   Wedgwood.

This bust is in black basalt. The height is thirteen inches. A fine engraving of it may be seen in Miss Meteyard's " Wedgwood and his Works," numbered Plate XVIII. One is owned by a collector in Chicago.

23. Washington.   Medallion.   Neale & Co.

An oval medallion in pottery with the head of Washington in high relief.

24. Washington.   Statuette.   Enoch Wood.

This statuette is fifteen inches high, and is identical in dress and figure with the statuette of Franklin, No. 46, save that the head of Washington is covered with white powdered hair or a white wig, instead of the dark natural locks that grace the Franklin statuette. The head and face only are colored, though the buttons, buckles, and coat ornaments or frogs are gilded. It seems rather unjust in Enoch Wood to put the head of Washington on Franklin's extremely rotund body. In the right hand of the figure is a scroll with vague lettering, and under the left arm a cocked hat. I know of but one of these statuettes with the Washington head ; it is in the Huntington Collection.

25. Washington. Statuette. Badin Frères.

This French statuette is about ten inches in height. Washington is dressed in a yellow coat and blue waistcoat, and carries a scroll marked " Patria." By his side is an American eagle crowing over a broken tablet painted with a picture of the British lion. On the pedestal in gilt letters, " Badin Frères, D'leurs, à Paris." Specimen in the Huntington Collection.

26. Washington. Statuette. Badin Frères.

Statuette of glazed pottery. Washington has his foot on a thoroughly subdued British lion and the British flag. He carries in his hand a scroll with word " Independence." Specimen in the Huntington Collection. The face of this statuette (as well as that of the preceding one, No. 25) bears more of a likeness to the Rembrandt Peale portrait of Washington than to any other.

27. Washington. Parian Pitcher.

An embossed full figure of Washington on a Parian pitcher in the Huntington Collection. Also designs of flags and spread eagles.

28. Washington. Bust. Ralph Wood.

Number G. 367, in the Catalogue of the Museum of Practical Geology in London. It is thus described :

" Bust of Washington, 10 inches high, in plain cream-colored ware, with impressed mark Ra. Wood, Burslem." Ralph Wood, whose name is stamped on this piece, was the father of Aaron Wood and grandfather of Enoch Wood.

29. Washington. Relief Portrait. Dresden.

Profile portrait of Washington in relief, gilded, on *bleu de roi* ground. On other side similar relief portrait of Franklin.

In front an American eagle. Dresden mark. One may be seen in the Trumbull-Prime Collection.

30. Washington. Medallion. Dresden.

Dresden china cup and saucer, gilded without and within. On the cup a blue oval medallion with exquisite head in white relief of profile portrait of George Washington. This beautiful piece is owned by Mrs. Nealy, of Washington, D. C.

31. Washington. Bust.

A bust of Washington in cream-colored oily pottery. It is about four inches in height and is one o fa set comprising busts of Clay, Webster, Calhoun, Lafayette, Franklin, etc. I think the date of manufacture was about 1850. They are common in America. Specimens may be seen in the Huntington Collection.

32. Washington. Mirror Knob.

A portrait of head of Washington, in a cocked hat, on a porcelain mirror knob. A transfer print in black; sometimes being printed in outline and filled in with pale colors. For description of mirror knobs see page 159 *et seq*.

33. Washington. Tomb. Wood.

This dark-blue design represents a bewigged man with knee-breeches at the tomb of Washington. In his hand he carries a scroll. This print is usually known as "Lafayette at the tomb of Washington." The face does not resemble Lafayette, and when Lafayette visited Washington's tomb he wore trousers, knee-breeches being out of date. It has been suggested that the solitary figure is intended for Jefferson. In the background is a view of a town and water, with shipping. The print is usually indistinct and poor, though the color is good. It is seen on all the pieces of tea and toilet services. Impressed mark, Wood.

34. Washington. Funeral Urn. Canton.

The pieces bearing this design are extremely beautiful in shape, quality, and decoration, every detail being perfect. The owner called it Lowestoft, but it is plainly Oriental in manufacture, being of very hard paste, and the character of the design (showing that it was executed after the death of Washington) would hardly point to the Lowestoft manufactory as its place of birth. The platters and plates have an open-work basket-design border lined with delicate threads of golden brown and gold. At each intersection of the interlaced border is a tiny embossed rosette colored in gilt or bronze, with a darker centre. The delicacy and beauty of this dainty border can hardly be described. In the centre of each piece, in various shades of gold—both dull and polished gold being combined—is a design of a funeral mound and an urn bearing the word "Washington," overhung by a weeping-willow. The leaves and branches of this tree are models of the gilder's art. On each piece are in gold the gracefully intertwined initials J. R. L., probably the initials of the person for whom the set was made. For beauty of design and workmanship these pieces excel any others I have ever seen bearing any so-called Washington design.

35. Washington Memorial.

This plate, with irregularly scalloped edge, is green in the centre, with red border. The decoration is a scene with a seated classical figure writing upon a tablet, and with a Greek temple in the background. The border contains four medallions of funeral urns and weeping-willows. On the back is stamped in red a funeral urn with the word "Washington," and the initials E. H. Y. S. The printing of this design is very clear and the lines very delicate, and the drawing is good.

36. Washington. Medallion.

A bowl of clear white china with plain band of gilt on the edge.

On one side, in blue, a medallion of Washington between two flags, surmounted by a spread eagle. Unmarked.

37. Washington. Funeral Urn.

Plate with pink flower border, centre in green. A statue of Washington and a cinerary urn with the word "Washington."

38. Washington. Portrait.

A portrait of Washington printed in black on a white stoneware pitcher—apparently modern. Crossed flags painted in colors. This pitcher may have been made to use in a hotel or on a steamboat.

Washington. Portrait.

On "Emblem of America" Pitcher. See No. 98.

Washington. Views of Mount Vernon.

See No. 195 *et seq.*

Washington. Portrait. Erie Canal.

See No. 166.

Washington. Portrait. Erie Canal.

See No. 170.

Washington. Inscription. Proscribed Patriots.

See No. 86.

Washington. Medallion. Staffordshire.

See No. 251.

XIV.

DESIGNS RELATING TO FRANKLIN

THE great popularity and long residence of Benjamin Franklin abroad would account for the many and varied ceramic relics relating to him that were manufactured in England and France during his lifetime, and that are still in existence, more varied in quality and shape even than those relating to Washington. Nor after his death did the production cease. I will place at the head of the list the most beautiful of them all.

39. Group of Louis XVI. and Benjamin Franklin. Niderviller.

This lovely statuette is of purest white porcelain bisque, and is about twelve inches in height, and ten inches in length. The face of the figure of Franklin is exceedingly fine, and is, in a degree, unlike any other portrait of him that I have seen. It has all the benignancy and sweetness of expression with which we are familiar, and an added nobility and intelligence which is more marked and more impressive than in any other likeness. It is an ideal portrait of Franklin, which must be regarded with pleasure and interest by every historical student. The figure of the King is also extremely fine and imposing. The face is beautiful, the carriage manly, and the half suit of armor, with the long royal cloak of ermine, form an impressive contrast with the simple fur-trimmed garment of Franklin, whose figure is slightly bent, but still

Neiderweiler Statuette.

impressive. The King holds in his hand a parchment book
or scroll bearing on one leaf in golden letters the words,
"Indépendance de l'Amérique," and on another leaf, "Li-
berté des Mers." This group was made to commemorate our
treaty with France in 1788. It is beautifully modelled and of
highest artistic merit, and must take rank as the most important relic of our country that has yet been figulated. It
bears the stamp "Niderviller," and was made at that factory
while it was owned by Count Custine. He had fought with
Lafayette in the war for American Independence, and doubtless knew Franklin. The statue was evidently modelled from
life. Count Custine also gave to Washington the beautiful
tea-service described on page 244 *et seq.* Three only of these
portrait groups of Franklin and Louis XVI. are known to
exist ; the only perfect one is owned by William C. Prime,
Esq., of New York, and will form part of the Trumbull-Prime
Collection at Princeton ; from it the illustration here given
was taken. Another imperfect one is in the possession of
William A. Hoppin, Esq., of Providence ; and a third and
mutilated specimen is in the Huntington Collection at the
Metropolitan Museum of Art.

40. Franklin. Medallions. Nini.

Some very good medallions of Benjamin Franklin were manufactured by Jean Baptiste Nini, who in 1760 entered the employ of M. Leray, or M. de Chaumont, at Chaumont. Nini
was a glass engraver of rare merit, and his work on these medallions was very beautiful. The fine copper moulds for his
medallions that he employed were melted down into ingots in
1820. His work may be known by the mark engraved in the
soft paste of "Nini," or "J. B. Nini F."—sometimes with the
date. He made at least six different sizes of medallions of
Franklin, some of which bear the date in relief.

Franklin, writing from Passy in 1779 to his daughter, Mrs.
Sarah Bache, speaks thus of these Nini medallions : " The

clay medallion of me you say you gave Mr. Hopkinson was the first of the kind made in France. A variety of others have been made since of various sizes ; some to be set in the lids of snuff-boxes, and some so small as to be worn in rings ; and the numbers sold are incredible. These, with the pictures and prints (of which copies upon copies are spread everywhere), have made your father's face as well known as that of the moon, so that he durst not do anything that would oblige him to run away, as his phiz would discover him wherever he should venture to show it. It is said by learned etymologists that the name of doll for the image children play with is derived from the word idol. From the number of dolls now made of him he may be truly said, in that sense, to be idolized in this country."

In several other published letters Franklin speaks of making gifts of these medallions to his friends, and states that they were made at Chaumont. Madame de Campan says that they were sold at the palace of Versailles, and bore this motto, " *Eripuit cœlo fulmen, sceptrumque tyrannis.*"

There are in the Huntington Collection several specimens of these Nini medallions, that collection containing in all eleven medallions of Franklin, many of which being unmarked it is futile to attempt to classify. A Nini medallion having a fine fur-cap portrait sold in the Governor Lyon sale for ten dollars. Mr. Huntington wrote thus to Hon. John Bigelow, of Nini and his medallions : " He must have had a certain vogue in his time, medallions of folks of the superior classes from his hand still turning up at sales and in curiosity shops. He did two Franklins—both at the Metropolitan Museum— dated and signed. The smaller one, with the cap, ' 1777 B. Franklin, Américain,' was among the earliest of the Franklin idols made here, and has been numerously reproduced by French, English, and other engravers. The larger, which is of the more usual size of Nini's work, is much rarer, has never been engraved from, as far as I know, and is to my notion

one of the most finely characterized of all the Franklin portraits—1799 (and in some copies MDCCLXXIX. ; you will find
specimens of both in the museum), with Turgot's lines for the
legend. In his letter to his daughter, Passy, 3d of June, B.
F. writes : ' The clay medallion of me you say you gave Mr.
Hopkinson was the first of the kind made in France.' This
must be the one with the cap. If the Ven. F. is correct in his
statement, it would curiously seem that his friend Chaumont
set Nini at him as soon as he caught the artist, to start (we
should now say inaugurate) his furnace at Chaumont with the
likeness of his friend."

41. Franklin.   Medallion.   Wedgwood.

This appears in Wedgwood's Catalogue of 1787 under the head
of "Illustrious Moderns." It was made in black basalt and
blue and white jasper. There appear to have been two of
these portraits ; for at the sale of the collection of Dr. Gibson,
in London, March, 1877, a blue jasper medallion of Dr.
Franklin, by Wedgwood & Bentley, was sold for £12 12s.,
while one with the fur-cap by Wedgwood sold for £11. Specimens can be seen in the Huntington Collection at the Metropolitan Museum of Art, and in the Trumbull-Prime Collection
at Princeton.

42. Franklin.   Cameo.   Wedgwood.

In Wedgwood's Catalogue of 1787. Made in white on colored
grounds, and in pure white.

43. Franklin.   Intaglio.   Wedgwood.

This is named in Wedgwood's Catalogue of 1787. It was
smaller, to be used as a seal, and was of black ware highly
polished. One may be seen in the Trumbull-Prime Collection.

44. Franklin.   Oval Plaque.   Bristol.

This medallion of Franklin is upon one of Richard Champion's
exquisite flower-plaques. This plaque is considered by

Owen to be "the most important" of Champion's work. Champion was an ardent admirer of America and Americans, and his special veneration for Franklin evidently impelled him to produce this elaborate work. It is eight and a half inches in length, and seven and a half in width, the portrait bust being surrounded immediately by a laurel wreath tied with a bowknot, and outside the laurel wreath by a rich wreath of roses and lilies in highly raised and most delicate work. Another specimen of the same medallion is known to exist upon a plain ground plaque, and has often been attributed to the Sèvres manufactory. One of these flower-plaques with the bust of Franklin was exhibited at the Loan Collection in New York, in 1889, by Dr. Caspar Wister Hodge, of Princeton, N. J. Rev. Dr. Hodge was the grandson of William Bache, the grandson of Franklin. Dr. Hodge's mother was born in Franklin's house in Philadelphia, and her account of the flower-plaque was that it was made at the Sèvres manufactory and was the gift of Louis XVI. to Benjamin Franklin; that it had been sent to America by private hands, in connection with a similar one of George Washington, which was surmounted by a gilt crown; and that the messenger, in officious democratic zeal, picked off the crown with his penknife before delivering the medallion.

Dr. Hodge said it was a complete surprise to him, and it could not have been a very pleasant one, when he offered the plaque for exhibition in New York, to be told that it was Bristol china, and was not unique. Of course these latter facts might be so without destroying the other part of the family tradition—that it was a royal gift; but it is far more probable that Richard Champion presented this choice specimen of his work to Franklin, for in a letter to Champion, written from Paris, January 2, 1778, the unknown writer speaks of a visit to Franklin, and says : " He begs his compliments and is much obliged for your present, which arrived in perfect safety. He says that there is a good likeness with Wedgwood

& Bentley's, only with this difference, that he wears his hair, which is rather straight and long, instead of a wig, and is very high in his forehead."

In the Lewis sale of Washington relics, held in Philadelphia, in December, 1890, there was sold an "oval porcelain plaque with a bust of Benjamin Franklin in a wreath of china roses and lilies, 8½ inches by 7½ inches." This I believe to have been the one which tradition in the Hodge family says came over to Washington. Some of the Bristol flower-plaques had a crown above the medallion ; one in Mr. Edkin's Collection is illustrated in Owen's "Two Centuries of Ceramic Art in Bristol." The Franklin plaque sold in Philadelphia for ninety dollars—a price to make an English collector groan with envy—while the one in Mr. Edkin's Collection (from which is taken the engraving in Mr. Owen's book) sold in England in 1874 for £150. Dr. Hodge had an insurance of one thousand dollars offered to him on his Franklin plaque when it was in New York.

45. Franklin. Medallion. Neale & Co.

The head of Dr. Franklin in pottery, by Neale & Co., Hanley. It is an oval medallion.

Franklin. Relief Portrait. Dresden.

See No. 29.

46. Franklin. Statuette. Wood.

This pottery statue is fifteen inches in height, and is neither very impressive nor well modelled. One in the Huntington Collection is colored, Poor Richard being gayly attired in gray coat, yellow waistcoat, and pink breeches. He carries his hat under his left arm, and a scroll in his left hand. Another in the same collection is precisely like it, save that the head only is colored. It is labelled, in gold letters, "General Washington." This mistake easily arose, for the statuette of Washington, described in No. 24, is exactly like this Franklin statuette except the head, which in the latter has flowing natural hair. A number of these Franklin statuettes bear the name of Washington, and it does not matter much, for they do not closely resemble either of the great Americans. This statuette is attributed to Ralph Wood or Enoch Wood, of Burslem. There are three of these figures in the Trumbull-Prime Collection, dressed in vari-colored garments, one being much smaller, about thirteen inches in height. But for the right arm being more extended, it would appear that the original mould had become worn and a new one cast, which in shrinking made this reduction in the size of this figure. One of these statuettes of Franklin in the S. L. M. Barlow Collection was sold in 1890 for forty-two dollars.

47. Franklin. Statuette.

In the Catalogue of the Museum of Practical Geology, Number G. 374, is described thus : "Statuette of Dr. Franklin painted in colors. Height, 13¼ inches. Mounted on square marbled pedestal with oval yellow medallions in relief ; unmarked. This may be a Salopian figure." One of these statuettes is in the Huntington Collection ; the medallions being in blue and white. Dr. Franklin wears in this case white breeches, blue waistcoat, scarlet coat, a blue ribbon with an order, and a long ermine cloak. This statuette is rather funny, though at first glance it is quite impressive. The Doctor, comparatively devoid of pendulous chin, stands erect and beautiful, with his head thrown back with a most imperious and even imperial air, to which the ermine cloak gives added weight and zest. He is so erect and so slender that we hardly know him. But when we glance at his feet, the impression of youthfulness and beauty vanishes. With feet several sizes too large for his figure, and gaudy light-green slippers several sizes too large even for those feet, we turn away to our familiar good old dewlapped man with the fur cap, and like him better than this splay-footed, ermine-cloaked plantigrade.

48. Franklin. Statuette.

Parian figure about seven inches in height. The likeness is good, though the feet are abnormally narrow and pointed; unmarked. A copy may be seen in the Huntington Collection.

49. Franklin. Statuette.

Pottery figure about seven inches in height, leaning on a pink pedestal decorated with raised white eagles. The coat is black, breeches yellow, and waistcoat pink. This gayly garbed slim young fellow does not at all resemble our own Franklin. The statuette is unmarked. A specimen may be seen in the Huntington Collection.

50. Franklin. Statuette.

This pottery figure is fifteen inches in height, and is in feature and figure and dress like No. 46, and was evidently modelled by the same hand. It is a poor thing, and bears but little resemblance to Franklin. A dilapidated specimen is in the Huntington Collection.

51. Franklin. Mirror Knob.

Print of Franklin in black on oval porcelain plaque in a mirror knob. For description of these knobs see page 159 *et seq.*

52. Franklin. Fur-cap Portrait.

Round plate with fluted border, with splashes of purple and yellow like No. 81. In the centre a good rendering of the fur-cap portrait of Franklin. In the Huntington Collection.

53. Franklin. Fur-cap Portrait.

Plate with pierced border like No. 82. Well-painted portrait in centre. In the Huntington Collection.

54. Franklin. Portrait. Dresden.

A Dresden plate with flower border and good portrait of Franklin. In Huntington Collection.

55. Franklin.   Bust.

Small bust of Franklin in bisque, mounted on a yellow and gold pedestal.   Marked "Francklin."   In Huntington Collection.

56. Franklin.   Bust.

A bust of Franklin in what appears to be modern majolica.   In Huntington Collection.

57. Franklin.   Bust.

White pottery bust glazed, about ten inches in height.   Around the base a wreath of laurel.   In Huntington Collection.

58. Franklin.   Bust.

White porcelain bisque bust, five inches in height, mounted on dark blue and gold stand.   In Huntington Collection.

59. Franklin.   Portrait.   Dresden.

A portrait of Franklin on a great cylindrical covered jar, twenty inches in height and eight inches in diameter.   The portrait is good, though the mouth is exaggeratedly small and the chin exaggeratedly remultiplied.   It is surrounded by a well-painted wreath of flowers.

Franklin.   Figure on Pitcher.

See No. 17.

Franklin.   Fur-cap Portrait.

See No. 13.

Franklin.   Emblem of America Pitcher.

See No. 98.

60. Franklin.   Tomb.

This design was printed in dark blue on dinner, breakfast, tea, and toilet services in vast numbers.   In such large numbers, in fact, that the pieces with this design are cheaper than any others bearing the names of any historical personages.   I have bought a large teapot for a dollar, cups and saucers for a dollar, etc. This might be classed among the Lafayette prints, but as we are not sure that the seated figure is intended for Lafayette, and Franklin cannot escape the formal

Tomb of Franklin Teapot.

witness of his inscribed tomb, we place it in this place in the list. A teapot bearing this print is here shown.

61. Franklin. Print. Fur-cap Portrait.

This print is in black on pitchers and bowls. It is the fur-cap portrait with the glasses. The legend reads : " Benj^a Franklin Esq. LL.D. and F.R.S., the brave defender of the country against the oppression of taxation without representation— author of the greatest discovery in Natural Philosophy since those of Sir Isaac Newton, viz.: that lightning is the same with the electric fire." See No. 18.

62. Franklin. Portrait.

A full-length print of Franklin on mug, with various maxims of Poor Richard's.

63. Franklin. Portrait.

A light-blue print of Franklin found on toilet services. The philosopher is seen flying his famous kite.

64. Dr. Franklin's Maxims.

Plate of cream ware with relief border of scrolls and scallops intertwined, with words in ornamental capitals, "Fear God : Honour your Parents." In the centre is a green print of a view of the inside and outside of a shop, with figures. Those within are working, those without are idle. Above, the words, " Dr. Franklin's Maxims." Below, the maxims, " Keep thy shop and thy shop will keep thee," " If you would have your business done, go ; if not, send." This plate is in the possession of Mrs. Nealy, of Washington, D. C.

65. Franklin's Morals. Staffordshire.

Dark-blue plate with waving edge, and dainty border of fruit, shells, and flowers. In the centre a man carrying a large key. Houses and a bridge in the background. On the back of the plate the words, " Franklin's Morals, ' The used key is always bright.' "

66. Franklin. House at Passy.

Upon a beautiful Sèvres vase at the Executive Mansion in Washington is seen a view of Franklin's house at Passy.

67. Franklin. Portrait Plaque.

Oval plaque of Italian majolica marked with inscription, " Cortoni Fab Alari. Beniamino Franklin, C. Brunacci Depinse." In the Huntington Collection. There are also three other majolica plates and plaques in this collection bearing portraits of Franklin.

I may say, in conclusion, what I have already shown in detail, that there can be no better opportunity of studying the face of Franklin, as shown in pottery and porcelain, than in the Huntington Collection. There are eleven relief medallions, eleven enamels, nine busts, six statues, and a large number of plates and plaques. You can also compare these ceramic portraits with innumerable bronzes, engravings, art gems, cameos, gold and silver and pewter work bearing the same serene, benignant face, and with some very funny though unintentional caricatures of Franklin by Japanese and Chinese artists, in some of which the well-known fur-cap has been transformed into a close crop of short woolly curls.

XV.

DESIGNS RELATING TO LAFAYETTE

I HAVE never seen in America any pieces of English pottery or porcelain bearing the name, portrait of Lafayette, or any reference to him that could be assigned to an earlier date of manufacture than 1824, the time of Lafayette's last visit to America. It is worthy of note, however, that the Lafayette pieces of crockery that were printed to commemorate and illustrate that memorable visit and that triumphal journey are, as a rule, in a much better state of preservation, freer from marks of fierce assaulting knives, barer of nicks and cracks, than other American historical pieces of the same date. The great veneration and affection felt by all Americans for the noble character of Lafayette, and their gratitude for his assistance in times of war, were doubtless the cause of the careful preservation of the pieces relating to him and printed in his honor. The fine platter shown on page 294, which is the clearest, darkest, "Landing" print I have ever seen, was always kept carefully wrapped in an ancient hand-woven "flannel sheet," and laid away in an upper drawer of a high chest, a "high boy," in a New-England farm-house, until it was ruthlessly removed from its honored seclusion of half a century, and hung on the wall of my dining-room.

During the triumphal journey of Lafayette through this country in 1824, ladies, in honor of him, wore sashes and belt-ribbons printed with his name and likeness, gloves with his portrait stamped upon the back, and medallions with laudatory inscriptions relating to him fastened upon their neck-ribbons and necklaces; while men and boys wore Lafayette medals, medallions, and buttons. Of all these tokens few now remain; but the various Lafayette plates and pitchers form lasting mementos of the visit of the "Nation's Guest." Few families in New England appear to have had more than two or three of the Lafayette pieces, but in the vicinity of New York persons purchased whole dinner services, especially of the "Landing" pattern. Mrs. Roebling owns the remains of an entire set purchased by her father, General Warren. Mr. William C. Prime also owns an entire service.

La Grange, the home of Lafayette, was a familiar scene to Americans, for many transparencies and paintings of the château were exhibited during Lafayette's tour in 1824, and two views of it appear on plates and platters. With these I continue the list of historical designs and subjects.

68. Lafayette. La Grange. Enoch Wood & Sons.

This is a dingy and poorly printed view of the gloomy entrance to the château, with its great fir-trees, an engraving of which is seen in Cloquet's "Recollections of Lafayette." The blue is good in tint, though the print is indistinct. It has a poor, confused shell border. On the back the stamp of Enoch

Wood & Sons, and the mark "La Grange, the Home of Lafayette." A plate with this design is here shown.

La Grange Plate.

69. Lafayette. La Grange 2. Wood. The superb platters with this print bear on the back, in a wreath of laurel, the stamp "Southwest view of Lagrange, the residence of Marquis La Fayette," also the impressed stamp of Wood. The color is of the richest dark-blue tint, a true "lapis to delight the world."

Across the top of the platter the border is formed in a graceful design of grapes and vine leaves. On the left the border is composed of finely drawn stalks of hollyhocks. On the right a tree and foliage form the border. On the lower rim is a design of fleur-de-lis and roses. The view of the château is different from No. 68, the whole front of the house being shown. A broad expanse of lawn fills the foreground, across which two dogs are running. Up a path on the left walk a man, woman, and child. I have never seen but two pieces bearing this design, both large platters twenty-three inches long. I purchased one for $12, which large price was unwillingly paid; but as I had never seen nor heard of any pieces bearing such a design, I could not bear to lose it when I believed it to be unique. Within a week after this purchase I saw the second and better platter and bought it for $1.50, and now I expect to find many another piece with this "Southwest view of Lagrange." I give these prices to show the impossibility of assigning a defi-

nite value to those " old blue " Staffordshire pieces. One of
these platters was obtained through the sale of the old dining-
room furnishings of Barnum's Hotel, in Baltimore.

70. Lafayette. Medallion.

This design is the head of Lafayette in blue on a white porcelain
plate, with the surrounding words, " Welcome, Lafayette, the
Nation's Guest and our Country's Glory." The plate has an
embossed border similar in design to that upon some New
Hall plates in my possession. It is unmarked. The portrait
is exceedingly ugly and mean.

71. Lafayette. Portrait.

A pitcher of stone-ware printed in blue, with a portrait of
Lafayette on one side, with this legend, " In commemoration
of the visit of Lafayette to the United States of America in
1824," and a wreath entwined with these words, " Lafayette,
the Nation's Guest." On the other side a head of Washington. Beneath the nose of the pitcher a spread eagle, and the
terse sentence, " Republicans are not always ungrateful."
One may be seen in the Trumbull-Prime Collection. I have
also seen several for sale in city " antique-shops."

72. Lafayette. Medallion.

Medallion portrait of Lafayette and similar one of Washington
on common white stone-ware mug. Some of these mugs also
have the date 1824, not the year of manufacture apparently,
but the date simply of Lafayette's visit to America.

73. Lafayette. Medallion.

A pitcher ten inches in height, bearing on both sides a good
portrait of Lafayette, with this legend, " General Lafayette
was born at Auvergne, in France. At 19 he arrived in America in a war-ship furnished at his own cost in 1777, & volun-
teered in our army as Major General. At Brandywine he was
wounded but refused to quit the field ; he assisted the army
with £ 10,000 from his own purse, and kept in service until

our independence was sealed and country free ; in 1784 he returned to France loaded with honors and the gratitude of the American people ; in 1824 the Congress unanimously offered a ship for his return, he declined the honor, but landed from the Cadmus at New York, August 24th, 1824, amid the acclamations of 60,000 freemen." In front of the pitcher is another portrait of Lafayette in vignette, with this legend above it, " General Lafayette, welcome to the land of Liberty," and below, " He was born at Auvergne in France, 1757, joined the American struggle in 1777, and in 1824 returned to repose in the bosom of the land whose liberty he in part gave birth to." This pitcher is globose in shape, is in a good shade of blue, and is unmarked.

74. Lafayette.   Cadmus.   Enoch Wood & Sons.

This was the name of the ship which brought Lafayette to America in 1824. The stamp " Cadmus " appears on a few only of the plates, and the others must be classified by the knowledge of, and comparison with, the marked ones, or with the illustration here shown. This is an exceedingly beautiful plate ; the graceful shell border is so rich and dark a blue, and the centre expanse of water and full-sailed ship and sloop are so distinct and bright, that it gives one the impression of looking out from a dark cave upon the sunny ocean. Every plate that I have seen bearing this design has been of the finest color, clearest print, most brilliant glaze, and in good preservation,

Cadmus Plate.

They have the stamp "Enoch Wood & Sons." The Cadmus was built for Mr. William Whitlock, and belonged to the
Havre line of packet-ships organized and managed by William
Whitlock, Jr., & Co., of 46 South Street. When this eminent
shipping-house learned that Lafayette had declined the offer
of a national vessel, the members at once put the Cadmus at
his service, declining to receive any remuneration therefor.
No other passengers were allowed on board save the General
and his suite, and the ship took no cargo. Captain Allyn
was the commander. Lafayette fully appreciated this initial
act of American friendship and hospitality, and the first private house at which he dined after arriving was at Mr. Whitlock's. The ship became in later years a whaling vessel.
The Long Island Historical Society have a portion of the
wood-work of the berths from the state-room occupied by Lafayette.

75. Landing of Lafayette. Clews.

Pieces bearing this print are perhaps more eagerly sought after
by collectors, patriots, and historical students than are those
bearing any other design. The prints are all in dark blue of
good tint (except a few rare polychrome prints of which I shall
speak), but vary in clearness and distinctness. It is said that
whole dinner-services and tea-services were printed with it,
but I have never seen either teapots or creamers. I have
found four sizes of plates, including the tiny cup-plates ; large
soup-plates, pitchers, platters, bowls, and vegetable-dishes,
and lovely little pepper-pots and salt-cellars. And I have
also seen an imposing toilet service proudly bearing in richest
blue the " Landing of Lafayette." The border is a handsome
design of what I think is intended for laurel leaves (but which
more resemble ash), clusters of flowers which are perhaps
laurel blossoms, and larger flowers which may be wild roses,
but look like jonquils. In the centre of the plates and on the
sides of the larger dishes is a spirited design bearing at the

base, in dark-blue letters, the words, "Landing of Lafayette.
At Castle Garden, New York, August 24th, 1824." In the foreground of this view are marshals or sentinels on horseback,
then comes a row of six smoking cannon, then the bay covered with beflagged shipping and small sail-boats, and two
clumsy, strangely shaped steamers, the Robert Fulton and
Chancellor Livingston, with their side-wheels quite up out of
the water. At the right, a small bridge over the water leads

Lafayette Landing Platter.

to an inclosed fort, over which floats the flag of the United
States. Over all is a sky of strongly defined clouds. On the
back is the impressed stamp, "Warranted Clews Staffordshire." A platter with this design is here shown. Plates of
this pattern sell for from four to ten dollars, according to clearness, condition, and size. This design has been seen in polychrome. A few years ago there stood in a barroom in New
York an enormous punch-bowl capable of holding many gallons. It bore printed or painted in high and varied colors

the " Landing of Lafayette." Plates and platters also have been offered for sale in New York with the design in many colors. Sometimes this design is found upon pitchers with a poor portrait of Lafayette.

Lafayette arrived in the Cadmus at Staten Island on Sunday, but postponed by request his entrance into New York until the following day. The landing at the Battery must have been a magnificent sight. The steamship Robert Fulton, manned by two hundred sailors from the Constitution, and her companion ship the Chancellor Livingston, " led in triumph rather than towed the Cadmus to the place of landing." Two hundred thousand persons welcomed the General with shouts, cannon thundered from the shore, the forts, the vessels. Flags, triumphal arches, decorations of various kinds adorned the streets and buildings. For those who, when they glance at their " Landing " plates, wish to find the image of the General there present, I will add that he was then sixtyeight years of age, was conceded by all to be far from a beautiful or heroic figure, with his small head, staring eyes, retreating forehead, and bad complexion, and he wore on that occasion "nankeen pantaloons, buff vest, and plain blue coat with covered buttons."

76. Lafayette. Faïence Patriotique. Nevers.

A plate of coarse pottery, with border of blue and yellow leaves. At the top two blue and yellow flags, and in the centre of the plate this legend in hand-painted, irregular letters of blue :

> " Cadet Rousette a des plats bleus
> Qui sont beaux, qui n'vont pas au feu ;
> Si vous voulez en faire emplette,
> Adressez-vous à La Fayette.
> Ah ! Ah ! Ah ! mais vraiment,
> Cadet Rousette est bon enfant."

1792.

This is a good specimen of the "Faïences Patriotiques." These revolutionary emblems were made at the Nevers Pottery, in France, in large numbers, at the time of the French Revolution. They were coarsely painted with patriotic, though frequently ill-spelled, designs and mottoes, and were designed to appeal to and influence the French peasantry. The great heat used in the firing prevented the potters from using red paint (since that color was destroyed by the high temperature), so in direct violation of all " rules of revolutionary iconology," the liberty cap was rendered in blue or yellow. It was in honor of the "Fayence of Nevers" that the poem of Defraney was written that begins,

" Chantons, Fille du Ciel, l'honneur de la Fayence !
    Quel Art ! dans l'Italie il reçut la naissance
    Et vint, passant les monts, s'etablir dans Nevers.
    Ses ouvrages charmans vont au delà des mers."

This Nevers plate is in the Huntington Collection at the Metropolitan Museum of Art.

77. Lafayette. Faïence Patriotique. Nevers.

Plate of coarse Nevers pottery with hideous profile portrait of Lafayette in yellow and blue, and date 1794. Border of blue leaves. Also in the Huntington Collection.

78. Lafayette. Faïence Patriotique. Nevers.

Plate of coarse Nevers pottery with scroll border of green, yellow, and blue. A full-face portrait of Lafayette in bright yellow, with purple hair. In the Huntington Collection.

79. Lafayette. Faïence Patriotique. Nevers.

Large plate of Nevers pottery, fourteen inches in diameter, with slightly scalloped edge. In the centre a design of a long-legged bird with man's head, saying, " La Fayette, Je tends mes filets." The bird tramples under foot, or under claw, a head marked " le Roi Soliveau," and is addressing his re-

marks to a head on a pole with a flag marked " Loi Martiale."
There is also a net-work or fence inclosing frogs. Above all,
the inscription, " Les grenouilles qui demandent un Roi, ou
le Roi Soliveau."

80. Lafayette. Portrait. Sèvres.

A Sèvres plate with an exquisitely painted portrait of Lafayette
in full uniform. A rich border of red, blue, and gold. In
the Huntington Collection.

81. Lafayette. Portrait.

Square plate with fluted border, with splashes of purple and
yellow, like No. 52. A spray of flowers in each corner. In
the centre a fine profile portrait of Lafayette in full uniform.
In the Huntington Collection.

82. Lafayette. Portrait.

Plate with pierced border like No. 53. In the centre the same
portrait as in No. 81. In the Huntington Collection.

83. Lafayette. Bust.

Bust four inches in height. One of same set described in No.
31. One can be seen in Huntington Collection.

84. Lafayette. Medallion.

White porcelain profile medallion about two inches and a half
in diameter. No mark.

Lafayette. At the Tomb of Franklin.

Were we sure that the figure in this design is Lafayette, it
would properly be placed here, but it is very uncertain
whether the seated mourner is Lafayette, or merely some
sombre-minded, non-historical, though patriotic citizen ; so a
description and illustration of this design will be found among
the Franklin Prints, No. 60.

Lafayette.　At the Tomb of Washington.

　　See No. 33.　The figure in this design may not be that of
　　　Lafayette.

Lafayette.　Portrait.　Erie Canal.

　　See No. 166.　The presence of Lafayette at the formal open-
　　　ing of the Erie Canal was naturally felt to be a great honor,
　　　hence the appearance of his name on many of the plates ;
　　　but as the other design is more prominent it is classed
　　　under that name.

There are many modern Parian busts of poor likeness and indifferent artistic merit, and occasional hand-
painted plaques of Lafayette, but they hardly come
within the intentions and purpose of this list.

XVI

PATRIOTIC AND POLITICAL DESIGNS

THE heroes and the naval battles of the War of 1812 furnished manifold subjects for the designs printed on a vast number of mugs and pitchers. They were made and printed at the Liverpool and Staffordshire pot-works to supply the American trade, and were imported in great numbers to this country. English potters appeared to have none of that form of patriotic pride and independence that would prevent them from celebrating and perpetuating the virtues and victories of their late enemies, or hinder them from printing inscriptions and verses insulting to their native land and their fellow-countrymen ; they were plainly and unsentimentally mercenary. These portraits, mottoes, and battle-scenes appear in various combinations of subjects, sometimes in juxtaposition with Washington designs. Occasionally a mammoth pitcher is found—a dozen pitchers rolled into one—decorated with a dozen different but generic prints. Such is the great heroic vessel known as the " Historical Pitcher of the War of 1812." It was made by Enoch Wood & Sons of Burslem, Staffordshire, England, about 1824, by the order of Horace Jones, Esq., of Troy, N. Y. It is now owned by his grandson, Horace Jones Richards, Esq., of the same city. It stands twenty inches in height, and measures twenty inches from the end of the spout to the extreme point of the handle. The body is eighteen inches in diameter—a foot and a half, and it holds eleven and a half gallons. It has an embossed border around the top, and is decorated with a coarse design in copper-lustre and green. On the front of the pitcher is the name of the purchaser, Horace Jones, and around the body are various prints that are often seen singly on other and smaller pitchers. In front, about five inches above the base of the pitcher, is a small projection or knob. This served as a second handle by which to carry the pitcher (for it is a great weight when filled—if it ever is filled), and it formed also a support to rest on the edge of a smaller vessel when pouring from the pitcher. On either side of this small handle are portraits of Washington and Adams. There are on one side of the great pitcher-body portraits of Captain Jones, of the Macedonian, Major-General Brown, of the Niagara campaign, Commodore Bainbridge, of the Constitution. Below these portraits a circle of prints representing the Constitution escaping from the British fleet; Commodore Macdonough's victory on Lake Champlain, and a large American eagle with the motto, " E Pluribus Unum." On the other side of the pitcher are the portraits of Commodore Decatur, Commodore Perry, and Captain Hull, of the Constitution; below are the engagements between the Chesapeake and Shannon off Boston Harbor, June 1, 1813, and Commodore Perry's victory on Lake Erie. Below the large handle on the right are two views of the manufactory and the names of the makers, and on the left a naval monument with flags and motto, " We have met the enemy and they are ours."

This pitcher arrived in Troy a short time before Lafayette made his visit to that city in 1824, and was first publicly used at the reception given to him September 18, 1824. Since then it has been used on many notable occasions. A bill was introduced to the State Legislature in Albany, in the spring of 1891, for the purchase of this pitcher and its preservation in the State Library. The purchase sum required was three hundred and fifty dollars. The bill did not pass. It is a pity it cannot be in the possession of the National Museum at Washington, since the State of New York did not care to preserve it as a relic.

There are some designs of the American eagle and flag, and a few relating to men of Revolutionary times, which may be assigned, though without any positiveness, to the period between the War of the Revolution and the War of 1812. With these prints I resume the list of American subjects.

85. John Adams.   Portrait.

A pitcher, eight inches in height, printed in black, with a very good, though coarse, portrait of Adams, and the inscription, " John Adams, President of the United States." Underneath is a design of two fat cherubs tying up a parcel and bundles— possibly an idealization of emigration. The print is signed " F. Morris, Shelton, Staffordshire." Strange to say, this pitcher was purchased in Chester, England.

86. Proscribed Patriots.   Liverpool.

A design printed in black on pitchers, and here shown. On the side a medallion with a willow-tree and monument. On

Proscribed Patriots Pitcher.

the monument the inscription, " G. W. Sacred to the memory of G. Washington, who emancipated America from slavery and founded a republic upon such just and equitable principles that it will" (remainder illegible). Around this medallion the legend, " The Memory of Washington and the Proscribed Patriots of America. Liberty, Virtue, Peace, Justice, and Equity to all Mankind." Under this, "Columbia's Sons inspired by Freedom's Flame Live in the Annals of Immortal Fame." Under the monument are portraits of Samuel Adams and John Hancock, and the letters S. A. and J. H.; and under these a beehive and cornucopia. On the front of the pitcher is the American eagle and shield, with inscription, " Peace, Commerce, and Honest Friendship with all Nations, Entangling Alliances with none. Jefferson. Anno Domini 1804." Under the handle, " Fame," in clouds.

87. William Franklin.   Medallion.   Wedgwood.

Two blue and white jasper medallions of the son of Benjamin Franklin. These medallions appear in Wedgwood's " List of Illustrous Moderns." William Temple Franklin was the last

Royalist governor of New Jersey, but his claim to fame rests
only on his being the son of his father.   Two of these medallions are in the Huntington Collection.

Samuel Adams.   Portrait.   Liverpool.

On Proscribed Patriots Pitcher.   See No. 86.

88. Jefferson.   Name in Inscription.

On a pitcher bearing a portrait of the American eagle, with
motto, " E Pluribus Unum," are these stanzas :

> " Sound, Sound the trump of Fame,
>   Let Jefferson's great name
>   Ring through the world with loud applause
>   As the firm friend of Freedom's cause.

> " Let every clime to freedom dear
>   Now listen with a joyfull ear.
>   With honest pride and manly grace
>   He fills the Presidential place.

> " The Constitution for his guide,
>   And Truth and Justice by his side,
>   When hope was sinking in dismay,
>   When gloom obscured Columbia's day,
>   He mourn'd his country's threaten'd fate
>   And sav'd it ere it was too late."

Jefferson.   Quotation.   Liverpool.

See No. 127.

Jefferson.   At Tomb.   Staffordshire.

See No. 33.

Jefferson.   Portrait.   Staffordshire.

See No. 166.

89. John Hancock.   Portrait.   Liverpool.

A black print on a mug.   On a ribbon scroll the inscription,
" The Honorable John Hancock."

John Hancock.   Portrait.   Liverpool.
  On Proscribed Patriots Pitcher.   See No. 86.

John Hancock.   House.
  See No. 157.

90. Montgomery.   Battle-Scene.   Liverpool.
  Black print on a pitcher of a battle-scene entitled " The Death
  of Montgomery."   One may be seen in the Trumbull-Prime
  Collection.

91. Warren.   Battle-Scene.   Liverpool.
  Black print on a Liverpool pitcher of a battle-scene, with name
  " The Death of Warren."   One may be seen in the Trum-
  bull-Prime Collection.

92. American Eagle.   Sailor Pitcher.   Liverpool.
  A Liverpool pitcher with an American spread eagle over the
  words " Herculaneum Pottery, Liverpool."   On one side
  waves and a full-rigged ship bearing American flag ; sometimes printed in black, and often coarsely colored by hand.
  This print is often seen on sailor pitchers with other prints of
  different designs.   On the other side, a sailor's ballad surrounded by wreath of flowers, with engraver's signature, " Job
  Johnson, Liverpool."

93. American Eagle.   Masonic Pitcher.   Liverpool.
  A Liverpool pitcher with American eagle and shield.   On the
  other side, Masonic emblems.   There were a vast number of
  these Masonic designs, one is shown on page 147, and as they
  were not specially American, though doubtless made largely
  for Americans, it is useless to specify them.

94. Ship Alligator.
  A pitcher with view of the ship Alligator on one side.   On the
  reverse a spread eagle, with a scroll border in gilt containing
  the names of fifteen States.

95. Mug.   Union to the People.

A mug of Liverpool ware printed with a group of three men
clasping hands.   They are supposed to be Hamilton, Madison, and Jay, but may be any other American statesmen.
Above the group, a liberty cap with the words " Union to
the People."   Below are branches with leaves and the legend,
" Civil and Religious Liberty to all Mankind."

96. Salem Ship-building.   Liverpool.

Two prints representing scenes of timber-rolling and ship-building, intended to commemorate the era of great prosperity in
Salem ship-yards.   They are accompanied with these verses :

" Our mountains are covered with Imperial Oak
    Whose Roots like our Liberties Ages have Nourish'd ;
But long e'er our Nation submits to the Yoke
    Not a Tree shall be left on the Field where it flourish'd.

" Should invasion impend, Every Tree would Descend
    From the Hilltops they shaded Our Shores to defend ;
For ne'er shall the Sons of Columbia be slaves
    While the Earth bears a Plant, or the Sea rolls its waves."

The finest specimen of Liverpool ware bearing these prints and
verses is a great punch-bowl, eighteen inches in diameter, in
the rooms of the East India Marine Society in Salem.   It also
bears on the inside of the bowl, in large letters, the name of
the Society and other inscriptions, and the date 1800.   Pitchers also are found with these prints, and also with the spread
eagle with the mark " Herculaneum Pottery, Liverpool."
One may be seen in the rooms of the Bostonian Society in
the old State House, Boston.   These prints are perhaps the
most pretentious of any made for commercial interests in this
country, and are usually very clear and good.

97. Plan of City of Washington.   Liverpool.

A Liverpool pitcher with black print of a map between two fe-

male figures.   Inscription, " Plan of the City of Washington."
On reverse is Washington design No. 13.

98. Emblem of America. Liverpool.

A Liverpool pitcher with a coarse black print of a female figure
holding the American flag, and facing two clumsily-drawn,
stumpy Indians.   In the background a group of oval portraits
labelled Raleigh, Columbus, Franklin, Washington, etc.   The
legend " An Emblem of America."   On the reverse a Washington design.

99. Crooked Town of Boston. Liverpool.

A Liverpool pitcher printed in black, red, or green, with inscription, " Success to the Crooked but Interesting Town of
Boston."   On the other side a long ballad, varying on different pitchers.

100. Liberty. Liverpool.

A Liverpool pitcher with black print.   Design, a seated figure
of Liberty with the legend, " May Columbia Flourish."

101. Infant Navy. Naval Pitcher.

This design is found on Liverpool pitchers of at least four sizes.
Under the nose of the pitcher is in large letters the inscription, " Success to the Infant Navy of the United States."   On
the side of the pitcher sometimes was seen a black transfer
print of a full-rigged ship, sometimes the American flag and
eagle, sometimes a large print of a naval battle with this
printed motto, " L'Insurgente French Frigate of 44 guns and
411 Men striking her Colours to the American Frigate Constitution, Commodore Truxton, of 40 guns, after an action of an
hour and a half in which the former had 75 Men killed &
wounded & the latter one killed & three wounded, Feb. 20th,
1799."   A very good pitcher with the latter design may be
seen at Washington's Headquarters, at Morristown.   See also
No. 18, and pages 141 *et seq.*

102. American Flag.

This print is found on pitchers and mugs, sometimes colored over the print. It is found on pieces with various other Washington and Sailor prints.

103. For America. Liverpool.

A Liverpool pitcher with the Farmers Arms, described on pages 153 *et seq*. Legend, " For America."

104. Peace and Prosperity to America. No. 1.

Liverpool pitcher printed in red, with scrolls of pink lustre. The design is a shield supported by two female figures ; the word " New York " on the top of the shield in large letters, and the names of twelve other States, including Boston, on a ribbon scroll. Legend, " Peace, Plenty and Independence." On the other side a shield supported by an eagle and an Indian. Legend, " Success to the United States of America, E Pluribus Unum." In front of pitcher the motto, " Peace and Prosperity to America."

105. Peace and Prosperity to America. No. 2.

A Liverpool pitcher with a wreath of ribbons and stars bearing names of eleven States, two of them being " Boston " and "Tenassee." In centre of wreath the words, " Peace, Plenty, and Independence." This wreath forms a medallion or shield supported by two female figures, each with a cornucopia. Above the medallion an eagle and flag. On the front of the pitcher, the motto, " Peace and Prosperity to America." This much resembles No. 104.

106. United States Soldier.

Liverpool pitchers and bowls with black or red print of United States soldier standing with his foot on the head of a British Lion. Legend, " By Virtue and Valor we have freed our Country, extended our Commerce, and laid the foundation of a Great Empire." In the background stand four Continental soldiers.

107. Liberty. Naval Pitcher.

A black print of ribbon scroll with names of sixteen States, enclosing verses beginning,

> " Oh Liberty ! thou goddess
>   Heavenly bright,
> Profuse of bliss,
>   And pregnant with delight."

On the reverse, a print of a ship with American flag.

108. People of America.

A Liverpool pitcher with a print of three men holding hands and elevating a liberty cap on a pole. Underneath, " People of America" on a scroll, and the words, "Civil and Religious Liberty to All Mankind." On the reverse, Liberty seated, and a soldier standing with a harp between the two figures. Beneath, the words " Tun'd to Freedom for our Country."

109. Historical Pitcher of War of 1812.

Described on page 299 *et seq.*

110. American Heroes.

Pitcher printed in copper lustre. On one side a full-rigged ship surrounded by a chain of elliptical links containing the names, Hull, Jones, Lawrence, Macdonough, Porter, Blakey, Beatry, Stuart, Washington, Perry, Rogers, Bainbridge, Decatur. Above are two clasped hands holding the chain. On the other side is the American eagle with " E Pluribus Unum," and a similar enclosing chain with clasped hands and the names Brown, McComb, Ripley, Pike, Porter, Miller, Bainbridge, Izard, Van Rensallaer, Adair, Lewis, Gaines, Scott, Jardson. This pitcher is globose in shape, and of fine quality of ware.

111. Naval Pitcher.   Liverpool.

This print of two men-of-war in a close engagement, appears
with various names.   A pitcher is here shown with the words
Macedonian and
the United States.

112. Perry.   Por-
    trait.

A white pottery
    plate with a black
    print of the por-
    trait of Commo-
    dore Perry, sur-
    rounded by a
    design of flags,
    c a n n o n, and a
    frigate ; a b o v e
    the name " Per-
    ry." The edge is
    scalloped, w i t h
    a black border.

Naval Pitcher.

Impressed mark, " Davenport."   This design appears on
pitcher described in No. 115.

113. Perry.   Portrait.

A white pottery plate with a black print.   In the centre, a full-
length portrait of Commodore Perry surrounded by a design
of flags, powder-kegs, cannon, and a full-rigged frigate.
Above the name " Perry."   The plate has a scalloped edge
with a black border.

114. Perry.   Portrait.

A portrait of Commodore Perry with the name O. H. Perry, Esq.
On a ribbon scroll, the legend, " We have met the enemy and
they are ours," the words of Perry's famous despatch.   Under

this, the words, "Hero of the Lake." See page 142 for description of Perry at this battle.

115. Jackson. Portrait.

A large globose pitcher with a portrait of Jackson, and the words "Major General Andrew Jackson." On the other side same portrait of Perry as No. 112. This print is also seen upon plates.

116. Decatur. Portrait.

A portrait of Decatur on a mug. Above, the words "Commodore Decatur;" below, on a ribbon, the famous war-motto, "Free Trade Sailors Rights." The old ballad says,

> "Then quickly met our nation's eyes
> The noblest sight in Nature,
> A first-class frigate as a prize
> Brought back by brave Decatur."

117. Lawrence. Portrait. Newcastle.

A portrait of Lawrence in copper-lustre on cream-ware pitcher, with motto, "Don't surrender the ship." His dying words, "Don't give up the ship," have become a national watchword. On the other side of pitcher, a portrait of Decatur, with his name.

118. Bainbridge. Portrait.

A mug with a portrait of Bainbridge, with words, "Commodore Bainbridge," and his characteristic words, "Avast, boys, she's struck!" Commodore Bainbridge commanded the Constitution—Old Ironsides."

> "On Brazil's coast She ruled the roost
> When Bainbridge was her Captain."

119. Hull. Portrait.

A pitcher bearing portrait of Captain Hull, and the words "Captain Hull, of the Constitution." On the other side, a portrait with the words, "Captain Jones, of the Macedonian."

120. Pike. Portrait.

A pitcher with the portrait of General Z. M. Pike ; above it the word " Pike ; " below, his noble words, " Be always ready to die for your country." On the other side, a portrait and name, " Captain Jones, of the Macedonian." A specimen can be seen in the collection of the Bostonian Society in the old State House in Boston.

121. Pike. Portrait.

Same portrait of Pike and same legend as No. 120. On the other side, portrait of Hull and legend, " Captain Hull, of the Constitution."

122. Jones. Portrait.

Plate with a portrait of Captain Jones printed in blue in the centre, with a ship on the left and flags on the right. Black shell border. Impressed mark, " Davenport." This description was given me by Mr. Prime.

Jones. Portrait.

See No. 120.

123. Preble. Portrait.

A pitcher with a good portrait of Preble, signed " D," with a figure of Fame on one side and the American flag on the other, and the name " Commodore Preble." On the other side of the pitcher, a well-drawn oval print of ships attacking fortifications. Above, the inscription " Commodore Preble's Squadron Attacking the City of Tripoli Aug 3. 1804. The American Squadron under Commodore Preble consisting of the Constitution 44 guns 2 Brigs & 3 Schooners 2 bombs & 4 Gunboats Attacking the City and Harbour of Tripoli Aug 3. 1804. the city was defended by Batteries Mounting 115 Pieces of heavy Cannon & the Harbour was defended by 19 Gunboats 2 Brigs 2 Schooners 2 Gallies and a Zebeck. the city Received Great Damage Several of the Tripolitan Vessels were sunk 3 of their Gunboats taken & a Great Number of Men Killed." On the front of the pitcher is the American spread eagle and the words, " Herculaneum Pottery, Liverpool."

124. Trophy.

Pitchers printed in lustre and purple with a trophy of arms and the verses,

" United & Steady in Liberties Cause,
We'll ever defend our Countries Laws."

Under the nose the legend,

" May the tree of Liberty ever flourish."

125. Macdonough.   Bombardment of Stonington.

A pitcher of cream ware with a black print entitled " The Gallant Defense of Stonington Aug 9th 1814." It represents that famous defence when the inhabitants of the town, with one gun successfully resisted the attack of the British force of several vessels, sinking one ship and driving off the others. Underneath, the legend, " Stonington is free whilst her heroes have one gun left." On the other side is the print of a ship with the words, " United States Frigate Guerriere, Com. MacDonough bound to Russia July 1818." Mr. Prime says that a citizen of Stonington who went to Russia on public service in the Guerriere ordered these pitchers in Liverpool. He may have made the drawing of the battle for the engraver.

Macdonough.   Victory on Lake Champlain.

Dark-blue print on Staffordshire ware.   See No. 188.

126. Naval Battle.

A globose pitcher printed in vermillion with a design of a naval battle. Underneath, the words " The Wasp and The Reindeer."

127. Militia.   Liverpool.

A Liverpool pitcher, twelve inches in height, bearing an oval medallion with design of cannon, flags, etc., with a man in full militia uniform. Above, this legend, " America ! whose Militia is better than Standing Armies." At base, within the medallion, " May its Citizens emulate Soldiers, its Soldiers Heroes." Below all, the lines :

" While Justice is the throne to which we are bound to bend
Our Countries Rights and Laws we ever will defend."

Under the nose of the pitcher is the spread eagle, with this legend, " Peace Commerce and honest Friendship with All Nations Entangling Alliances with None ; Jefferson." This pitcher is printed in black and is painted in colors. It was made in 1808, in Liverpool, for a Narragansett sea-captain.

DeWitt Clinton. Portrait. Erie Canal.
See No. 166.

DeWitt Clinton. Monogram.
See No. 172.

DeWitt Clinton. Eulogy.
See No. 168.

128. Steamship.
Printed in red on a cream-ware tea-service. On the large pieces are two views, one a steamship at sea, with land and a fort in distance. The ship floats American flag, and has the smoke-stack nearly as tall as the mast. The other view, a ship flying American flag over the British, approaching a shore upon which lies an anchor. An American eagle on the shore holds a laurel branch among the stars. The scroll border is in purple lustre. This is apparently Newcastle ware. Specimens can be seen at the rooms of the Essex Institute, in Salem.

129. Liberty Medallion. Head.
Embossed head of Liberty on Castleford teapots. The same head used on gold coins of United States of 1795.

130. Liberty Medallion.   Figure.

Embossed figure of Liberty seated.   Found on Castleford wares.

131. American Eagle.   Medallion.

Embossed eagle and shield on Castleford wares.   Same as die
on United States gold coin of 1797.

132. Harrison.   Pitcher.   American Pottery Co.

This pitcher is the most interesting piece of American pottery
bearing an historical design that I have ever seen.   The
dealer who offered it to me asserted that only six were ever
manufactured.   He also said that he could easily procure
dozens of Washington pitchers that were *two hundred years
old*, but that I would find it hard to get a *colonial* pitcher
with a picture of Harrison on it.   To this latter assertion I
warmly agreed.   It was six-sided, bulging in the middle to a
diameter of about nine inches, about eleven inches in height,
and with a foliated handle and scalloped lip.   It was of
coarse-grained brownish pottery, darker in shade than Liverpool ware.   On four of its sides the pitcher bore a view of a
small log-cabin above a good portrait of Harrison, with the
words, "The Ohio Farmer W. H. Harrison."   Below all, a
spread eagle.   On the bottom of the pitcher was printed in
black, "Am. Pottery Manfʸ Co., Jersey City."   It is the
only piece of American ware with printed decorations similar
to Liverpool ware that I have ever seen.

133. Columbian Star.   Jno. Ridgway.

This plate, which is printed in light blue, is popularly known as
the "Log-cabin" plate.   In the centre is a domestic scene
of a log-cabin with open door, and a woman and child are
seated outside watching a man who is ploughing a field in
the foreground.   A "lean-to" joins the house, beneath which
stands the cider barrel of "hard cider."   A man in the background is chopping stumps.   A small river bears a canoe
with a single figure.   Across the stream is a flagstaff with an

American flag. Pine-trees are grouped near the cabin, and abundant smoke rises from the chimney. The border is composed of large stars set in a firmament of small ones. The inscription is, " Columbian Star. Oct. 20, 1840. Jno. Ridgway." It will be remembered that William Henry Harrison was elected President in the fall of 1840. This plate is owned by Mrs. Nealy, of Washington, D. C.

XVII.

STAFFORDSHIRE WARES

NO ceramic specimens are of more interest to the American china collector than the pieces of dark-blue Staffordshire crockery that were manufactured in such vast variety of design, and were imported in such great numbers to America in the early years of this century. Their beauty of color—the color called by the Chinese "the light of heaven," a blue like the lapis the Bishop wished for his tomb at St. Praxed's, a tint unexcelled and hardly equalled in modern wares—makes them a never-ceasing delight to the eye ; and the historical character of their decoration frequently adds to their interest and value. Mr. Prime wrote in 1876 of these pieces of crockery, "they have ceased to be common, are indeed becoming rare, and collectors will do well to secure good specimens." Since that year specimens have become rarer and more valuable still. The Staffordshire pieces that date from the year 1830 to 1850, though still printed with American views, are lighter and duller in tint of blue, and are more frequently stamped in green, pink, sepia, chocolate, black, or plum color. The designs, as well as the colors, are weaker, as if fading gradually and dying into the vast expanse of dead-white crockery and china which spread its uninteresting level over the tables of country folk for the quarter of a century that elapsed before the Centennial Exhibition of 1876, that turning-point in household art decoration in America.

The shapes of the pieces of table-ware also became degraded, and were not so graceful as the Staffordshire tea and dinner sets of the first quarter of this century. One specially pretty piece that came with many dark-blue dinner sets of the latter-named date was the low fruit-dish with its tray, both with pierced basket-work borders. The pickle leaves also were gracefully shaped. The pitchers, both of the table and toilet sets, were graceful, and "poured" well, that most important, and ofttimes lacking, attribute of pitchers.

Pickle Leaf.

Both basins and pitchers of toilet sets were, however, inconveniently small. There was also not the monotony of design which we find nowadays on sets of china. I mean that all the pieces of a set were not stamped with the same design. I am convinced that the tea sets, such as the familiar Tomb of Washington and Tomb of Franklin design, seldom were furnished with a set of plates bearing the same decoration, but consisted only of teapot, waterpot, creamer, slop-bowl, sugar-bowl, and occasionally two cake-plates. The copper-lustre china tea sets of the early part of the century seldom had tea plates like the rest of the sets.

It was only the most popular and universally widespread designs, such as that of the Landing of Lafayette or the Pilgrim, or the Boston State House, that were found on all the pieces of dinner services and sold together. Sets were formed, usually having the same border, with different designs on the different-sized plates. We found in the summer of 1891, under the eaves of an old farm-house in Worcester County, a painted blue sea-chest which contained a sight to make a china hunter both smile and weep. The dust of years covered the chest, the floor, the ladder-like stairs that led to the attic. Every step of the staircase had to be cleared for our climbing entrance of the accumulated and forgotten autumn stores of what had been ears of seed-corn, but were now only rat-nibbled cobs, bunches of cobwebbed herbs, broken chairs, dried and withered gourds and pumpkins. The house-mistress frankly acknowledged that she hadn't "been up garret for years," she had been "so poorly and tissicky." We smiled when we opened the lid of the chest and saw the familiar and much-loved color, the color of our guiding star in our search, the rich, dark blue. But we grieved as we lifted the pieces out, for fully half of them were broken. There was an entire dinner-service of the "Beauties of America," set of J. & W. Ridgway. All had the same medallion border that is here shown on the Philadelphia Library plate. As the chief beauties of America in those days were not fair maids, but almshouses, all the larger dishes and tureens bore monotonously ugly views of square and many-windowed almshouses. The views on the gravy tureens, with their little accompanying platters, were all of the Exchange at Charleston; the large platters were of the Capitol at Washington; the smaller, of the Boston Hospital. The twelve dinner-plates bore a view of New York City Hall; the breakfast-plates were of the Philadelphia Library; the soup-plates all bore the view of the Boston Octagon Church; little plates six inches and a half in diameter had a view

Philadelphia Library Plate.

of the Boston Insane Hospital; the pickle leaves and handleless bowls of the ladles were still different, bearing a small, unnamed house with the same border. Tumbled in a crushed heap in the corner of the chest was the saddest sight of all, a superb old Worcester cream-pitcher, four pieces of Plymouth porcelain, an India china tea set, three Pilgrim plates, all broken, surmounted by two heavy tankards which the owner thought were pewter, but which were solid silver. They are all there still, huddled in sad fragments in the old blue chest; and the Staffordshire dinner set also, for the owner, though ignorant of the value of the crockery and china, of their number even, and their condition, still "couldn't spare them" when we asked to buy the whole pieces and thus rescue them from the sad fate of their brothers. The wife was deaf and poor and sick, and the husband looked sicker and poorer still, but both were stubborn, good-temperedly stubborn, in their assertion that they "couldn't spare them." We sat down in the dust of the floor and begged; we raised our offer to city prices; we offered to send another dinner set of French china to replace the Staffordshire one, but all in vain; we drove away and returned again to use fresh entreaties; the owner did not care for the "old crockery;" scorned the assertion that the tankards were silver, and threw them carelessly back into the chest; had no association with the pieces, no sentiment against selling them; but he "couldn't spare them."

It is difficult to find a full dinner set of the old Staffordshire dark-blue ware. The scattering of families and consequent division of property, the destruction through every-day careless use, have seldom left so full a set as the one just described. The Ridgways issued another set of views of the various colleges and buildings of English universities. The stamp on the back was in blue, a pointed oval, about three inches long, with words, "Opaque China, J. & W. Ridgway;" in the centre of the mark was the individual name of the building in the design.

A great number of these pieces appeared in the antique-shops in the winter of 1890, through the sale of the dining-room furnishings of an old hotel in Baltimore, which must have consisted largely of this set of college views. The owners sold all the old blue and white table crockery, the old substantial and beautiful Sheffield plated trays and tea sets, and bought nice new American "hotel ware" and shining electro-plated silver.

The name Cambridge on many of these University plates enabled some unscrupulous or ignorant dealers to palm off the college views of that University to a few thoughtless buyers, at high prices, as views of Harvard College, in Cambridge, Mass. Views of private residences in London are frequently found in America with the same border as the University pieces, a wreath of convolvulus broken by pretty cameo-like medallions of boys playing with goats.

All these English views are exceedingly useful for wall decorations, especially for high shelves, or as a background for lighter-colored bits of china, where it is not necessary that the design of the decoration should be carefully distinguished ; and their vast variety makes them a constantly interesting subject for investigation and purchase. I have seen one collection of over two hundred Staffordshire plates bearing each a different English view, and I have seen many scores—perhaps hundreds—still different.

Some of the richest pieces of color are the dark-blue plates printed with the "Wilkie Designs," such as the well-known Letter of Introduction, and the much-sought after Valentine design. The Don Quixote series is also good. Equally glorious and resplendent in color are pieces bearing the Dr. Syntax designs. I have seen only plates and tureens with the latter. These Syntax plates have an additional source of interest in the wit of the humorous scenes that they represent. "Dr. Syntax's Noble Hunting Party," "Dr. Syntax Upsets the Beehive," "Dr. Syntax Painting the Portrait of his Landlady," "Dr. Syntax Star-Gazing," "Dr. Syntax Reading his Tour." These I have seen, and there are doubtless many others. They were printed from a set of pictures drawn by Thomas Rowlandson, one of the most celebrated designers of his day of humorous and amusing subjects. They were drawn to illustrate a book published by William Combe, in 1812, called "Dr. Syntax's Tour in Search of the Picturesque." A second tour, "In Search of Consolation," appeared in 1820. This was also illustrated by Rowlandson. A third tour, "In Search of a Wife," was printed the following year. These books had an immense and deserved popularity. Not only did these Staffordshire plates appear, but a whole set of Derby figures were modelled—"Dr. Syntax Walking"—"In a Greenroom"—"At York"—"Going to Bed"—"Tied to a Tree"—"Scolding the Landlady"—"Playing the Violin"—"Attacked by a Bull"—"Mounted on Horseback"—and were sold in large numbers. The Staffordshire plates have survived in greater variety in this country. Doubtless they were imported in larger quantities than were the Derby figures.

Strangely enough, no Biblical scenes are represented on these Staffordshire plates, save one with a print of the Flight into Egypt.

Other interesting forms of ware manufactured in Staffordshire were the old drinking-mugs known as

"Tobys." They were seated figures of rummy, old, red-nosed fellows with drinking-mugs in their hands. They wore usually cocked hats, the hat forming the lip of the mug. They were gayly dressed in high colors, and were sometimes twelve and even fourteen inches in height. A terrible damper has been put, within a few years, on the joy of collecting these " Tobys," by the fact of their reproduction in vast numbers after precisely the old models, and in precisely the same colors. Of course, the modern Tobys are very shining and new, and upon ex-amination are easily distinguished from the old ones; but when a closet-door in an antique shop suddenly and most unadvisedly swung open, the sight of a row of twenty or thirty Tobys, all precisely alike, did not seem to enhance the value of the asserted-to-be-unique speci-men on the shop shelf, nor make me very warm about purchasing further specimens, were they old or new.

It is impossible to obtain any information in England about this dark-blue earthenware, or " semi-china," which was made for so many years in such vast quantities for the American market. The Staffordshire pottery works have all changed owners; the plates from which these wares were printed have all been lost or destroyed ; the present owners of the works are ignorant of the exist-ence even of these printed American pieces. There are almost no specimens to be seen in English collections, not even of pieces bearing English views; none for sale in English shops; and even in so exhaustive, extended, and careful a treatise on the ceramic art of Great Britain as that of Mr. Jewitt, he does not speak of them, and evidently is ignorant of the wares, the stamps, and marks. A careful search throughout the Staffordshire region developed absolutely not one fact about these " American historical pieces;" and I may add that a collection of Staffordshire ware bearing both American and English views is now being gathered in America for presentation to the Museum at Burslem, and consequent enlightenment of English collectors and manufacturers. Hence it is plain that each American collector must be a law to himself with regard to marks; or rather, American collectors must unite and form a new table of marks of "American pieces." I will specify a few that I find on my Staffordshire pieces.

A circular impression about an inch in diameter, with an inclosed circle having in the centre the word " Warranted," and a spread eagle bearing a thunderbolt and laurel leaf. In the quarter-inch ring inclosing this inner disk are the words, in capital letters, " T. Mayer. Stone Staffordshire." Accompanying this impressed stamp is always found (on my pieces) a very spirited rendering in dark blue of the American eagle, bearing a laurel branch in his right claw, and a bunch of arrow-like thunderbolts in his left. He measures two and three quarters inches from tip to tip of wings, has an American shield on his breast, and a ribbon bearing the word " E Pluribus Unum " in his mouth. The lighter clouded background has thirteen white stars. This mark is the richest in color and best in drawing of any that I have seen. This T. Mayer was, I judge, the Thomas Mayer who had the Dale Hall Staffordshire

works from 1829, and of whom Shaw speaks as having
made the best specimen of solid earthenware ever produced at that time—a vast table. This stamp and mark
are given by neither Chaffers nor Jewitt, nor Phillips
and Hooper. The marks E. Mayer, and E. Mayer &
Son, are frequently seen. These firms were in existence
from 1770 to 1830 in Hanley.

A distinct circular impression an inch in diameter; in
the centre appears a spread eagle with shield on his
breast, and below him the words " Semi China; " surrounding all the words " E. Wood & Sons, Burslem.
Warranted." In conjunction with this impressed stamp
appears often a dull-blue mark, an oblong panel an inch
and a half long and about three-eighths of an inch wide,
inclosing the name of the view on the face of the plate.
On this panel stands an eagle with laurel branch in his
right claw, and in his beak a written scroll attached to
a small United States shield, and bearing the words
" E Pluribus Unum "—the whole on a clouded background. Many of the pieces bearing both of these
marks are confused in outline, as if the dies or plates
from which they were printed were worn out. And
they also have the poorly drawn, ugly shell border.
This stamp and mark are not given by Chaffers or Jewitt. The ware also varies greatly, the earlier plates
being of much lighter weight. The impressed circular
mark appears alone on some very richly colored, clearly
printed, and beautifully drawn pieces decorated with
spirited marine views and clear and graceful shell borders. These were evidently made for the American

market, for on all of them appears prominently a full-rigged ship bearing the American flag; yet they cannot be classed as "American views." The names given to some of these views are "A Ship of the Line on the Downs," "In a Full Breeze," "Christianeburg," "Danish Settlement on the Gold Coast, Africa," "York Minster."

The name "Wood," alone, appears impressed, and often accompanied by an impressed crescent. The date of this mark is apparently about 1818, when the firm was no longer Wood & Caldwell, and Enoch Wood's sons had not been taken into partnership. All the pieces with this stamp are rich in color and clear in outline, as if the dies or plates were fresh and new.

The mark " E. W. & S." on lighter-blue pieces I have also fancied stood for E. Wood & Sons.

A circular stamp, impressed, of a crown, surrounded by words "A. Stevenson, Warranted Staffordshire." This stamp appears with a mark printed in blue of an eagle holding a tablet, with the name of the view on the face of the plate; or sometimes with a blue printed mark of an urn festooned with drapery, on which is printed the name of the view, which is usually of an English scene. The Cobridge Works were erected in 1808, were owned for a few years by Bucknall & Stevenson, and afterward by A. Stevenson alone. The works were closed in 1819, hence pieces bearing this mark can have the date quite definitely assigned. The circular mark is given by Chaffers as appearing once on a painted faïence plate. The impressed mark of name Stevenson in capital letters is found on many " American historical pieces," usually on plates with a beautiful vine-leaf border and white impressed edge.

A circular stamp of concentric rings, impressed, about one inch in diameter. In the centre a crown, and in surrounding ring the words " Clews Warranted Staffordshire." After 1819 the Cobridge works passed into the hands of Mr. James Clews, who continued them until 1829, when they were again closed and remained so until 1836, when they were opened under another firm name. Mr. Clews came to America, and an account of his enterprise here is given on page 97 *et seq*. This mark is not given by Chaffers, who calls the firm J. & R. Clews, and says they made " pale cream-colored ware." During the ten years that Mr. Clews owned these Cobridge Works some of the richest pieces of dark-blue color that were ever made by any potter took the form of pieces bearing American historical designs, and bear the last-mentioned stamp.

The mark of an open crown surmounting the words " Clews Warranted Staffordshire " appears on a set, " Picturesque Scenery." Upon the back of each piece appears also the colored stamp which was placed by the manufacturers to designate this set, all of which were printed with American views. It is a little landscape of pines and a sheet of water with a sloop. This scene is crossed diagonally with an oblong stamp bearing the words " Picturesque Views," and the name of the special view printed on the face of the piece ; for instance, " Penitentiary in Allegheny nr Pittsburgh Pa." This set of views of "Picturesque Scenery" was of much later date than the rich dark-blue pieces, being printed in sepia, green, chocolate, or plum color, thus showing the degraded taste of the second quarter of the century.

An impressed mark of Rogers appears sometimes in conjunction with an eagle stamped in blue. Occasionally, also, the eagle is seen without the Rogers mark. Sometimes the chemical sign for iron is found with these marks. The firm of Rogers was in existence in Burslem until 1849.

A circular impressed mark, one inch in diameter, with a star in the centre, surrounded by words "Joseph Stubbs Longport." This mark is not given by Chaffers, nor the name of the manufacturer or manufactory. Jewitt, who gives no marks, says that he was a successful potter at Dale Hall from 1790 to 1829, preceding T. Mayer at his pottery, and thus proving that pieces with the Stubbs mark are the earlier of the two. The circular mark of "Stubbs & Kent, Longport," also unknown in England, appears on many pieces; for instance, the dark-blue basket and rose, and the milkmaid designs so common on toilet and dinner services. Still another impressed mark of "Stubbs" alone, in capital letters, appears on many American historical pieces, particularly on the ones with what is known as the eagle, rose, and scroll border.

A large number of pieces were printed, with views of public buildings in America, by the firm of J. & W. Ridgway. These pieces bore on the back an oblong stamp inclosing the name of the building and its location, as, for instance, "City Hall, New York;" above this the words "Beauties of America," below, J. & W. Ridgway. One of the set is shown on page 319. The pieces bearing this stamp are only medium blue in tint, though the color is good and some of the shading is dark. These pieces are disfigured by the border, which has the effect of oval medallions inclosing alternately a single stiff rose and a six-petalled flower—a myrtle blossom, perhaps. This border is poorly shaded and far from graceful in designing. I cannot definitely assign the date of these pieces; the firm succeeded Job Ridgway & Sons in 1814, and was in existence in 1829. This mark is not given by Chaffers. Another Ridgway mark is an oval medallion with the initials J. R. under a crown, and with the names of the pattern in a scroll. Still another has the initials J. W. R., another Jno. Ridgway, and another W. Ridgway.

A large number of very beautiful English views, printed in dark blue, are found on dinner services of Staffordshire ware, bearing the mark in blue of a spray of rose leaves with a double scroll and name "Riley," and name also of the view—for instance, "Goggerdan, Cardiganshire." The firm of John & Richard Riley rebuilt in 1814 the Hill Works, that had formerly been owned by Ralph Wood, and ran them until 1839. The prints of this firm are clear and distinct, and really artistic in drawing, the borders being specially graceful. The only mark given by Chaffers is "Riley Semi-China" on blue willow-pattern ware. This I have also found, the words appearing within a circular belt. The impress Riley also is seen.

R. Hall's wares were imported to America in large quantities, especially his "Select Views." I do not know whether this is R. Hall who ran the "Sytch Pottery" in Burslem until 1830, or whether he was Ralph Hall who owned the Swan Banks Works, Tunstall, during the first quarter of the century. Chaffers does not mention either Hall, and Jewitt gives no marks. The stamp most frequently seen is an oval ring in blue; at the top, "R. Hall's Select Views;" below, a sprig of flowers and the words "Stone China." The ring inclosed the name of the view, Biddulph Castle, Staffordshire, and Pains Hill, Surrey, being the most frequent. I have seen hundreds of Pains Hill plates in New England, fully half the country houses that I have entered had a few on cupboard or pantry shelves.

Still another Hall mark is a crown-shaped blue stamp with "Hall" and the name of the set—for instance, "Quadrupeds." Another, a blue stamp in an irregular shield, at top and bottom "R. Halls Picturesque Scenery," in the middle the name—for instance, "Fulham Church Middlesex." Another is an irregular shield, with scrolls with words "Oriental Scenery, I. (or J.) Hall & Sons;" and also "Italian Scenery, I. Hall & Sons;" and "Indian Scenery, I. Hall & Sons." The views, of course, on these pieces are indicative, respectively, of the marks on the back.

The views of Oriental scenery were taken from the illustrations of Buckingham's Travels in Mesopotamia, of the date 1828.

A very interesting mark is a wreath of blue flowers

inclosing the words "Bristol Flowers," and accompanied either by impressed initials in capitals, E. & G. P., or an impressed cross like the Bristol stamp. This mark has been seen only on pure white "semi-china," decorated in clear blue, with a design of fruit and flowers in which the passion-flower predominates.

Still another blue mark, on pieces a trifle lighter in tint, is a fine spread eagle; above, the word "Ironstone;" below, "Sydenham J. Clementson." Chaffers does not mention this name or mark. Jewitt gives no marks, but says Clementson became proprietor of the Sydenham works about 1832, and manufactured for the American market.

The impressed mark of "Adams Warranted Staffordshire" appears in a circle around an American eagle. And the initials R. S. W., in a graceful scroll with a branch of leaves, appear on many beautiful American views. I have been told that this was the stamp of R. S. Warburton, but can give no proof nor further information. It may be the stamp of some member of the Wood family, so many of whom were potters.

When we examine all these special American marks on English pottery, it seems odd to read Mr. Jewitt's statement, that marks were frequently omitted on the English china sent to America, "on account of the jealous dislike of the Americans of that day to anything emanating from the mother country."

With the pieces of Staffordshire wares bearing American designs, and a few pieces which cannot be classed elsewhere, I conclude my list.

134. Albany.

 View of city of Albany printed in black on plate. Date of view
 apparently about 1840.

135. Albany.

 View of Albany in bright dark-blue. E. Wood & Sons.
 Marked on back, " City of Albany State of New York," and
 spread eagle with E Pluribus Unum. In centre the Capitol Hill with old Capitol. On the river a steamboat and sailing vessels. Cows grazing in foreground. Shell border.

Albany. Capitol.

 See No. 166.

Albany. Theatre.

 See No. 170.

Albany. Canal.

 See No. 171.

Alleghany.

 See No. 241.

136. Anti-Slavery Plate.

 This design is printed in a purplish and rather light blue on
 various pieces of dinner and tea services. The plates are
 most frequently found. One is here shown. They have
 slightly scalloped edges and a scroll border dotted with stars.
 Four American eagles and shields are in the border, and four
 medallions. The upper one contains the figure of Liberty
 standing beside a printing-press, while a negro kneels at her
 feet. Around the design are the words, " The Tyrants Foe
 —The People's Friend." In the lower medallion is the design of the scales of Justice. In the medallion to the right are
 the words, " Of One Blood are All Nations of Men." In the
 medallion to the left, " We hold that all men are created
 equal." In the centre of the plate, against the background

of a sun-burst, are these words : " Congress shall make no
law respecting an establishment of religion, or prohibiting the

Anti-Slavery Plate.

free exercise thereof; or abridging the freedom of speech, or
of the press, or the right of the people peaceably to assemble
and to petition the government for a redress of grievances.
Constitution U. S." On some of the pieces—pitchers and
teapots, for example — there also is seen this inscription,
" Lovejoy—the First Martyr to American Liberty. Alton,
Nov. 7th, 1837." It is asserted that the pieces bearing this
design were the gift of the English Anti-Slavery Society to
the American Abolitionists, shortly after the death of Lovejoy ; that they were sold at auction in New York, and the proceeds devoted to the objects of the Society of Abolitionists.
If this account is true, these plates are certainly among the
most interesting relics of those interesting days.

Battery.   New York.
  See No. 217.

137. Baltimore.   Battle Monument.

A plate printed in black, dark brown, or green, with border of
flowers.   In the centre a view of the city of Baltimore with a
monument in the foreground.   Name on the back, "Battle
Monument Baltimore."   This monument, which stands in
Battle Square at the intersection of Calvert and Fayette
Streets, is commemorative of those who fell defending the
city when it was attacked by the British in 1814.   It has a
square base twenty feet high, with a pedestal ornamented at
the four corners with sculptured griffins.   On each front is an
Egyptian door with bas-reliefs and inscriptions.   A column
eighteen feet high rises above the base and is surrounded by
bands inscribed with the names of those who fell in battle.
The column is surmounted by a marble figure typical of the
city of Baltimore.

138. Baltimore.   Exchange.

View of Exchange building, in dark blue.   This plate is very
rare.

139. Baltimore.   Court-House.

A dark-blue plate with a rose and fruit border.   In the exact
centre of the plate is the Court-House in an open square.
Pedestrians are walking to and fro.   The design of this plate
is very stiff and ugly.   The mark on the back is a scroll of
blue, with words "Baltimore Court House;" also a circular
impressed mark, smaller than the Clews mark, with words
"Warranted Staffordshire"

140. Baltimore & Ohio Railroad.   Wood.

Plates printed in dark blue with rich shell border, with a train
of little cars like stage-coaches, and the stumpy little locomotive which it is said was designed by Peter Cooper, and which

was originally intended to have sails like a boat to help propel it along. The corner-stone of this railroad was laid in Baltimore, July 4, 1828, by Charles Carroll of Carrollton, the last surviving signer of the Declaration of Independence. This event was considered of so great importance that it was celebrated by a great trades-procession in Baltimore, during which the cordwainers made a fine pair of satin shoes which were at once sent to the idolized Lafayette, and were placed in the museum at La Grange.

In 1830 the first locomotive was placed on the road. Peter Cooper thus describes it :

" The engine was a very small and insignificant affair. It was made at a time when I had become the owner of all the land now belonging to the Canton Company, the value of which, I believe, depended almost entirely upon the success of the Baltimore & Ohio Railroad. When I had completed the engine I invited the directors to witness an experiment. Some thirty-six persons entered one of the passenger cars, and four rode on the locomotive, which carried its own fuel and water ; and made the first passage of thirteen miles over an average ascending grade of eighteen feet to the mile, in one hour and twelve minutes. We made the return trip in fifty-seven minutes."

The locomotive on these blue plates is not like the Tom Thumb locomotive in an old print which I possess ; it is more like the " Stourbridge Lion," the first engine made in England for America, which arrived in New York in 1829. Marks on plate both E. Wood and Wood.

141. Baltimore & Ohio Railroad. Down Hill.

This plate is in dark blue with a shell border. It has a stationary engine at the top of a hill, with a number of small freight cars running down a very steep grade, with the cars at a very singular angle. Both Baltimore & Ohio plates are here shown.

There were several of these down-hill tram-roads built at an early date in America. One on the western slope of Beacon

Baltimore & Ohio Railroad Plates.

Hill, in Boston, was constructed in the year 1807. It was used for transporting gravel from the top of the hill down to Charles Street, which was being graded and filled. The descent of the heavy gravel-loaded train drew up the empty cars—thus the machinery was worked without horse-power. In 1810 a similar one was built in Ridley, Pa., for transporting stone. In 1825 a third road was built, in Nashua, N. H., to carry down earth from a hill to fill up a factory location on a grade below. In 1826 a road three miles long at Quincy, Mass. carried in the same manner granite to the Neponset River. In 1828 the coal-mines at Mauch Chunk, Pa., had a road nine miles long to the Lehigh River. The empty cars were drawn up by mules. In 1828 the Delaware & Hudson Canal Company, and the Bunker Hill Monument Company, had similar tram-ways or roads.

Other views of early railroads and locomotives appear, and are often sold as of the Baltimore & Ohio Railroad. They are probably views of English railways.

142. Boston.   Almshouse.   J. & W. Ridgway.

This view is upon the cover of an enormous soup-tureen, described in No. 178.   The set medallion border is shown on page 319, and is found on all pieces of this "American Beauties" set.   Stamp on back in oblong disk, "Beauties of America.   J. & W. Ridgway.   Almshouse, Boston."

143. Boston.   Common.

Comparatively modern print in black of a view on Boston Common.

144. Boston.   Hospital.   Stevenson.

Dinner set printed in dark blue with view of the Hospital. Trees in foreground, and a smart chaise with man and woman driving.   Border of vine leaves on dark blue.   White impressed or fluted edge on some specimens.   Mark in blue on back, "Hospital, Boston."   Impressed mark, "Stevenson." There is said to be another view of this hospital with a canal in the foreground.

145. Boston.   Insane Hospital.   J. & W. Ridgway.

Printed in dark blue on various pieces of a dinner service. Small building in centre with high fence in foreground.   Same medallion border as shown on page 319.   Stamp on back in blue, "Beauties of America.   Insane Hospital, Boston.   J. & W. Ridgway."

146. Boston.   Octagon Church.   J. & W. Ridgway.

A plate printed in dark blue, with view of the church and of other buildings.   In the foreground a curious covered coach or carriage with two horses, one carrying a postilion.   The same medallion border as shown on page 319.   Stamp on back, "Beauties of America.   Octagon Church, Boston.   J. & W. Ridgway."   This Octagon Church was often known as the New North Church, and was built in 1815.   A description of it is given in Drake's "History of Boston," page 552.

147. Boston.　State-House.

Print in dark blue, on dinner and toilet services, of a view of the State-House and surrounding buildings, including the John Hancock house. Trees and the Common in foreground, and a group of grazing cattle. Three poplar-trees appear at the right; also a man with a wheelbarrow. The border is a pretty design of roses and forget-me-nots. The mark on the back is different from any stamp I have seen—simply the American "spatch-cock" eagle in blue. This State-House plate is popularly known as "the one with John Hancock's cows." One is here shown. The "New State-House" was built on a portion of John Hancock's field, where not only his cows, but those of many of his fellow-townsmen, found pasturage. During the memorable visit of D'Estaing and his officers to Hancock, the latter's servants milked all the cows on the Common to obtain milk enough to supply the visitors. This pasturing of cows on the Common in front of the State-House continued until the year 1830, when accidents from bovine assaults upon citizens became so frequent that the cows were exiled from their old feeding-ground. The pitchers printed with this view are very handsome, often having an extended view of Boston in the vicinity of the State-House encircling the body of the pitcher. I have

State-House Plate.

seen one with the initials R. S. W. on the base, though I have
always attributed this view to Rogers.

148. Boston.   State-House.

Print in rather light blue of a view of the State-House.   Surrounding buildings do not show in this design.   In the foreground is a horse and chaise with driver.   No maker's stamp.
Border of roses.

149. Boston.   State-House.   Jackson.

View of State - House with group of persons in foreground.
Printed in pink.   Mark, "Jackson."

150. Boston.   St. Paul's Church.

Blue and white plate with view of St. Paul's Church.

151. Boston.   Athenæum.   J. & W. Ridgway.

This dark-blue design is on plates of different sizes, and possibly on other pieces of dinner services.   It has the set medallion border shown on page 319.   Mark on the back, "Boston
Athenæum.   Beauties of America.   J. & W. Ridgway."   In
the present Athenæum building may be seen one of these
plates with this note : "This building stood in Pearl St., and
one-half was given by Mr. James Perkins, the other half
bought of Mr. Cochran in 1822, and the whole occupied by
the Athenæum until 1849."

152. Boston Court-House.   J. & W. Ridgway.

This design is on platters, plates, and dishes in dark blue.   It
has the set medallion border shown on page 319, and in the
centre a view of the Court-House.   Mark on the back, "Boston Court-House.   Beauties of America.   J. & W. Ridgway."

153. Boston.   Lawrence Mansion.

Though all the plates, pitchers, and basins which bear this
beautiful dark-blue design are unstamped and unmarked, it
is well known that it is a view of Mr. Lawrence's handsome
house, which stood on Winter Street, Boston.   It is a view of

a large three-storied double mansion, surmounted by a steeple which at first sight seems a part of the house, but which is intended for the steeple of the Park Street Church in the background. A garden is on one side of the house. It has a clear vine-leaf border.

154. Boston. Warehouse. Adams.

This is a rich plate printed in clear dark blue, with a design showing Boston streets and buildings. A large warehouse stands at the right, on the left a block of buildings, and in the background the wharves and harbor with shipping. The beautiful border is formed on the top and sides by a design of trees with foliage. On the back is the stamp, in blue, "Mitchell & Freemans China and Glass Warehouse Chatham St. Boston Mass.; " also the impressed mark, "Adams." No doubt these plates were made at the order of the Boston firm whose name they bear. I have known of but four pieces with this design. A plate may be seen at the rooms of the Bostonian Society, in the old State-House in Boston.

155. Boston. Almshouse.

A view printed in dark blue of the old Almshouse on Leverett Street. The border is the beautiful design of vine-leaves like that on No. 144, and the plates and platters have a white edge. Mark on back, "Almshouse Boston."

156. Boston Mails.

Plate printed in brown or black. The border contains the figures of four steamships with these names severally printed under them—Acadia, Columbia, Caledonia, Britannia. In the centre is a view labelled "Gentlemen's Cabin." Mark on the back, "Boston Mails." These plates were doubtless printed to commemorate the opening of the first line of steamships between Liverpool and Boston. I have seen the date of the first trip given as July, 1840, when the Britannia arrived in Boston.

157. Boston. John Hancock's House.

This print is seen in red, blue, or green on cups and saucers, or on slightly scalloped plates. One of the latter is here shown. This historic house is not now in existence. It was the intention of Governor Hancock to present the handsome and sub-

John Hancock's House.

stantial mansion, with its elegant furniture, by bequest, to the Commonwealth of Massachusetts, to be preserved as a memorial of great historical events, and to be used, if necessary, by the Governor of the State during his residence in Boston through his term of office. Hancock died without signing this bequest, and his heirs then offered it to the Government for a modest purchase-sum. After many years of indecision, half-acceptance, and final refusal on the part of the State, this fine old house was in 1863 pulled down. In it Washington, Lafayette, and scores of other distinguished men were visitors. There D'Estaing made his home in 1778, and with forty of his officers dined with hospitable welcome every day for many weeks. It was during this visit that the event occurred of which Madame Hancock complained—that D'Estaing went to bed overcome with Hancock's good wine, and tore her best satin bed-spread in pieces with his spurs, which he had been too drunk to remove.

158. Brandywine Creek.

View of Gilpin's Mills on Brandywine Creek. Dark blue. Mark on back of scroll, eagle and E Pluribus Unum.

Brooklyn. View from.

See No. 208.

Bunker Hill Monument.

See No. 164.

159. Burlington. Richard Jordan's House. J. S. & Co.

View of a commonplace frame house and outbuildings, and an inclosed door-yard, with a broad-brimmed Quaker and a cow in foreground. Mark, "Richard Jordan's House. J. S. & Co." This house was in Burlington, N. J. The design is printed in pink or black on tea services, and appears to have been a popular one in New Jersey and Pennsylvania.

Cadmus.

See No. 74.

Cambridge. Harvard College.

See No. 179 *et seq.*

Capitol at Washington.

See No. 259 *et seq.*

160. Catskills. Pine Orchard House.

This is a pretty landscape in dark blue, with hotel in the distance, and a man on horseback in the foreground. Mark on back, "Pine Orchard House, Catskills." It is doubtless made by E. Wood & Sons.

161. Catskills.

Print in rich dark blue of a mountain-scene with cliffs, peaks, and pines, and a solitary figure. A confused shell border. Mark on the back, of eagle with E Pluribus Unum, and an oblong stamp with the words, "In the Catskills;" also a confused impressed stamp, probably E. Wood & Sons.

162. Centennial.

Various pieces of ornamental and useful nature were made of a clear white china for the Centennial of 1876. The stamp on the bottom was, "Manufactured solely for J. H. Shaw & Co., New York. Trade Mark, Philadelphia, 1876." Each piece bore the words, "A Memorial of the Centennial, 1876;" also in high colors a medallion with portrait of Washington and two United States flags surmounted by an eagle. These modern pieces deserve mention among the historical china, since a single piece is usually desired by collectors. Views also were made of the different buildings at the Centennial Exhibition of 1876, on porcelain plates, with ugly purple and brown border.

163. Charleston. Exchange. J. & W. Ridgway.

This is one of the few Southern views. Dark-blue print, with medallion border shown on page 319. Stamp on back, "Exchange, Charleston. J. & W. Ridgway. Beauties of America." This historical building was erected in 1767, at a cost of £60,000. It was used as a "provost" during the occupation of Charleston by the British during the Revolution Prisoners were confined in the cellars. Colonel Isaac Haynes, an American officer, spent, in 1781, the last few months of his life in confinement within its walls, and from thence he was taken to his execution amid the protests of the entire populace.

His death so enraged the officers of the American army that they joined in a memorial to General Greene, proposing measures of retaliation on captive British soldiers and officers, thus subjecting themselves to a certainty of like death in case they were captured by the enemy. After the Revolution the Exchange was used as a Custom-House and Post-Office, and is now used in the latter capacity. It is still standing. The cupola has been removed.

164. Charlestown, Mass.

A view in black of Bunker Hill Monument at Charlestown, Mass.

Chief-Justice Marshall. Steamboat.

See No. 185.

City Hall. New York.

See No. 211 *et seq.*

City Hotel. New York.

See No. 218.

Columbus. Landing of.

See No. 186.

Constitution of United States.

See No. 136.

165. Conway. New Hampshire.

A pink or red print. In the centre a view of dwellings, including a log-cabin with sheds; mountains, highway, pine-trees, and people. Marked on the back " View near Conway N. Hampshire." A plate bearing this design is usually considered to be worth about a dollar and a half.

Deaf and Dumb Asylum.

See No. 178.

166. Erie Canal. A. Stevenson.

This print is in dark blue on plates. In the centre of the plate is a view of buildings, among them a church with a high fence. These are said to be intended to represent the Capitol grounds and surroundings at Albany. The border is of oak leaves and acorns, broken by five designs, four being the portraits of Jefferson, Washington, Lafayette, and Governor Clinton, with their respective legends, "Jefferson," "President Washington," "Welcome Lafayette The Nations Guest," and "Governor Clinton." The fifth design, at the bottom of the plate, is the picture of an aqueduct with the words, "View of the Aqueduct Bridge at Rochester." Mark, impressed, "A. Stevenson warranted Staffordshire," in circle, with crown in centre. Another mark printed in blue is of an urn, wreath, and the words "Faulkner Ware." This plate is in the possession of A. G. Richmond, Esq., of Canajoharie.

167. Erie Canal. Utica.

The plate bearing this design is usually known as the "Utica Plate." In the centre is printed these words, "Utica, a village in the State of New York, thirty years since a wilderness, now (1824) inferior to none in the western section of the state in population, wealth, commercial enterprise, active industry, and civil improvement." This inscription is inclosed in a laurel wreath. The border of this plate has two views of a canal lock and aqueduct, and two of a canal-boat. The print is also seen on pitchers.

168. Erie Canal.

Same border, with designs of canal-boats and locks as No. 167. In the centre the words, "The Grand Erie Canal, a splendid monument of the enterprise and resources of the State of New York. Indebted for its early commencement and rapid completion to the active energies, pre-eminent talents, and enlightened policy of DeWitt Clinton, Late Governor of the State." I have seen pitchers bearing this design and the design described in No. 167.

169. Erie Canal at Buffalo, N. Y.

This print is in black upon a plate marked " R. S." (Robert Stevenson.)

Erie Canal.

This entry might properly come under the head of either No. 166 or No. 167, since it describes a pitcher which had both of those decorations in blue, and also an American eagle with the words " E Pluribus Unum."

170. Erie Canal.

Black print upon a pitcher. On the right of the handle is a large view of an aqueduct, river, hills, and buildings, and the words, " View of the Aqueduct Bridge at Little Falls." At the left of the handle a building, with the words " Albany Theatre 1824." Below the spout a front view of the head of Washington, and words, " President Washington." This piece is not marked with maker's name.

171. Erie Canal. Clews.

Entrance of the Erie Canal into the Hudson at Albany. Marked " Clews." It is a pretty view of a canal lock with boats, and with high-wooded hill in the background. In foreground, groups of men fishing. This design is seen on dinner and toilet services. The border is of roses. The color is rich and dark.

172. Erie Canal.

Oval platter of Oriental china of greenish tint, decorated in gay colors, with a gold edge, and the monogram D. W. M. C. (DeWitt and Maria Clinton). In the centre a landscape with the Erie Canal. This odd and interesting piece sold at the Governor Lyon sale for $10.

Fairmount Park.

See No. 227 *et seq.*

173. Fishkill.

This is one of the sets of Clews Picturesque Views. Marks are
described on page 327. Printed in red, green, black, and
brown. The name on back, "Nr Fishkill Hudson River."
This is a pretty view of an old Dutch house and kitchen on a
high bank. In the background, poplar-trees and a manor-
house. By the side of the water fishermen are stretching
nets.

Fort Gansevoort, New York.

See No. 215.

Gilpin's Mills.

See No. 158.

Girard's Bank.

See No. 231.

174. Harper's Ferry. W. Ridgway.

Print of landscape view in black or sepia. Mark on back,
" Harper's Ferry from the Potomac side. W. Ridgway."

175. Hartford, Conn. State-House.

Print in dark blue of the old State-House, with two stiff poplar-
trees on either side.

176. Hartford, Conn. Mount Video.

Print in dark blue of Mount Video, now known as Wadsworth
Tower.

177. Hartford, Conn. Mount Video. Jackson.

Print in black of view similar to No. 176. Mark, "Jackson
Ware."

178. Hartford, Conn. Asylum. J. & W. Ridgway.

Print in dark blue on enormous soup-tureen and other pieces of
a dinner service, of a view of the Deaf and Dumb Asylum at
Hartford which was established by Dr. Gallaudet. Same
medallion border as shown on page 319. Mark on back,

"Deaf and Dumb Asylum, Hartford. J. & W. Ridgway. Beauties of America."

179. Harvard College. R. S. W.

A very finely printed plate in dark blue of the College buildings. Only three halls are shown. The trees in foreground are un- usually well drawn. The clear border of oak leaves and

Harvard College Plate.

acorns is on a stippled background. Mark on back, in scroll with rose branch, "Harvard College," and some specimen also R. S. W. A plate is here shown.

180. Harvard College. E. Wood & Sons.

Black print with flower border marked "E. Wood & Sons."

181. Harvard College. E. W. S.

A clear and beautiful print in medium shade of blue on white ground. The edge has a white beading. The border is most artistic design of flowers and fruit, with a pretty spray of blackberries. In the centre a well-drawn view of four college buildings. A pond is in the foreground, with tree at right and left. By tradition this platter once formed part of the table-furnishing of the College dining-hall. Mark on back, " Harvard College. E. W. S."

182. Hoboken. New Jersey.

A view of the old Stevens mansion, marked on the back " View at Hoboken New Jersey."

183. Hudson, N. Y. Clews.

View of the town of Hudson as it looked in 1823, printed in black, with rose and vine border. On the back or underside of this dish are views of Stockport, a few miles above Hudson. It is said that engravings were sent abroad by Hudson residents, from which these views were copied.

184. Hudson River. Baker's Falls.

Black print of view of Baker's Falls.

Hudson River, near Fishkill.

See No. 173.

Independence of Texas.

See No. 254.

Jordan, House of Richard.

See No. 159.

185. Hudson River. Steamboat. E. Wood & Sons.

This is a view in dark blue of a steamboat on the Hudson River taking passengers from the shore in a small boat attached to a rope which is wound around the steamer's wheel. Accidents became so frequent from this means of transfer that the method was quickly abandoned. There are two of these sets of plates, precisely alike, save that on one on the wheel-house of the boat is the name " Chief Justice Marshal Troy," and on the other the words " Union Line." On another flag, which is seen on both plates, are the words " Troy Line." They are marked "E. Wood & Sons." I have seen three sizes of plates bearing these designs. One is here shown.

Steamboat Plate.

186. Landing of Columbus. Adams.

A plate stamped in pink or black with a pretty design of the landing of Columbus. He stands with his two captains dressed in Spanish costume; Indians peer out from behind the trees; the three Spanish ships lie anchored off the shore. A scroll and flower border inclosing four medallions of quadrupeds. The stamp is "Adams." The name "Columbus" is on an anchor.

Landing of the Fathers.

See No. 240.

Landing of Mayflower.

See No. 240.

187. Lake George.

A beautiful view printed in dark blue on platters and plates, with shell border. Mark on back "Lake George, State of N. Y." This is doubtless by E. Wood & Sons.

188. Lake Champlain. Macdonough's Victory. Wood.

This is a rather confused view of a naval encounter representing the battle of Lake Champlain. It has the clear, beautiful shell border, and the color is invariably rich and dark. It appears on all the pieces of tea and dinner services, and must have been sent to America in large numbers. On a rock in the foreground are the words " Commodore MacDonough's Victory." On the back, the impress mark " Wood." A plate is here shown.

MacDonough's Victory Plate.

Lawrence Mansion. See No. 153.

189. Lexington. Transylvania University. E. Wood & Sons.

A plate with a view of Transylvania University in the centre. On either side are rows of stiff poplar-trees, and in the foreground a man and woman walking. The print is in a good shade of dark blue, and has the poor shell border. It is marked on the back with an eagle, shield, and " E Pluribus Unum," and words " Transylvania University Lexington." Also the impressed mark of E. Wood & Sons. I have rarely seen this plate—one lot of three only, and all three were rather indistinctly and poorly printed; still they may be plentiful in the South or in the neighborhood of the University.

190. Lexington. Transylvania University.

Transylvania University A print in black or light blue of a smaller representation of the University and grounds. Apparently quite modern.

Little Falls. Erie Canal. See No. 170.

191. Louisville.   Marine Hospital.

A rich dark-blue plate with shell border.   Stamp on back,
"Marine Hospital, Louisville, Kentucky."   This is doubtless
by E. Wood & Sons.

Macdonough Victory.

See No. 188.

Marine Hospital.   Louisville.

See No. 191.

192. Maryland.   Arms of State.   T. Mayer.

A large oval soup-tureen and plates, printed in dark blue, with a
handsome and spirited version of the arms of the State of
Maryland.   The stamp of T. Mayer and the blue mark of an
eagle that appear on these pieces are fully described on page
324.   The border is a beautiful design of trumpet flowers and
roses, while the extreme edge of the plates is ornamented with
a conventionalized laurel wreath broken at intervals of about
six inches with a star.

Mayflower.   Landing of The.

See No. 240.

193. Mendenhall Ferry.   Stubbs.

A print in clear dark blue of a landscape with cattle in the foreground and a comfortable house, a story and a half high, a
Lombardy poplar and an elm-tree, and a narrow river.   In
the background, on the opposite side of the river, hills with
several dwelling-houses.   The main point is the ferry—a
cable stretching across the river, and by which boats were
taken from side to side.   The ferry-boat is shown.   The border is a scroll, with eagles with half-spread wings and flowers,
such as is shown on page 354.   Though these pieces have
no maker's stamp, the impressed mark on pieces bearing the
same border is "Stubbs."   The only mark on this piece is
the name Mendenhall Ferry in an oval medallion.   Menden-

hall is an old Pennsylvania name, but I do not know where the ferry was located. Joseph Mendenhall owned a farm of a thousand acres on the Brandywine, below Shadd's Ford, in Chester County, and it is very probable that the ferry was there.

Merchants' Exchange. New York.

See No. 204.

194. Millennium.

A plate printed in blue, plum, green, black, and pink. In the centre a design of a lion led by a child, while lions and lambs lie peacefully at their feet. Above, the words, "Peace on Earth," surmounted by a dove with olive branch. Below, the words, "Give us this day our daily Bread." The border is a design of wheat sheaves and fruit, broken at the top of the plate by an eye and a Bible open at Isaiah. Mark on back, "Millennium." One is shown on page 24.

Mitchell & Freeman's Warehouse.

See No. 154.

195. Mount Vernon.

This view of Mount Vernon is in black on a cup and saucer of white china. It is the front view of the house, and in the foreground a negro is leading a prancing white horse. At the top is this inscription, "Mount Vernon, Seat of the late Gen'l Washington." Inside the cup is a dotted border. It has no stamp or mark of maker. I have also seen this print upon a cup and saucer of cream-colored Liverpool ware.

196. Mount Vernon.

Landscape in dark blue. Marked "Mount Vernon nr Washington. J. & W. Ridgway."

197 Mount Vernon.

Dark-blue plate with Mount Vernon in foreground and city of Washington in background. Mark, " View of Washington from Mt. Vernon." Geographical and topographical laws were naught to English potters.

198. Mount Vernon.

Stamped in pink. In the centre a group of visitors at a monument ; the border a good floral design. On the back of plate the mark, " Virginia."

Mount Video.

See No. 176 *et seq.*

199. Nahant. No. 1. Stubbs.

This plate is ten inches in diameter, of a rich dark-blue color, and is very handsome—as are all the plates with its border, a

Nahant Plate.

scroll containing alternate e a g l e s and roses. In the centre is a view of the Nahant Hotel, with the ocean and rocks in the foreground. On one rock are a dog, and a man firing a gun ; on a second, two women fishing ; on a third, a man and woman walking. On the right of the foreground is an old - fashioned c u r r i c l e with two horses harnessed tandem. On the back of the plate is an oval blue stamp with the words, " Nahant Hotel near Boston." One of these plates is here shown. This hotel was built of stone in the year 1818, by the Hon. Edward H. Robbins, at a cost of sixty thousand dollars.

It was enlarged by a wooden addition until it contained three hundred rooms. It was burnt on September 12, 1861, and has never been rebuilt. The view on the plate shows only the old stone part of the hotel. It has been suggested that these plates were decorated for and used in the hotel. There is no evidence to prove this, nor is it probable. I have never seen any pieces save plates with this design.

200. Nahant. No. 2. R. S. W.

Same view of the hotel at Nahant, with a large tree in the foreground at the left, and no curricle. The border is the oak leaf and acorn design, shown on page 361 ; the stamp on the back, " Nahant Hotel nr Boston R. S. W." The plates bearing this design are about an inch less in diameter than the ones described in No. 199.

201. Natural Bridge. Virginia.

A poor and small view of the Natural Bridge, printed in lightblue or pink in the centre of a white plate. Sometimes the plate has a weakly drawn flower border.

202. Newburgh, on the Hudson River. W. R.

This is a black print on a white china plate twelve inches in diameter. On the back an impressed shield and eagle, and an oblong stamp surmounted by an eagle and having a pendent festoon of flowers. The name " View from Ruggles House in Newburgh Hudson River," and the initials W. R., are on the stamp. There is no border. In the centre of the plate is a pretty view of the Hudson River with the familiar mountains in the background. The water is dotted with sloops and little boats, and a large tree is at the left of the foreground.

203. Newburgh, on the Hudson River.

Black print on dinner set of a view of Washington's Headquarters at Newburgh. Confused rose border.

204. New York Fire, or Ruins of Merchants' Exchange.

This plate is ten inches in diameter, in a brown or dull-blue
print. A view of the ruins of the Merchants' Exchange, with
the front still standing, is in the centre of the plate. A safe
and books and papers, and a group of persons, are in the foreground, also a squad of four soldiers with an officer. Sentries
patrol in front of the Exchange; groups of lookers-on are on
either side; and flames and smoke in the background. The
border is divided by eight scrolls bearing alternately the
words "Great Fire" and "City of New York." The spaces
contain alternate subjects; one a group of old fire-imple-
ments, a fire-engine, fireman's hat and trumpet, and underneath the date, 1833; the other space contains a phœnix with
flames behind, against a background of old city buildings, and
underneath the date, December 16th. On the back of the
plate, the same phœnix over the stamp "Ruins Merchants'
Exchange," and in fine letters the mark "Stone-Ware."

This plate was printed to commemorate the terrible fire which
devastated the business portion of New York in 1833, burning
over thirteen acres in extent and causing a loss of seventeen
million dollars. The fire extended from Coffee House Slip
along South Street to Coenties Slip, thence to Broad Street,
along William Street to Wall Street, burning down the south
side to the East River, with the exception of the buildings
from Number 51 to 61. The Merchants' Exchange was one of
the last buildings to yield to the flames.

This beautiful marble building had a front of one hundred and
fifteen feet on Wall Street, was three stories high above the
basement, and was considered at the time the handsomest
building in the United States except the New York City
Hall. The Post-Office had been established in its basement
in 1827. The letters and mails were removed to a place of
safety, but the noble marble statue of Alexander Hamilton,
which stood in the Rotunda, was crushed by the falling side-

walls. The Seventh Regiment (then called the National Guard) kept guard over the ruins, and the funny fur-capped sentries shown on the plate are doubtless of this regiment. A fine view of the front and rear of the ruins of the Merchants' Exchange is shown in William L. Stone's "History of New York ; " but the old stone-ware plates form an equally faithful, and much more curious and interesting, memorial of the great conflagration.

205. New York. Arms of State. T. Mayer.

The arms of New York with seated figures, instead of standing figures as in the present coat of arms ; also the motto "Excelsior" and name New York. On the back is printed in blue the American eagle, with motto "E Pluribus Unum," also the impressed mark of "T. Mayer, Stone, Staffordshire." Both marks are described on page 324. There were doubtless dinner-services with the arms of all the existing States of the Union, but I have seen only the plates and platters with arms of New York, Rhode Island, Pennsylvania, and South Carolina, and the soup-tureen with the arms of the State of Maryland.

206. New York. Arms of State.

I have seen in many collections, the Trumbull-Prime Collection being one of the number, pieces of Lowestoft china bearing a poor and crude rendering of the Arms of State of New York. These must have been decorated in China in large numbers, to be so wide-spread and numerous.

207. New York Bay. Clews.

This view of the Bay is taken from Castle Garden. In the centre is the fort on Governor's Island. A side-wheel steamer and frigate are among the shipping. The stamp on back is "View of New York Bay."

208. New York. Stevenson.

A dark-blue print of a view of New York from Brooklyn

Heights. In the foreground is a pretty old Dutch homestead
view, low sheds, a well, and a man on horseback. On the river
is some shipping and a small steamboat. In the background
the lower portion of New York, showing Trinity Church spire.
The border is a rose pattern. On the back is the mark
" View of New York from Brooklyn Heights by (or for), Wm.
C. Wall Esq." Also the impressed mark of "Stevenson
Warranted." A plate with this print is in the rooms of the
Long Island Historical Society, in Brooklyn.

209. New York. Jackson.

A view of Castle Garden, with a tree to the right, printed in
brown. Marked "Jackson's Ware."

210. New York. Scudder's Museum. Richard Stevenson (?).

A dark-blue plate with a design in the centre of the plate of a
house with the sign "American Museum," and a garden in
front. The border is a pretty design of oak leaves. On the
back, in a scroll, the mark "Scudder's American Museum
R. S." This museum stood in a garden on the corner of
Broadway, where now is the great *New York Herald* building.
It was a famous place of amusement in its day, and afterward
passed into the possession of P. T. Barnum ; there he laid the
foundation of his fame and fortune.

211. New York. City Hall. Jackson.

This is a black or brown print with a flower border. In the centre is the City Hall with flag flying from the staff on the roof ;
in the foreground a horse and wagon, men and boys. Stamped
on the back " City Hall New York ; " and " Jackson Warranted."

212. New York. City Hall. J. & W. Ridgway.

A plate printed in dark blue with a view of the New York City
Hall. In the foreground are large trees and a wondrously-

attired man, woman, and child standing facing the building, to which the man points with his cane. The border is the ugly set medallion border of flowers shown on page 319. Mark in blue on the back, " City Hall New York. Beauties of America. J. & W. Ridgway." The corner-stone of this building was laid in 1803, and the edifice was completed in 1812. It stood with the bridewell on the west, the almshouse behind it,

City Hall Pitcher.

and the jail on the other side. It cost half a million dollars—a most reasonable expenditure when compared with the twelve million dollars for its neighbor the Court-House—and was at that time the handsomest structure in the United States. The "three fronts," as they were called, are of Stockbridge marble. It is still standing, a good example of pure design and style. A very simple way of dating the various City-Hall prints is found in the presence in the design of the clock in the cupola ; this was placed in its position in 1830. Some prints show the dial very distinctly.

213. New York. City Hall. Stubbs.

Same view of City Hall as No. 212, but the park in the foreground is intersected with paths and the trees are different. The border is of scrolls, roses, and eagles, shown on page 354. Color, dark blue. Mark on back, "City Hall New York." This view is taken, I think, from a drawing by W. G. Wall, which was published December 20, 1826.

214. New York. City Hall.

Same view of City Hall as No. 213, with no trees in the foreground. Oak-leaf border with outer edge of white. Color dark blue. Probably by Stevenson. A pitcher bearing this view is here shown.

215. New York. Fort Gansevoort.

Printed in dark blue on various pieces of a dinner-service. A view of the fort with water and sloop in foreground. A confused leaf border. The pieces I have seen bore no maker's mark.

216. New York. Almshouse. J. & RidW gway.

A view printed in dark blue of the ugly Almshouse on Blackwell's Island. One of the Beauties of America set, with same marks and border as shown on page 319.

217. New York. Battery.

A view of the Battery in common black print.

218. New York. City Hotel. R. S. W.

A plate printed in dark blue, with a view looking down Broadway, and including Trinity Church. In the foreground, in the middle of Broadway, in front of a hotel, a man is sawing wood on an old-fashioned saw-buck. The clear oak-leaf and acorn border, and scroll mark on back, with R. S. W., as in No. 219.

219. New York. Park Theatre. R. S. W.

A view of the Park Theatre, including the lower end of City Hall Park with its ancient brick posts, where now stands the Post-office. In the distance the spire of the Old Brick Church, where Dr. Spring preached. A clear oak-leaf and acorn

border, and scroll and leaf mark, with initials R. S. W. A
plate is here shown. The first Park Theatre was built in
1797. It stood in Park Row, about two hundred feet from
Ann Street. It was opened on January 29, 1798, the first play
being "As You Like It;" $1,232 were taken in at the first
performance. In May, 1820, it was burned to the ground. In

Park Theatre Plate.

1821 it was rebuilt, and opened with "Wives as they Were
and Maids as they Are." It was burnt on December 16, 1848.
An original water-color drawing of the interior is in the rooms
of the New York Historical Society, with a key to the members of the audience, for the figures are portraits. Many of
the men are sitting with their hats on. In this theatre
appeared Thomas A. Cooper, Charles Mathews, the Keans,
Charles and Fanny Kemble, Malibran, Celeste, Fanny Ells-
ler, Madame Vestris, Clara Fisher, Julia Wheatley, Master

Burke, the Ravels, Mr. and Mrs. Wood, Charlotte Watson, Charlotte Cushman, Ellen Tree, Taglioni—what prettier memento of the old New York stage can there be than the old Park Theatre plate?

220. Niagara.

A view of Niagara Falls in a pink print on small plate.

221. Niagara.

Print in medium shade of blue. A large house and trees in foreground and diminutive semi-circular waterfall in background. On back the stamp " Niagara."

222. Niagara.   Table Rock.

This beautiful dark-blue plate has the rich shell border of Wood, though it does not bear his impressed mark, and has only the stamp with eagle and motto " E Pluribus Unum " and words " Table Rock Niagara." The view is taken from the foot of Table Rock looking upward, and is very artistic. Entire dinner services bearing this design were exported to America.

Park Theatre.   New York.

See No. 219.

Passaic Falls.   Trenton.

See No. 256.

223. Peace and Plenty.   Clews.

A medium-blue plate decorated with border of fruit and flowers. In centre, a Roman husbandman crowned with grain and surrounded by sheaves of wheat ; in his right hand a sickle, and in his left a basket of fruit ; by his side a shield with the American eagle and the motto " Peace and Plenty." Made by Clews. Two plates bearing this design sold at the Governor Lyon sale for three dollars each.

Penn, Wm.   Treaty with Indians.

See No. 267.

224. Pennsylvania. Arms of. T. Mayer.

A very spirited and beautiful rendering of the arms of this State, printed in dark blue on platters and plates, with border and marks like No. 190. Marks fully described on page.

225. Pennsylvania Hospital. J. & W. Ridgway.

In dark blue, marked " J. & W. Ridgway. Beauties of America." Border shown on page 319.

226. Philadelphia. View.

This print is in dark blue upon a plate six inches in diameter. The border is a confused scroll with roses. The spires of two churches are seen, and in the foreground is a wharf with a derrick, and a sloop alongside. Some of the plates have upon the back the stamp " View of the city of Philadelphia." Also the impressed stamp of a star like the Worcester mark.

227. Philadelphia. Fairmount Park. Stubbs.

A view of Fairmount, with a large tree in the foreground, and a man and woman in the dress of the early part of the century. On the opposite and further shore of the lake are two of the handsome dwelling-houses which stood there at that time. The border is the handsome design of scroll, roses, and eagles. The medallion stamp on back " Fairmount near Philadelphia." Impressed mark, Stubbs. A plate with this design is here shown.

228. Philadelphia. Upper Bridge. Stubbs.

This is one of the four Fairmount Park views. It bears on the back the impress and the oval blue stamp " Upper Bridge over River Schuylkill." The border is the same as shown on page 364. On the left of the foreground of the view is a large tree, and under it is a group of persons, one of whom is sketching. At the left is an old covered Pennsylvania wagon with six horses. The view of the ferry bridge is clear and

Fairmount Park Plate.

good, and the color is a good blue, though not rich and dark. Impressed stamp on some specimens, Stubbs.

229. Philadelphia. Library. J. & W. Ridgway.

Plate printed in dark blue with set medallion border. In the centre a view of the Library at Philadelphia. Mark on the back, "Philadelphia Library. Beauties of America. J. & W. Ridgway." One of these plates is shown on page 319.

230. Philadelphia. Stoughton Church. J. & W. Ridgway.

Plate printed in dark blue with set medallion border shown on page 319. In the centre a view of the old church which stood on Filbert Street above Eighth. The church looks like an old Grecian building. Mark on the back, "Stoughton Church. J. & W. Ridgway, Beauties of America."

231. Philadelphia.   Girard's Bank.   Jackson.

A view, printed in pink or black, of Girard's Bank.   Mark on back, " Jackson Warranted."

232. Philadelphia.   United States Hotel.

A view of the hotel in rich dark blue, with a border composed chiefly of the foliage of two trees standing at the right and left and meeting overhead.

233. Philadelphia.   Woodlands.   Stubbs.

View of a low building like a lodge and landscape in dark blue. Scroll, eagle, and rose border shown on page 364.   Stamp on back, " Woodlands near Philadelphia."

234. Philadelphia.   Washington Church.

235. Philadelphia.   Race Street Bridge.   Jackson.

Print in black, brown, or pink, marked on back with name of view and " Jacksons Warranted."

236. Philadelphia.   Race Street Bridge.   Stubbs.

Eagle, rose, and scroll border like No. 225.   Impressed mark, " Stubbs."

237. Philadelphia.   Waterworks.   R. S. W.

Low building with dome in centre of the plate, fountain at right, and trees, fence, and an old-time covered emigrant wagon in foreground.   Distinct oak leaf and acorn border, like No. 180.   Clear dark blue in color.   Mark on back in scroll with leaves, " Philadelphia Waterworks.   R. S. W."

238. Philadelphia.   Waterworks.   Jackson.

Same view as No. 237, but smaller, and printed in black. Mark on back, " Jacksons Warranted."

239. Philadelphia.   Bank of the United States.   Stubbs.

A plate in dark blue with street and buildings in the centre. Eagle, rose, and scroll border shown on page 364.   This is the bank which was in 1833 forced into bankruptcy by President Andrew Jackson.

240. Pilgrims. Enoch Wood & Sons.

This Plymouth Rock decoration is found on plates and pitchers, and the pieces are perhaps more highly prized than any other historical Staffordshire wares, especially by all descendants from and lovers of the Pilgrims. The print is clear and good, though the blue color is not very dark.

Pilgrim Plate.

In the centre of the plate is a print representing a "rock-bound coast" with the Mayflower and a small boat overfilled with Pilgrim Fathers landing on Plymouth Rock, upon which are inscribed the names Carver, Bradford, Winslow, Brewster, Standish. Two Indians are also perched on the rock. Above this print is the small-lettered inscription " The Landing of the Fathers at Plymouth, Dec. 22, 1620." The border consists of a handsome design of eagles and scrolls, broken by four medallions or shields. The upper one contains the words " America Independent, July 4, 1776 ; " the lower the words, " Washington born 1732, died 1799 ; " on the right a little view of two full-rigged ships with names Enterprise and Boxer (?) ; on the left a part of the print on No. 128—a steamer, rock, and eagle. On the back is the blue stamp " Enoch Wood & Sons Burslem." One of these plates is here shown   In spite of the presence of the steamship, the name of Washington, and the date 1799, I have been gravely informed by country owners that these plates were two hundred years old, and once even that they " came over in the May-flower." We have often been told that the plates were "made for the dinner at the laying of the corner-stone of Bunker Hill Monument, in 1824, when Daniel Webster spoke." This account was obviously improbable, since nothing in the design on the plate bore reference to that occasion, and the probability seemed equally clear that the celebration was instead the bi-centennial celebration of the Landing of the Pilgrims, which was held in Plymouth in 1820, and at which Webster, clad in silk gown and satin small-clothes, made the address which laid the foundation of his reputation as an orator. I was glad to receive confirmation of my belief from Mr. T. B. Drew, Librarian of Plymouth Hall, at Plymouth. He says, " The Pilgrim plates you refer to were made in England by order of John Blaney Bates, a well-known contractor and builder of his day, who in 1820 was building the Plymouth County Court House. He had it so nearly completed that the dinner of the celebration was provided in that building. It was, as you say, the bicentennial of the Landing of the Pilgrims, but often termed by us the Webster celebration, on account of Daniel Webster being the orator of the day. There were two sizes of pitchers and two of plates, and one of the plates has on the rock the names as you describe. After the dinner the wares were sold either at auction or private sale, and the different pieces became distributed quite widely through New England. I know of no publication that gives any account of what I have been telling you, but the facts were well known and have been told by aged people who remember the circumstances." To this information I can add in one respect. There are six sizes of plates, one being deep like a soup-plate. An old lady still living in Plymouth, asserts that while the plates were furnished by Mr. Bates, her husband, seeing their popularity and ready sale, ordered the pitchers, as she remembers, from Holland. As the print on the pitchers varies from that on the plates, being encircled also by a narrow ribbon scroll with the words " The Landing of the Fathers," and as the former do not bear the stamp of Enoch Wood of Burslém, this reminiscence is probably correct, except possibly the point that the pitchers came from Holland. These plates are usually found one in a family, but from one household, near Worcester, Mass., were purchased by a china-hunter eight tea-plates, and from another family two soup-plates, four tea-plates, seven saucers, and ten " cup-plates." By cup-plates I mean the little flat saucers in which our grandmothers set their tea-cups when they poured the tea in the deep saucers to cool.

Pine Orchard House.

See No. 160.

241. Pittsburg Penitentiary.

This is upon large and small platters and plates in purplish-pink, blue, brown, and black prints. The ware is stone-ware of good quality. The border is a pretty scroll-work design with roses and other flowers and eagles. The edges are slightly scalloped. This Pittsburg plate has a clear unperspectived drawing of the Penitentiary, with high hills at the background. Stiff little houses and trees are scattered around. In the foreground a man in knee-breeches is holding a horse which is harnessed to a chaise. The building in this print is the Western Penitentiary of Pennsylvania, at Alleghany City. It is an enormous stone building of ancient Norman style of architecture, that was built in 1827.

242. Pittsburg.

Print in pale blue, brown, or black of a view of Pittsburg, with the Iron Mountain in the background and two large steamers named respectively "Home" and "Pennsylvania" in the

foreground. Mark on the back, "Picturesque Views, Pittsburg."

243. Pittsfield. Clews.

A winter view of the town common at Pittsfield, Mass., with the
church and other public buildings. In the foreground an
elliptical enclosure with a skeleton elm-tree, intended to represent the famous great Pittsfield Elm. The author of "The
China-Hunters' Club" quotes from a newspaper of 1864, that
the trunk of this tree was made into bowls and other relics, and
that "about 1825 Mr. Allen, a merchant of Pittsfield, had a
view of the elm and park, as they then appeared, taken and
sent to England, where it was reproduced on blue crockery
ware." As the fence which appears in the view on the plate
was not placed around the elm until 1825, this date is
probably correct. Before that the tree had been entirely un-
protected ; it was sadly nibbled by the farm horses that were
frequently hitched to the iron staples that were driven into
its trunk. When the elm fell in 1861, a great number of these
staples were found imbedded in the wood. The design of the
church appears in four medallions in the border of the plate.
It is marked " Clews" and the name " Winter View of
Pittsfield Mass." I have also seen this same view with a
vine-leaf border.

Plymouth Landing.

See No. 240.

244. Quebec.

Dark-blue print of view of the heights at Quebec. Mark on
back in blue scroll " Quebec," also the impressed stamp of a
Greek cross.

245. Quebec. Falls of Montmorency.

Dark-blue view of the Falls, with a shell border. Stamp on the
back " Falls of Montmorenci near Quebec." This and the
previous number are the only views of Canadian scenery that

I have ever seen on old Staffordshire plates. Persons who have gathered china in Canada tell me that they have found no other views there.

246. Rhode Island. Arms of State. T. Mayer.

Dark-blue print marked "T. Mayer Stone Staffordshire." Same border as No. 192. Marks fully described on page 324.

247. Richmond, Va. College.

View of college printed in light blue.

248. Savannah. Bank. J. & W. Ridgway.

View of the Bank at Savannah. It has the same set medallion border shown on page 319. Mark on back "Bank, Savannah, Beauties of America. J. & W. Ridgway."

Scudder's Museum. New York.

See No. 210.

249. South Carolina.

A plate with a palmetto-tree in the centre, and a ship in the distance, on either side a flag. A shield with the date July 4th and the motto of the State of South Carolina. Flower border like plates of E. Wood & Sons.

250. South Carolina. Arms of State. T. Mayer.

Dark-blue plate. Marked "Stone Staffordshire T. Mayer." Same marks and border as No. 192, and a very clear rendering of the State arms.

251. States. Clews.

This design is the larger plate shown on page 9. It is found on all the pieces of a dinner service, but I have never seen a tea set. The dinner plates are exceptionally large. The print is in a rich shade of dark blue. In the centre is a medallion of what is said to be the White House, at Washington, with sheep or cattle grazing in foreground. It is supported on one side by a kneeling figure with plumed helmet and bearing a

liberty cap—labelled Independence.   On the other side the
figure of a woman kneeling on her ankles with the bandage of
justice on her eyes, and Masonic emblem on her apron.   She
holds a portrait medallion labelled Washington.   On the pedestal at her ankles, the word " America."   The border is of
flowers and a scroll with names of fifteen States, and with fifteen stars.   On some pieces these stars are simply crosses.
Impressed stamp " Clews Warranted Staffordshire."   On the
larger pieces, such as tureens, the centre view is often of an
English castle—the White House view not being large enough,
apparently, to fill the space.   Some of the platters have in the
centre a view of a two-story house, while in the foreground are
two men and a sheet of water with a sloop.   This is sometimes called the Washington Masonic Plate.

252. Steamship.

A dark-blue print of a side-wheel steamship, bark rigged, under
full sail, and flying the American flag.   Impressed mark of
" E. Woods & Sons."   This may commemorate the Savannah,
the first steamer to cross the Atlantic, in 1819.

Stevens Mansion.

See No. 182.

Stoughton Church.

See No. 228.

Table Rock.   Niagara.

See No. 222.

253. Temperance Plate.

This curious and finely printed plate is very rare.   It is made
of a soft yellowish paste, and the decoration is printed in
black.   The edges are slightly scalloped and have a little line
of black.   In the centre of the plate is a shield supported by
the figures of a man and woman ; the man bearing a banner
inscribed with the word " Sobriety," and the woman a similar

banner with the words " Domestic Comfort." By the side of the man is a small figure of a boy seated reading ; on the opposite side that of a girl sewing. The shield is surmounted by a crest—an oak-tree—and above that a scroll containing the motto " Firm as an Oak." Below the shield are clouds and two shelves of vases and jars of antique shapes ; and beneath all a scroll with the motto " Temperance, Sobriety." The shield is divided by perpendicular lines and transverse bars. In the spaces thus formed are designs. That of a beehive has on the bar beneath it the word " Industry ; " that of a farmer working in a field, the word " Health ; " that of a sailor, the word " Freedom ; " that of a pile of money, the word " Wealth ; " that of a cornucopia, the word " Plenty ; " that of a snake, the word " Wisdom ; " in the lower space are an open Bible and the letters I.H.S. There is no stamp or mark on the back. It is probably a Masonic design, but is called the " Temperance Plate."

254. Texas. J. B.

English stone ware with blue or pink prints. Trophies of war in the corners, and on the sides symbolical figures of Peace and Plenty. In the centre, a fight between Texans and Mexicans, marked " Gen. Taylor in Texas." It was doubtless printed to commemorate the Independence of Texas. Marked on the back with initials J. B. A large platter bearing this design sold in the Governor Lyon sale, in 1876, for $7.50.

255. Texan Campaign.

Plates with a small, poor print in sepia green, red, or black, of a scene with troop of soldiers with mounted commander. Border, a scroll with trophies of arms and flags. Stamp on the back " Texan Campaign."

Transylvania University.

See No. 189 *et seq*.

256. Trenton Falls.

This plate is eight inches in diameter, of a rich dark blue. The handsome shell border indicates it to be one of Clews manufacture (as Mr. Prime asserts) ; the impressed stamp on the back cannot be deciphered. The view in the centre of the plate is a pretty group of pine-trees with the Passaic Falls in the middle. On the back is a blue stamp of an eagle with the scroll and the words " E Pluribus Unum," and the name " View of Trenton Falls."

257. Troy. Clews.

A view of Troy, N. Y., from Mount Ida, marked Clews.

Union Line. Steamboat.

See No. 184.

United States Bank.

See No. 239.

United States Hotel.

See No. 232.

Utica.

See No. 167.

Virginia. Natural Bridge.

See No. 201.

Virginia.

See No. 198.

258. Virginia. J. W. Ridgway.

Print in black or brown with floral border. In centre a landscape view. Mark on back " Virginia. J. W. Ridgway." The house bears a close resemblance to Arlington House.

Wadsworth Tower.

See No. 176.

Washington's Headquarters.

See No. 203.

Washington, D. C.　View of.

　See No. 197.

259. Washington, D. C.　Capitol.　J. & W. Ridgway.

　A view of the Capitol in dark blue with man and woman on
　horseback in the foreground.　Medallion border shown on
　page 319.　Marked "J. & W. Ridgway.　Beauties of America.
　Capitol Washington."　This appears usually on large platters.

260. Washington, D. C.　Capitol.　R. S. & W.

　A very beautiful dark-blue plate with slightly scalloped edge,
　with view of the Capitol, large tree in foreground.　A vine-

Capitol Plate.

　leaf border.　Mark on back in shield "Capitol Washington.
　R. S. &. W."　One is shown here.

261. Washington, D. C.　Capitol.　Stevenson.

　Dark-blue print of same view.　Vine-leaf border and white
　fluted edge.　Impressed mark, Stevenson.

262. Washington, D. C.　Capitol.　E. Wood & Sons.

　Dark-blue plate with view of the Capitol.　Confused shell bor-
　der.　Mark "E. Wood Warranted Staffordshire."

263. Washington, D. C.   White House.   Jackson.

This is a view of the Executive Mansion at Washington, with garden to the left and a group of figures to the right.   It is printed in black and marked " Jackson."

264. Washington, D. C.   White House.

Another view printed in black of the White House.   Scalloped edges and wide ornate border.   Marked on the back " White House Washington."

265. Washington, D. C.   White House.   Jackson.

Pink and white printed plate marked on the back "Presidents House Washington," and mark " Jacksons Warranted." Same border as No.

White House.   Washington.   States.

See No. 251.

266. West Point.   Clews.

View of West Point, with river and steam-boat and row-boat. Mark on back " Picturesque Views.   West Point Hudson River," also impressed mark " Warranted Clews Staffordshire."

267. William Penn.   Treaty with Indians.   Jackson.

Print in black or brown on dinner service of a view with William Penn, in Quaker garb, talking with an Indian chief. At their feet a box of treasure, including a string of beads which an Indian woman is examining.   Border a stencil design.

Woodlands.

See No. 233.

XVIII.

CHINA MEMORIES

WHAT fancies we weave, what dreams we dream over a piece of homely old china! Every cup, every jar in our china ingatherings, has the charm of fantasy, visions of past life and beauty, though only imagined. I like to think that the china I love has been warmly loved before—has been made a cherished companion, been tenderly handled ere I took it to be my companion and to care for it. It is much the same friendly affection that I feel for an old well-read, half-worn book; the unknown hands through which it has passed, the unseen eyes that have gazed on it, have endeared it to me. This imagined charm exists in china if it be old, though we know not a word of its past, save that it has a past and is not fresh from the potter's wheel and the kiln. The very haze of uncertainty is favorable to the fancies of a dreamer; I summon past owners from that shadowy hiding-place; weave romances out of that cloud; build past dwelling-houses more quaint, more romantic than any in whose windows I have gazed, whose threshold I have trodden in my real china-hunting. Victor Cousin says: "If beauty absent and dreamed of does not affect you more than beauty present, you may have a thousand other gifts, but not that of imagination."

If you have no imagination you may have none of these china dreams—these "children of an idle brain," but you still may have china memories. Fair country sights does my old china bring to my eyes; soft country sounds does it bring to my ears, the sound of buzzing bees, of rustling branches, "the liquid lapse of murmuring streams," of rippling brooks where we dipped the old blue crockery mugs and cups the day we found them, and drank the pure but sun-warmed water. When I look at this queen's-ware creamer, I hear the sweet, clear, ear-thrilling notes of the meadow-lark, "in notes by distance made more sweet"—who sang outside of the farm-house where I first saw the dainty shell of china. Sweet scents, too, does the old china bear. When I found that old yellow Wedgwood dish in the country tavern, it was filled with tiny fragrant wild strawberries —I smell, nay, I taste them still. That flaring-topped vase was full of sweet white honeysuckle when I espied it in a farm-house window—I carried away the scent of the honeysuckle when I bought the vase. This old mottled stone-ware jug, with the hound handle, stood in the deep shade of a stone wall by the side of a sunny hay-field when first it met my view. It was filled with honest home-brewed beer for the hay-makers. We sat fuming and sizzling in the hot sun, watching them spread and turn the fragrant hay until the beer had all been drunk (and we did not have to wait long), and we bore the jug off in triumph, breathing to us forever the scent of new-mown hay with, to speak truthfully, a slight tinge of stale beer.

A halo of "sweet Sabean odors" fairly envelops all family china. In those blue and white Canton sugar-bowls, and in that great jar with the red lacquered cover, my grandmother kept her fragrant spiced rose-leaves—there are rose-leaves in them now. In that tall pitcher she always placed the first lilac and cherry blooms—and lo ! as I look at the poor cracked thing, "sweet is the air with budding haws and white with blossoming cherry-trees." More prosaic and homely, but equally memory-sweet, what a penetrating aroma of strong green tea rises out of that copper-lustre teapot ! What a burnt and bitter, but wholly good-smelling steam arises from that old flip-mug, the steam from many a quart of flip brewed from New England rum, and home-made beer, stirred with the red-hot iron loggerhead.

Like Charles Lamb, I was born china-loving. " I am not conscious of a time when china jars and saucers were introduced into my imagination." When I was a little child the dearest treasures of my doll's house were a small cup-plate of purest porcelain, delicately bordered with a diagonal design of tiny berries and spike-shaped bachelor's buttons and fine lines of gold, and a nicked India china tea-caddy, cork-stoppered, and filled with precious rose-water — rose-water of my grandmother's own make, distilled in the old rose-water still that stood, when unused, a cumbrous and mysterious machine under the dusty eaves of the garret. I suspect that still had been employed in early colonial days to manufacture a less innocuous liquid than rose-water, but now only the petals of the Queen of the Prairie, the

sweet-brier, the cinnamon roses, went into its innocent
limbec; and its sweet-scented product was intensified by
the contents of one of the long, thin, gilt glass bottles
of ottar of roses that my great-uncle, Captain Royal, who

Crown Derby Plate.

' followed the sea," brought home in such vast numbers
from China. One day there poured out from the door
of my doll's house a penetrating fragrance of roses; I
peered within—the keen anguish of that moment fills
me even now; the tea-caddy had fallen—nay, had been
knocked on my precious little plate, and both were
broken. There on her back, drenched with my cherished
rose-water, lay the iconoclast, my miserable maltese kit-
en, in mischief still, pulling down with her sharp,
wicked claws my proudest masterpiece, a miniature

chandelier of wire and glass beads over which I had spent many a weary hour. I burst into a loud wail of hopeless despair; the bedraggled kitten rushed frightened from my side, shedding odors of Araby as she bounded away,

> " An amber scent of odorous perfume
>   Her harbinger."

Ah! never again, even at sight of housemaids' broken spoils, have I felt such heart-breaking grief. To this day, when I look back at the plate here shown and the little coffee-cans of the blue Tournay sprigged set which I now know to be Crown Derby, and to have been bought by Uncle Royal in a sudden streak of extravagance (perhaps he, too, was china-mad); to this day I grieve for their companion, the little broken cup-plate, and again I smell the sweet, cloying fragrance of rose-water.

These old dark-blue plates also tell a tale. They are known to us as "the doctor's pie-plates," not from the comical figure of Dr. Syntax with which they are decorated, but so called in derision. An old New England physician, a pie-hater, stole, one Thanksgiving eve, twenty-eight carefully made pies that his patient wife and daughters had provided for his Thanksgiving guests. He rose stealthily in the dead of night, threw lemon and apple, quince and cranberry, mince and "Marlborough" pies to the pigs, and hid the blue pie-plates in an old rat-nibbled, cobweb-filled, musty, dusty coach that had stood for half a century in his carriage.

house, and in which his English grandmother had journeyed in state throughout New England. Thirty years later, after his death, at the destruction of the old coach, these hidden pie-plates were found by his descendants. They are therefore not simply "good pieces of blue," they are ceramic monuments of the household tyranny of man.

Shall I ever forget my first view of my largest and choicest Washington pitcher? It stood filled with dried grasses and pressed and varnished autumn leaves, and painfully covered with an ignominious shell of decalcomanie and scrap-book pictures, on a table in a lonely light-house. Only by its shape did we know it, the old watermelon shape of Liverpool ware. Not a vestige of its early decoration could be seen, but we bought it as a hazard of fortune. Oh, the delight I felt when I reached home and scraped off Pauline Hall's smirking and high-colored countenance, and saw with a thrill of friendly recognition the black-lined face of my own solemn and immaculate Washington surmounting her full-blown, rosy shoulders and scarlet and gold bodice. Never do I look at my fully restored pitcher but I see him again, as then, with his dignified head turned very much aside, as if sadly shocked at the position and dress he found himself in.

The clear blue letters on these old Delft apothecary jars speak not to me of the drugs and syrups, of the lohocks and electuaries that were contained within them in olden times; they are abbreviations of various Biblical proverbs, such as "Every fool will be meddling," and "Let him that thinketh he standeth take heed lest he fall." The little, ill-drawn blue cherubs that decorate

these jars seem always to wink and smirk maliciously at me, and to hold their fat sides as though they were thinking of the first time they gazed at me and jeered at me out of the window of the gray old farm-house in Narragansett, as I stood entrapped by the sudden crushing in of a peaked-roofed hen-house upon which I had climbed to peer within a window at the hidden Delft treasures. There I stood on broken eggs and piercing splinters for one hour, with only distracted hens and scarcely less distracted thoughts for company, until the owner of henhouse and Delft jars returned and kindly chopped me out of my absurd and well-deserved stocks. Severe and unceasing monitors are my old apothecary jars.

When I stick gillyflowers and clove-pinks in the pierced tops

Delft Apothecary Jars.

of these three-legged India china "posy-holders," I am, like Marjorie Fleming, "all primmed up with Ma-

jestick Pride"—the honest pride of a successful china-
finder who has snatched her prize from before the
very face of a dozen other collectors. These "posy-
holders" stood for forty years on the high-towering man-
tel-tree of a country parlor, a parlor that was viewed
yearly by scores of inquisitive and curiosity-seeking summer visitors, visitors too dull-visioned to recognize these
china treasures. Perhaps the high-shelved station of the
china, a foot only from the ceiling, helped to hide them.
Perhaps the gruesome row of oval silvered disks that
stood in their company, tarnished coffin-plates bearing
the names of past and dead dwellers in that home, may
have chilled and repelled investigation. Perhaps the
scarlet, blue, and gold dragons and shrimps on the posy-
holders were dulled by the greater glories of their surroundings, for this parlor shone resplendent with glowing color. The walls had been painted by a travelling
artist in the early part of this century, and lavish was his
fancy and his sense of color. Above the high black
mantel-shelf a yellow ochre sun threw his rays over vermillion and purple clouds. These rays of light were
gilded and curved in various directions, and gave Phœ-
bus the appearance of a good-tempered, smiling octopus,
withal somewhat intoxicated. At either side of the fireplace sprung a great palm-tree that bore at the base of a
spreading cluster of leaves luscious bunches of great
hanging pineapples. Around one tree a frightful serpent
coiled, his striped folds most beautifully diversified with
gilded spots. Behind the other tree lurked a crouching
tiger. On the plastered wall were painted two portraits

with fine simulated gold frames, apparently held in place by heavy cord and tassels ; one was of George Washington, the other the past owner of all these glories. It was curious to see the marked and comic likeness a fair young daughter of the house, the village school-mistress, bore to the hard-faced, non-perspective old daub of a grandfather on the wall ; had you dressed her in a brass-buttoned blue coat and a high stock, she would have been far more like the portrait than most portraits are like their originals. One large space was decorated with a full-passengered coach with four prancing horses ; the other bore a marine view—fierce waves, and a strangely rigged brig, with gilded cannon, and fine flags and pennants all blowing stiffly against the wind that filled the sails. A steamboat, too, sailed these waters blue—the greatest triumph of the painter's art. Robert Fulton's invention was in its infancy when this steamboat was evolved, and it was plainly constructed from the artist's imagination. The cranky hull bore two brick chimneys ; it rested on crossbars like a wagon, and had four great wheels that sat well up out of the water. The floor of this room was painted a dull drab color, and in brilliant yellow was displayed a diagram of the solar system, planets, moons, and orbits, sadly worn and defaced, however, by the footsteps of three generations of New Englanders.

Do you wonder that the china posy-holders were overlooked in all this blaze of glory? I recount the gaudy decorations with grateful praise. Through them my treasures stood, ever " eye-sweet and fair," but unnoticed, for years, humbly awaiting my china-loving and china-spying vision.

These dainty egg-shell cups and saucers have also their memory, their lesson—a word softly spoken but clear ; they were once owned by two silver-haired " antient maides" of Chippendale elegance and Pilgrim blood, who lived under the moss-covered, decaying roof-tree of a pallid, gaunt, old colonial home in New England. These " last leaves on the tree " kept their dainty, shallow, apse-shaped china closets in a state of snowy purity, of precise and unvarying order, of unspotted contamination, which might be taken as an emblem of their narrow, pure, and monotonous lives. No thick, substantial modern wares, no gayly painted crockery, no vessels of common clay, stood on their well-ordered and softly shining shelves, just as no modern notions, no knowledge of the common, the evil things of life, had ever entered their simple minds, had ever shocked their fair souls. Fragile, graceful, antiquated, pale in decoration, were their weakly sprigged, lavender-bordered, delicately fluted cups ; looking like their own softly wrinkled faces, their meagre, bent figures, their slender hands. Worn was the gilt on the china, faded was the furniture of their rooms, as ill-health had worn their gentle spirits. Rather scantily filled were their china shelves, as were thin and few their garments, as was sparsely filled their larder. Deep green shadows fell on the glass doors and white shelves of their china closets from the thick-branched old lilacs that close-screened each small-paned window, from the dark century-old cedars that overhung their home; death and loneliness and scanty means had shadowed their lives. My pure, dignified, and silent old cousins, no sweetly-perfumed, softly-tinted, strong-growing blossoms of New England life were you, but rather the sad, white, scentless " life everlasting " that waved like summer snow-drifts over your own sterile, rock-filled fields. These fragile porcelain emblems of your colorless life shall not be carelessly handled and rudely gazed at in their new home, but, close-hidden away in an old apple-wood beaufet which once stood beside your virginal china closets, shall forever teach to me the lesson of contentment, simplicity, and resignation which you showed in your gentle lives, the lesson which through your old china still lives—the lesson of peace and rest.

A halo of mysterious ghost-seeing, an eternal radiance of poesy, surrounds this copper-lustre pitcher. We found this irradiated pitcher when we went a-spinet-hunting. We found the ghost also, a tall, pale, terrifying apparition, who stealthily entered our room at midnight as we slept in the old Pardon tavern, who mysteriously and quietly carried off our gowns, but who proved in the cold disillusionizing daylight to be our landlady's daughter, an amateur dressmaker of unbounded ambition and few resources. And our poet! we found him also, a unique and untutored son of the gods, a rare product of New England soil. We prosaically hired this Yankee Walt Whitman to drive us to the Maybee farm—the house which we had been assured held both china and spinet. Our dearly-remembered poet was a tall, wiry New Englander, whose only visible attire was a moth-eaten fur

hat, a woollen shirt, a pair of heavy boots, and faded
overalls, held in place by a single suspender. He looked
too thinly clad for the raw spring weather, but seemed
perfectly comfortable
and contented in his
light clothing. Poet-
like, his hair was long.
Four little wintry
curls blew out from
under the old hat.
We had been warned
that he did not call
himself a farmer, but
proudly avowed and
named himself a poet;
and it was hinted that
he was a little "luny."
He had begun his

Copper Lustre Pitcher.

rhyming career with the composition of epitaphs for all
the village inhabitants, both living and dead; and from
hence had advanced to the constant use of rhymes in
every-day life and hence had acquired the name of
"Rhyming Darius." He "lisped in numbers for the
numbers came;" and proudly did he display his God-
given talent to us prosy city folks. He also combined
with his vocation as poet the additional talent of em-
ploying intensely legal forms of speech; for he had at
an early period of his life been a witness in some country
trespass case, and had since then always spent a day "in
court," whenever the rare days of idleness of a New

England farmer would permit. As a result, he always cross-questioned everyone with whom he had any conversation, and adopted, as far as he could remember, a lawyer's phraseology and legal terms. He had a wily manner of evading questions, and seldom gave a direct answer; so between questions and answers we held "open court" all the way to the Maybee farm.

Our poet also made a strange introduction of the letter "u" into words—which use he evidently regarded as something extremely eloquent and scholarly, but which produced some very astonishing variations in our vernacular speech. He was much excited at the nocturnal abstraction of our gowns and he poured forth a perfect volley of rhymed questions upon the subject to us as he drove, seated sidewise, fixing us "with his glittering eye:"

> "Why didn't she apply to ye purs-u-nal
>   An' ask ye fur the garment?
> Did she retain the artucle
>   Long enough to bring a warrant?
> Did she take it with malice of forethought
>   Or unpre-med-ure-tated?
> Did she terrure-fy ye very bad
>   A-purloinin' as ye stated?
> What air ye goin' to do?
>   Did her mother know it too?
> Why didn't ye holler out?
>   An' ask her what's she's about?"

At last, to stop his flood of inquiry, we began to question him, to draw him out about the spinet and china.

"Do you know the Maybees well?"

"Wall—I may perhaps assert
    And assure-vure-rate I do ;
At any rate I know him
    And I s'pose I know her too."

"Is it an old farm, and an old house?"

"It ain't so old as some,
    And it's a little older 'n others.
The farm 's older 'n the house ;
    It used to be my brother's."

"How long have you known them?"

"Oh—quite an in-ture-val,
    But I ain't known 'm all my life ;
I've known him sence I was two year old,
    And a leetle longer his wife."

"Do you know whether they have an old spinet?"

"I'll tell you in a minute
    If you'll tell me what's a spinet?"

"It is like a little old-fashioned piano. Have they
got such a one? Is it old? Is it small? Describe it
to us."

"They 've the funniest thing you ever see ;
    It's just as cur-u-ous as it can be ;
How to dure-scribe it just beats me ;
    Spinet's the name for it down to a T.
It ain't so big as some pianures,
    And it ain't so small as othures ;
'Tain't so old as some you'd see,
    And 'tain't so new as it might be ;

That is all that I can say.
I heard old Maybee tell one day
He'd a mus-ure-cal com-bure-nation
He'd be glad to sell for a very small sum ;
'Twas as old and mean
As any he'd seen,
And he'd like to sell it, he says,
Before it drops to pieces."

We looked at each other in amazement at this strange specimen of Yankee humanity—that is, we did it whenever his gaze was averted long enough to give us any chance to look at each other. We sank back in despair of ever receiving a definite description of the spinet, and above all of any china—that most indescribable of country possessions. We feebly tried to parry him with some of the skill which he himself displayed, but failed ignominiously under the scathing sharpness of this " lawyer " of thirty years' experience. We finally answered his rhyming questions with as much directness and truth as the chief witness in a murder trial. As we alighted from the wagon and were about to enter the Maybee door, Darius pulled me back by the sleeve and whispered :

" Ye mustn't mind Miss Maybee
If ye find her a leetle cross ;
She ain't at all e-lab-ure-ate,
Any more than my old horse.
She won't show any man-ures
When you ask to see her pianure."

A sharp-featured young woman advanced to meet us. Her hair bore two partings, an inch apart, and the middle lock was strained painfully back. Her face was curiously mottled with yellow patches which showed plainly that dyspepsia and biliousness had marked her for their own. She looked so sour, so sharp, so devoid of " man-ures " that we quailed visibly before her keen black eye. What new specimen of humanity had we here ? Into what world was our china and spinet-hunting carrying us ? "

We began the conversation very mildly by saying that we had heard that Mrs. Maybee had some china that she wished to sell.

" Then you've heard a lie," the acrid voice broke in.

" But surely we have heard that you have a piano to sell ? "

" Well, I ain't. I've got a musical combination, but I ain't so awful anxious to sell it."

For minutes we stood there, facing this resentful being, who showed no desire to have us seat ourselves, while we pleaded, we praised, we cajoled, we apologized, and we questioned, until, at last, she allowed us to see her precious spinet. We entered the gloomy " best room " where it stood, gave one glance at it, and sank on the haircloth sofa. It was a *melodeon*—a forlorn, broken-down, old *melodeon*—to which some farm-tinker had added an oblong frame strung with catgut and wire strings, in the apparent hope of forming some instrument of the nature of an Æolian-harp.

Tears of disappointment fairly sprang to ɔur eyes ; but the contrast, the revulsion of feeling, the sense of the ludicrous, was so keen, that we gave way to hysterical laughter; we could not suppress it. Where, alas! were our "manners?" I was the first to recover my self-possession. I turned to Mrs. Maybee, who stood before us speechless with angry astonishment, and said pacifically: "You were very good to let us see it. It is not quite what we expected to find. It is so much newer than an old spinet! I fear my sister could not afford to buy it, as she has one piano already. It is very curious and very ingenious, and no doubt you will sell it to someone." We were walking slowly toward the open door in the hope of immediate escape; but we were not to escape so easily, not without punishment for our adventurous raid. As we drew back, Mrs. Maybee advanced; and it seemed for a while that we should be obliged to buy the old melodeon and take it off with us. But I seized upon a diversion, a godsend, in the shape of a row of window-plants in the kitchen. One fine geranium flourished in this "copper-lustre" pitcher, which had had a hole knocked in the bottom, to permit the water to drain out. I immediately began to admire that geranium, and offered Mrs. Maybee a dollar for the pitcher and plant. This diverted her mind from the unfortunate "spinet;" and after much sharp talk and bargaining we paid her one dollar and seventy-five cents for the geranium and pitcher, rushed from her inhospitable door, and drove away with our poet. "The True Story of the Life, Temper, and Adventures of Orvilla Maybee," related to us in legal verse by "Rhyming Darius" on our homeward drive, made us wonder that we escaped unharmed from that New England vixen.

So our broken lustre pitcher was all that we had to carry home with us from our "spinet hunt." And I will close this little tale of New England experience with a simple statement of the cost of the pitcher and the geranium (which died when transplanted).

Two fares to Pardon and return	$4 00
Bill for supper, bed, and breakfast for two	1 50
Wagon, poetry, and legal advice	1 00
Paid Mrs. Maybee for pitcher	1 75
Total cost of pitcher	$8 25

As I have since seen a fac-simile of our pitcher (only whole and unbroken) in a bric-a-brac shop, ticketed $2, we cannot consider the trip financially successful; though, truth to tell, it was far more so than many another expedition we have made. But a golden lustre, the memory of our legal poet, englamours forever in our eyes our copper pitcher. When we look at it we hear again the strident voice, the bizarre pronunciation, the voluble rhymes of our poet of the soil, our Darius, as he exclaimed in amazement :

> " Ye don't hang 'em on the wall,
>   Them cracked old kitchen dishes !
> An' keep a frac-tured pitcher
>   As if 't was act-ure-ly precious !
> They say that city folks
>   Is mighty extrav-ure-gant,
> But with such test-ure-mony
>   I'm willin' to swear they ain't.
> There ain't a party in this town
>   So stingy an' such a non-com

As to hang that pitcher on the wall,
  Lookin' 's if 't was jest goin' ter fall,
An' the hole showin' in the botturm."

Many ghosts has our china-hunting revealed to us; the ghosts of the past, the visions and dreams that never become realities, the inexorable fate, the sad kismet of New England life. Such was the story of the house of Hartington, a story sadly typical of many New England homes; a story which the sight of these little lettered and escutcheoned cups always retells to us.

A description had been given to us of an old town with old houses and old people and old china, and after a gloomy night in a hideous country hotel we started out to find some townsman of whom we could hire a horse and carriage of some or any sort to carry us to Rindge and Anthony Hartington's house — the oldest house of all.

A thin, auburn-haired, freckle-faced Yankee, about twenty-one years old, answered our questions with the greatest interest, and finally offered us the use of his own horse and open wagon for the whole day for two dollars. "And I'll drive fer ye, too," he added, with enthusiasm. "Ye'd never find old Hartington's if ye took the hoss yerself, an' I do' 'now as I can neither, without some pretty tall huntin' and questionin'."

So off we started on the back seat of an open country "express wagon" to find "old Hartington's farm." The warm October sun streamed down upon us, the great red and russet rock-broken fields stretched off into the beautiful lonely purple mountain, "heeding his sky affairs," the dying brakes and weeds sent forth their sweet nutty autumn fragrance, the soft yellow and brown leaves fluttered down on us, and the ripe chestnut-burrs fell rustling by our side as we rode through the narrow wood-roads. The hard New England landscape was softened and Orientalized by the yellow autumn tints. The half-sad stillness of dying nature and the warmth of the Indian summer inclined us to ride quietly and thoughtfully along the country roads, but that neither Mr. Simmons, nor his new wagon, nor Jenny, his steed, would for a moment permit. She had the unpleasant habit, so common among country horses, of "slacking-up" suddenly at the foot of every hill. The wagon was a "jump-seat," so the back seat was not fastened in securely. At every hill (and the New England hills are countless) we and the seat were pitched forward on Mr. Simmons's back. He seemed to expect this assault and rather enjoy it. To quite counterbalance this sudden stoppage of progression, Jenny would spring forward with much and instantaneous speed whenever she caught sight of Mr. Simmons's short whip. This whip he used as a pointer in his many and diffuse explanations, so whenever our attention was called to an old house, or a poor "run-out" farm, or "the barn òld White hung himself in," Jenny emphasized the explanation with a twitch of our necks that brought into active play muscles little used before.

At last the long hill leading to the Hartington house was reached, the longest and steepest yet seen. The road was almost unused, a mere track, and spoke to our china-hunting instincts most favorably of the little intercourse held by the Hartingtons with the rest of the world. Slowly plodded Jenny over the fringed gentians, for here the road was full of them, as open and blue as the October sky over our heads. We had never seen this lovely delicate flower growing elsewhere than sparsely by a brookside or in damp ground, but here, on this rocky hill-side, in this poor soil, it opened its blue eyes in such luxuriance that the road was as full of its azure bloom as in September the fields are yellow with golden-rod, or in June white with daisies. As we turned in from the main country road we passed an elderly man with bowed head, ragged clothes, slouching gait, and a general appearance of extreme depression and sadness more marked even than is usual in the carriage of the New England farmer. As he did not lift his head to look at us, nor nod with the cordial common country form of recognition, we did not speak to him, and he slowly followed us up the hill.

The Hartington house was a mansion, a brick manor-house. We were met at the great door by a young untidy woman, whose clear pink-and-white complexion and curly hair could not, however, compensate for her lack of good teeth, several front teeth being missing and the others discolored. This poor care and poor condition of the teeth is most common among New England women in the country. Nearly every woman over thirty years of age will show when speaking two rows of blue-white porcelain disks so evidently false that they hardly seem like teeth, but look like a "card" of cheap buttons. We thought her the daughter of the house; she proved to be its mistress, the wife of Anthony Hartington. A more desolate, unhappy, hopeless home I have never seen. The elderly gloomy man, who now entered, proved to be Anthony himself. He spoke but little, and from the young wife, who seemed in a feverish state of excitement at our visit, we learned the forlorn and desolate story of the household.

Anthony had married early in life and had had nine children, all of whom, with his wife, had died of that fell curse of New England—consumption. The last child, a daughter, Luriella, had died in June. This young wife had been her school friend and had married the forlorn old man two years ago, in order to come to live there and nurse her friend through her last illness, thus giving a touching example of the life-sacrifices and self-abnegations so sadly frequent in New England country homes. "We didn't think she'd live through the winter," she said, "but she did, and died in June. I was glad she lived till it was warm. It is so cold here in winter," she added apologetically.

A heavy gloom settled on us as we walked from room to room, and I was additionally overwhelmed by the uncanny, unreasoning sense that I had been there before, had lived there. It was all so familiar to me, so strangely well known, that I could scarcely speak, but walked bewildered and frightened through the rooms I had known a hundred years ago. I have never felt at any other time that sense of pre-existence, but I know that nothing about that old house was new to me.

The upper part of the windows were of small panes of greenish "bull's-eye" glass, rarely found in the country now; the lower panes of cheap, modern glass, some being broken and pasted over with dirty bits of calico and paper, and all as opaque with dirt as the ancient upper panes. Outside the windows lay an unkempt tangle of lilac bushes, shrubs, weeds, straggling withered flowers, box borders, and thistles, that once had been a lovely, well-kept garden, but had evidently been unentered and unheeded for years. It stretched down the hill-side to the well-tenanted family graveyard with its moss-grown and chipped slate headstones with their winged cherubs' heads and crossbones. I had often gathered flowers in that garden; I remembered it well, and had walked and played among the gravestones.

Inside the four great parlors hung cobwebs and dust —and wasps! the floors were sprinkled with them; thousands lay dead in the two-feet-wide window-seats, while swarms of live ones buzzed loudly at the dingy windows. "They won't touch you," she said, as we drew back. "He thinks there must be a nest somewhere." A nest! A colony of nests rather—a hundred nests, the accumulated nests of years.

The parlors had few pieces of furniture, and all were broken except a modern marble-topped table and a "what-not." "I bought these," she said, "when I was married, to please Luriella; I didn't want to spend much, for fear she would need medicine. But she didn't take much at last; she thought it didn't do any good."

A set of painted book-shelves in a corner held a few

books, two or three china dogs, some common sea-shells, a large ginger-jar, and a number of really beautiful pewter porringers with handles. My companion had already conveyed to " him " our wish " to buy any old pieces of furniture or china you may wish to part with," and though we had not heard a word nor seen a gesture of assent, the wife told us that " he " was willing to sell. Yet, when we said we would like to buy the little handled porringers, he walked out of the room without a word.

All the wood-work in these parlors—the wainscoting, the high mantels, the panels of the doors, the heavy window-frames—were ornamented with a curious design, a row of half-pillars joined at the top in a series of pointed arches, with carved sunbursts in the spandrels. It was most graceful and odd—I have never seen it elsewhere—yet it was perfectly familiar to me; I could almost remember, yes, I could remember, counting the number of pillars in the room.

The two kitchens were enormous rooms. One, entirely closed away and disused, disclosed a horror of dirt and rubbish, old pots and pans, and tubs, and wheels, thrown, a shapeless mass, into the fireplace, and scattered over the floor. In the smaller kitchen the chimney-nook, the great fireplace, had been boarded over, and a small rusty kitchen stove placed for daily use. I seemed to remember when I sat by this ingle-side, and great logs lay on this broad hearth, and the roaring flames surged up the great chimney and threw their cheerful light into the now desolate room.

Through this kitchen there wailed a moaning noise from the empty chimney, which made even my cheerful companion look solemn and depressed. She " didn't like to hear it, either," our guide said, quietly.

Two bedrooms and a " living-room " completed the number of apartments on the ground floor. But the living-room was not lived in ; the two bedrooms were the only apartments that bore signs of occupation. There was not a carpeted floor in the house, but to these two rooms, braided rag rugs and strips of home-spun carpet gave an appearance of comparative comfort. The " rising-sun " and " twin-sister " patchwork quilts on the untidy beds added to the effect.

The most incongruous, most inadequate apartment on this floor was the pantry, a little dark box of a closet, to which one small greenish glass window dispensed a dingy light. We had intended to ask for our dinner, since it was then "high noon," but a sight of this cooking sanctum dispelled all thought or wish for dinner. It was so cobwebby, so dusty, so poor-looking that we could not wish to eat any dinner that could issue from its dark shadows. We found afterward, beyond the disused kitchen, a large square room which, in the early days of the prosperity and good cheer of this house, had doubtless been a pantry, but was now filled with broken grindstones, crushed Dutch ovens, fragments of crockery, pails and pans, " peels " and " slices," yarn-winders, and part of an old rose still. Indeed through this entire house, nothing could ever have been wholly destroyed or carried away, but was thrown, in its broken, grimy desuetude, into some neglected closet or room to gather years of dust and dirt, as if the owner, too poor to buy new furniture, still clung to the shattered remnants of past plenty.

We rescued from the dingy little pantry, from among the litter of broken cups and plates and knives, bunches of dried herbs, empty spice-boxes, cracked woodenware, and greasy pans, a few treasures which we spread out on the kitchen table—half a dozen " Pain's Hill " plates (a favorite pattern throughout New England), two open-work bordered Leeds platters, a dear little boat-shaped queen's-ware creamer with dainty twisted handles, two helmet pitchers, two tea-cups, and half a dozen plates of a set of old Lowestoft china bearing a pretty armorial device and initials. We hardly dared ask to buy the latter pieces until we saw the evident contempt the farm-wife had for them. Nothing so American as a Lafayette or Pilgrim plate was to be seen.

One large dresser in the kitchen was found to be literally filled with battered and broken brass and pewter candlesticks, glass whale-oil lamps, snuffers, pewter saveaIls, extinguishers, and trays, and brass chimney hooks for shovel and tongs. We rescued from this medley several candlesticks, two curious Dutch hanging-lamps, and a really beautiful but broken candelabra of Sheffield plate. These we placed with the china on the kitchen table. I wished to add the pewter porringers found in the parlor, but the wife softly drawled in her nasal voice : " He won't sell 'em—they were hers

—she used to make mud-pies in 'em when she was little." And pretty playthings they must have been—fifteen dear little shallow pewter posnets and porringers with flat pierced handles, varying in size from one large enough to hold a pint to a true doll's or a " 'prentice " porringer an inch and a half in diameter. They were full of little, common, colored pebbles and shells, dried seeds, and old purple glass beads, perhaps just as " she " had last played with them. Other and more distant memories, too, may have clung to the old porringers—of days when the old man was a boy and took his " little porringer " and ate his supper of bread and milk from it ; and perhaps, in the far years when the old man was a baby, his mother had had served to her in one of these old porringers her " dish of caudle," that rich mixture of eggs, spices, bread, milk, and wine which was thought years ago to be the proper diet for a sick person.

Then we mounted the spiral staircase to the second floor, the chambers. Through this dreary expanse we walked slowly — the dusty half-furnishings growing shabbier and shabbier—still stumbling over broken furniture on the uneven floors, until we entered a south room that was such a blaze of cheerful, yellow, tropical light that we exclaimed with delight. Walls and ceilings were hung solid with long yellow ears of corn, left to dry for use in the winter. Even the old cherry four-post bedstead was draped with them. Such a color! Such a glory ! " She used to like to see them too," the low voice murmured.

A third story, a gambrel-roofed attic, was too dusty

and repelling to enter, but in one of the deserted bed-rooms we found, whole, though black with dust, a dressing-table which had been the lower portion of a high chest of drawers. As is common now in New England farm-houses, the top drawers had been lifted from this table portion and set upon the floor to use as a bureau; not half so tidy and cleanly a fashion of furniture as when it stood on its high legs and let a broom or brush sweep freely every portion of the floor under it. The upper portion of this high chest was seen afterward in the outer wood-shed full of strips of leather, broken harness, nails, and pieces of iron. It had been gnawed by rats and whittled by knives till it was valueless. The lower or table portion was whole. It had three shallow "jewel drawers," three deep drawers with brass handles and carved "sunbursts." It proved, when dusted, to be of curled maple; and after long discussion with Mr. Simmons we decided to take it with us. Its bowed legs ended in claw-and-ball feet that would just set within the carriage sides. "If one on ye don't mind settin' in front with me, the other can set in the back seat with the table in front of her," he said.

This young wife had not once shown the usual country curiosity about us, but as she turned away to find some newspapers to wrap around the plates, I said to her, "There is much here we should like to buy and take away with us, but it would cost so much to move the pieces so far, and they are so out of repair." Then we told her who we were, whence we came, what we should do with the china, and that we should often think and speak of her when we looked at the plates this coming winter. "I can't bear to think of the winter without her," she answered, softly.

Jenny had been fed and watered and "hitched up," and we prepared to start. I clambered into the back seat of the wagon, then the dressing-table was lifted in and placed in front of me. Luckily its legs were long enough, so the weight did not rest on my legs, else I could never have taken it. Our laps were filled with the frail china; the candlesticks, lamps, and two warming-pans were placed on the floor of the wagon, and we started, leaving the two dreary figures and the dreary house behind us. All the way down the steep hills I had to hold the table to keep it off the occupants of the front seat, and all the way up the steep hills it lay heavily in my lap; but at last we reached the country station and packed our china and brass in two market-baskets which Mr. Simmons brought us from his "store." We could hear the sallies of country wit from the loafers at the station at Mr. Simmons and his strange load, and his indignant and most offensively personal and profane answers in return. Then we received a baggage-check for the dressing-table, and finally entered the train rather conscious that two warming-pans and two newspaper-covered market-baskets are hardly ordinary or desirable travelling luggage.

A few days later, when cleaning the inside of the dressing-table, the following letter was found. It had been caught and held by a splinter of wood under the top of the table, and had evidently lain untouched for years. It was folded in the old-fashioned way, dated May 12, 1810, and addressed to Madam Janet Hartington. It read thus:

D^R AND RESPECT^ED MOTHER The letter which I wrote you some three months ago on the s'bj'ct of my proposed marriage was answered by you, and the answer duly rec^d by me.

The two letters I wrote you since on the same s bj'ct have rec^d no answer.

And now it is too late to receive any further advice on the matter, for I wish to most Respectfully inform you that I married the object of my choice a week past today in Kings Chapel in Boston. There were but few present, as was Oriana's wish.

The plans you wrote me, most Respect^ed Mother, for the advancement and future prospects of our family, interested me much, and I quite concur in them all.

And no one could be more fully fitted to assist me in my career than my Oriana. Her graceful and ladylike deportment fit her to adorn any circle no matter how exalted.

She is quite ready to become a most dutifull and obedient daughter to you and I trust, my Dr Mother, the fact of her being an orphan will open your heart to her ; and then the wish you have always had, viz, to have a daughter, may thus find its fullfillment.

I know not from what source you obtained the strange advice that her Father did amass his fortune in the African Slave Trade. I have never wounded her tender heart by inquiry as to the source of her Fathers wealth (tho' 'tis a calling & trade has been followed by many citizens apparently much respect^ed). But the thought of his " ill-gotten gold " need no further trouble you. Thro' ill advice and knavery, her fortune has dwindled to a thousand dollars, and now her wealth is only in her beauty and her amiable disposition. She has however much good furniture and china which will grace well our home.

I regret much to hear that my bills and debts in College have cóst you so much, and that the Farm is so run behindhand. This, with the debts my Father left behind him, make it most advisable for me to give up my intention to practice as a lawyer, and have decided me to return to manage your Farm.

It is quite opportune and most Providential that your Farmer is dead, since he managed so ill.

With your wise instructions and counsels, we can no doubt retrieve the money that has been lost, and carry out my Grandfathers plans to make our house and name one of the most powerful in the State.

Thus shall I assume the position in town and county that you always wished me to take.

We shall leave by coach for Ringe in a week, our household goods and furnishings to follow us in waggons.

I know, Dr Mother, that you will admire and praise my Oriana, as who could do otherwise ?

I have talked much to her of your aspirations and ambitions, and she hopes most Respectfully to help to carry out any plans you may have.

With most affectionate greeting from Oriana and myself, I am

Your Loving and Honour^{ed} Son

GEORGE HARTINGTON.

In due time the table was scraped, cleaned, and polished, and with its cheerful mottled golden color and shining brass handles, was most thoroughly attractive and satisfying. The pretty Lowestoft china cups were set on it and used for petty toilet purposes. An old canopied mirror was hung over it, and every night after I had lighted the candles in the repaired and resilvered candelabra, I sat there looking at the china, thinking of the blue-fringed gentians, the old house. of the lonely empty rooms, the poverty, the dreariness ; then of the high hopes and ideas of George Hartington, and ambitions of his mother, and, above all, the strange familiarity I had had with my old home.

At last I wrote to the wife at the farm, telling her of the old letter; asking of the career of George Hartington, his success, his life, his fate. I thought he must be Anthony's grandfather or granduncle. The answer came, written in a stiff, uneven hand, but showing more intelligence than her conversation : "George and Oriana Hartington were my husband's father and mother. My husband is seventy-five years old, and was their only child. George Hartington died three years after he was married. My husband remembers his mother as a feeble, sickly woman who didn't have much to say on the farm, and seemed always afraid of Madam Hartington. She died of consumption when he was twelve years old. That was her china you bought with the O on it. His grandmother lived to be ninety-two years old. He is not very well this winter, he has a bad cough. If you know of any good cough medicine, I could buy it with the money you gave us for the table and china," etc.

And this is the end of all Madam Hartington's ambitions—a broken-down, broken-hearted, childless old man. It is the New England kismet.

Sad often are many of the memories, sad are the pictures, brought to my mind by my old china. It speaks to me too often of deserted farms, of unthrifty farmers ; of shabby homes, the homes of drunken fathers and sickly mothers; of rasping young Philistines, haters of old things and old ways ; of miserly old women and extravagant young ones; of gloomy widowers and miserable bachelors; of the hopeless round of toil of New England farm-wives, those human beasts of burden, bending grievously under the heavy load of loneliness and labor; it speaks sadly to me of the pinched ways and poor living, the *res angusta domi* too frequently to be seen, alas! in my beloved New England. All these shadows, however, are softened and lessened by the lapse of time, just as in my memory the days of my china-hunts have all been sunshiny and bright; it never rained, nor was it cold nor windy, nor was it ever sultry or dusty when I have been a china-hunting; all china days were Emerson's

> "   .   .   .   charmed days
> When the genius of God doth flow.
> The wind may alter twenty ways,
> A tempest cannot blow;
> It may blow north, it still is warm;
> Or south, it still is clear;
> Or east, it smells like a clover-farm;
> Or west, no thunder fear."

XIX.

CHINA COLLECTIONS

IN past years any stray china-lover who wished to see and to learn had to search well to find any public collections, or even specimens of old china, in America. In town-halls, in the curiosity shops of eccentric old women, or in the "museums" of land-stranded old sailors, a few pieces might be seen—not saved nor shown because they were china, but because "Parson Boardman, who preached forty-nine years in this town, owned this tea-set;" or "this china was taken out of the cabin of an English frigate in 1813;" or "these mugs were used when George Washington passed through the town." In this class of discursive and disjointed collections, though of course in a superior and highly honored way, might be placed the china of the Museum of the East India Marine Company in Salem, of whose arrangement Eleanor Putnam wrote, "it was as if each sea-captain had lounged in and hustled down his contribution in any convenient vacant space." In that old museum, as I remember it a decade ago, elaborate models of Chinese junks and American merchant vessels bore on their miniature bowsprits strange additions to their rigging, and shadowed by their dusty hulls queer and varied trophies, queerer then than now—sharks' teeth, Turkish pipes, sandal-wood beads, Italian crucifixes, Peruvian pottery, and South Sea shells and savage weapons. Teak-wood furniture and miniature palanquins and pagodas sheltered many curious china treasures which I vaguely recall, queer in name and shape—nests of egg-shell saki-cups and saki-bowls galore ; ink-stones of green celadon with their accompanying water-bottles and little cakes of gilded India-ink ; perfume flasks of painted Japanese wares ; bottles of purest porcelain for Oriental hair-oil, or, rather, hair-glue ; pottery jars full of unpleasant-looking mouldy mysteries, which might be preserved fruit or might be mummies ; " plaster boxes " lettered in Chinese ; strange triangular bits of blue and white Persian porcelain " to clean out shoes with ; " old Liverpool mugs taken from a wreck and wildly labelled "from Ceylon ; " and, chief of all, two vast soup-tureens of purest white Canton porcelain, duck-shaped, six feet in length from beak to tail by *memory's* measurement. In the cold light of recent and more mature inspection these two great East India birds of good cheer, like many another remembered object of the good old times, shrank to about half their ancient size ; but are still impressive relics of the great days and great dinners of the old East India Marine Company, the dinners where, filled to the wings with some hot, well-peppered Indian broth, the twin tureens graced the board around which gathered all these old treasure-bringing and treasure-giving Salem mariners.

A recent visit to my dearly-loved and warmly-remembered old museum grieved my heart ; its charm was gone. Great, light, airy rooms have been added to the old building; an arranger, a labeller, and a model cataloguer have ruthlessly invaded the dusty cases and weeded out the boxes of dried-up and shrivelled fruits, the skins of moth-eaten birds, and of seedy and disreputable fishes. The Chinese paper-fans and woven baskets, once rare enough to be carefully treasured in a museum, now seen in every dry-goods shop in the land, seem wholly to have disappeared. The iconoclasts have prosaically separated each old sea-captain's relics into parcels and placed them in wonderfully well-arranged and classified cases, labelled Madagascar, Alaska, Sumatra, or whatever the land of their early home may be. I suppose the shoe-cleaners and hair-oil bottles are there somewhere in their properly assigned places, but I did not search for them. I glanced at my old friends, the punch-bowls, and the great duck-tureens, but the old-time glamour, the "unstudied grace" of the museum was gone.

In many public buildings at the present day, among treasured colonial relics, may be seen fine specimens of old china. A neighbor of the East India Marine Company, the Essex Institute, has a small but interesting and well-labelled collection of old Salem china.

The Bostonian Society displays in its rooms in the old State House in Boston a number of old Liverpool pitchers and about twenty Staffordshire plates and platters with American designs, as well as some pieces of the china of John Hancock and a few other good Boston citizens.

In the rooms of the Historical Society of Pennsylvania, in Locust Street, Philadelphia, may be seen a number of interesting pieces, including a set of Dresden

cups and saucers, presented to Benjamin Franklin by
Madame Helvétius, of Auteuil, that extraordinary friend
of Franklin's whose behavior so shocked Mrs. Adams.
By the side of this Dresden set are the beautiful coffee-
cups, teacups, saucers, teapot, creamer, bowl, and choc-
olate-pot presented to Mrs. Robert Morris, wife of the
United States Minister of Finance, by Luzerne, the
French Minister; a cup and saucer said to have been
used at the wedding of George Washington; a punch-
bowl made for the Society of the Cincinnati by order
of Colonel Hampden; several Washington pitchers; a
Perry pitcher, and an Erie Canal pitcher.

In the Deerfield Memorial Hall, in the rooms of the
Connecticut Historical Society, of the various societies
of antiquity, and local associations throughout New
England, may be seen good pieces of old pottery and
porcelain, often with an interesting and doubtless authentic story attached, but too frequently wildly and
amazingly labelled as to place of manufacture and date.

Many rich private collections exist. Vast stores of old
colonial treasures are preserved in private houses in our
Eastern States. The Washington pieces of pottery and
porcelain in the Huntington Collection are far outdone
in beauty and in rarity by many private collections,
such, for instance, as that of Miss Powel, in Newport; of
Mrs. Russell, in Cambridge; while the varied collection
of old china at the house of the Washington Association
of New Jersey, with the exception of the historical interest which attaches to it through the story of various
past owners of renown, and excepting, of course, the

rare and beautiful punch-bowls, is equalled and excelled
in many a New England home. In Hartford the collections of Mr. Trumbull, of Dr. Lyon, would make envious
any English china-buyer. In Albany, in Philadelphia,
in Worcester and Providence, in New Haven and Washington, in New York and Brooklyn, many a closet and
room full of well - preserved colonial china show the
good taste and careful judgment of loving owners. In
Boston the collection of Mr. Wales is of unbounded interest and value.

There is but one public collection in America which I
have seen that is of positive and unfailing worth to the
American china-collector—the Trumbull-Prime Collection. I mean for the china-collector for whom these
pages are written, the gatherer of household wares of
colonial times and of the early part of this century. It
is much deplored by residents of New York that this
beautiful and instructive collection has not found a
home on shelves neighboring the Avery Collection of
Oriental porcelains in the Metropolitan Museum of Art.
But it has been placed where it will serve a nobler purpose than contributing to the pleasure or profit even of
china-lover or china-collector—where it will instruct the
china-maker. In the spacious cabinets of the beautiful
art building of Princeton College, it is near the great
china factories of Trenton ; and may the owners of
those factories soon learn the lesson of beauty and variety of form, color, and paste, that is so plainly shown in
the china treasures gathered by Mr. and Mrs. Prime.

It has been easy for anyone, for everyone, who had

any idea or knowledge of old china, to form a collection of china in America. Of course, the value of the accretion was variable, not so much resulting from the length of the purse of the gatherer as from his judgment and care in buying. It is still possible to obtain such a collection. The old china is not yet all discovered and culled from country towns. One china-hunter found in Northampton, that besearched city, in a summer week in 1891—found and bought and bore away in triumph— a large States pitcher, a Boston State House pitcher, a Trenton Falls plate, a Capitol plate, two State House plates, several pieces bearing the design of McDonough's victory, a dozen or more plates with English views, two helmet-pitchers, several pepper-pots, and, in addition to the " treasures of clay," a tall clock and four harp-backed chairs that once were Jonathan Edwards's, a Chippendale table, and various trophies of pewter and brass. Dealers might have visited these Northampton folk in vain, but this beguiling china-hunter bore away his cart-load of old furniture and crockery for a sum total as small as in days of yore.

It is for such slow and careful collectors that these pages are written, for the collectors who having read and studied all the foreign text-books and histories and manuals of pottery and porcelain still know very little of the china within their gates, the china to be gathered in America. The number of such china hunters is steadily crescent. In Chicago, St. Louis, Cincinnati, china collections are being formed ; and many of the finest specimens of American historical china that have been

A Beaufet.

offered for sale in New York and Boston "antique shops" during the past year have been purchased and sent to California.

It is a matter of course that this old china should show to its best advantage in an old-fashioned house, or in a new house built in " American colonial" style of architecture. But whatever the house may be in which all these loved china waifs are assembled and cherished, it should not conceal them, as in Charles Lamb's "great house," in a china-closet. A suitable resting-place for the old pieces is in the sheltering home in which it passed its early days—in a corner cupboard. This was in olden times called a "beaufatt," or "bofet," or "beaufet," or "bofate," or as Cowper wrote of it—

> " This china that decks the alcove
> Which here people call a buffet,
> But what the gods call it above
> Has ne'er been revealed to us yet."

A corner cupboard seems to be, like all old-fashioned furniture, well adapted for the express purpose for which it was made. It is not a modern pattern combination china-closet, washstand, and refrigerator all in one, but for the simple purpose of china-holding and china-showing it is perfect. The old china never looks prettier (except when on the table) than in its wonted home —a corner cupboard or beaufet. The narrow scalloped or crenated shelves with their wider rounded projections at the extreme back seem expressly shaped to show each piece to its best advantage. Even the Gothic small-

paned glass door, when present, does not hide the daint
pieces. The apse-shaped, shell-fluted top with its pillare
frame and carved sunbursts, and its surmounting bras
eagles or balls, seems a fitting roof to shelter the fragil
in-gatherings.

The old china seems always to look better and mor
at home in an old-time setting. On page 44 is show
a shallow dresser, an adaptation of an old kitchen fash
ion, with narrow ledges of shelves hung with old pew
ter porringers, which proves also a delightful way t
show to plain view the rows of blue and white plate:
especially the dainty gems of "cup plates," which are s
treasured and loved by the china-hunter that ther
never seems to be any spot altogether worthy to hol
and display them quite as they ought to be shown. C
course, large articles—what were called in olden time
"hollow-ware"—cannot be placed on a dresser; tin
pepper-pots, salt-cellars, tea-caddies, very small creamer:
and plates and platters set on edge must form the dress
er's only burden.

Another old-fashioned resting-place for china may b
adopted in modern times for the sustentation of an
broken-nosed, handleless, nicked, cracked, or scorche
treasure, "the broken teacups wisely kept for show,
which no true china-hunter will despise, but whic
will not bear the too close examination of scoffers, an
to which distance lends a haze of enchantment and ve
of perfection. I mean a "crown of steps," or "shelf c
steps," or "china steps," as they were variously calle
One is here shown, but as they are so rare nowaday

China Steps.

perhaps the term needs some explanation. On top of a high chest of drawers, a "high-boy," was placed in olden times a three-tiered, graduated platform of "steps" to hold and display china. The lower tier of the platform was about eight or ten inches shorter and five inches shallower than the top of the "high-boy." This left free a shelf of about five inches wide upon the sides and front of the top; the tier was four or five inches high. The second tier, or step, was made shorter and narrower in the same proportion, thus leaving a second ridge or shelf. The top tier, or platform, was smaller still. Thus when the china was arranged around the three sides of the "crown of steps" it made a pretty pyramid of pitchers and teapots and jars, and each piece could be plainly seen. Rather high up in the air they were, perhaps, for purposes of close examination or for freeing from dust, but safe from danger of breaking. Very rarely an old "high-boy" will now be seen with a fixed or permanent "crown of steps," but usually this set of china-shelves was separate, and frequently was only made of stained wood. Such were probably the "Steps for China Ware" of Abraham Blish, of Boston, in 1735, which were worth only two shillings. Such also were "the steps & some small China thereon" of John Proctor in 1756, since they were worth only five shillings and fourpence. Another inventory has this item: "1 Japan Chest Draws and Steps for China."

On such a "shelf of steps" the china is "out of the way;" and for the same virtue I like to hang china on the wall—pitcher, jugs, cups, as well as plates—they are

so safe and yet so plainly visible in that position.   Then
you can do away with "the dozen little teetery tables"
that litter and obstruct our rooms and make man's life
a burden.   There is a certain restfulness in the spacious
parlors of some old houses that I know, a sense of room
in which to move, of liberal elegance, of substantial good
taste, that is owing largely to the absence of small litter-
ing chairs and tables.   Everything is upon the walls that
can be hung or placed there ; decoration is profuse, but
not in the way.   I would rather keep china anywhere
than upon a table.   Perhaps the upsetting of a tea-table,
with its burden of eighteen teapots, and the utter anni-
hilation of teapots and depression of spirits that resulted,
may have conduced to this feeling.   For the purpose of
hanging plates upon the wall come various little wire
frames or holders; but when you have fifty or one hundred plates in your dining-room, even these cheap holders are quite an expense.   Mr. Prime gives in his book
an illustration and the details of the manner of making a
wire frame or holder by which to hang plates on the
wall.   This invention of his is very ingenious and very
good ; many a one have I in my home ; but it requires
for its manufacture a wire-workman or a tinker, either
amateur or professional, and tools of various kinds, and a
neatly made spiral cylinder of wire.   This places the
possibility of manufacturing Mr. Prime's holder quite
out of the reach of the average woman.   I, too, have
invented a holder, and it can be made by any woman,
since she need employ but one tool—her own distinctive
instrument—a pair of scissors.   The materials, too, are

peculiarly feminine—picture-wire or strong twine, and dress-hooks. I will say for the benefit of the masculine china-hunter who may read these pages that both white and black dress-hooks can be purchased for a few cents a dozen, and of various sizes, from the heavy cloak hooks, which are strong enough to hold a thick Delft plaque, to the tiny hooks that are sufficient to sustain a fragile saucer. And the process of manufacture of my plate-holder is so simple! You use your tool but once—to cut off the length of wire. Then place four of the dress-hooks at equal distances around the rim of the plate, slipping them firmly over the edge. String your wire on the back of the plate through the two loops at the end of each of the four hooks and draw it tight. Twist the ends of the wire firmly and neatly together, make a little wire loop by which to hang it, and your plate-holder is done. A man may use a pair of " cut-nippers " to cut the wire, and a pair of pincers to twist it if he so will ; but a pair of scissors is all that is really necessary, and will answer every purpose, though the usage is not thoroughly conducive to the welfare of the scissors. I will not say that this holder is better than Mr. Prime's, though I point with pride to the facility and simplicity of its construction ; but I think l can boast that it is cheaper.

The dark blue Staffordshire plates especially should be thus hung on the wall, where they form so rich a point of color that they put to shame all the thin water-colors and pale French china in their vicinity, and make us fully appreciate Oscar Wilde's sigh of " trying to live up to his blue and white china."

But let me no longer dwell on the charms of our widely gathered possessions, lest it be said of me as was of Horace Walpole—

> " China's the passion of his soul,
>   A cup, a plate, a dish, a bowl
>   Can kindle wishes in his breast,
>   Inflame with joy or break his rest ; "

but end with the assurance that I fully concur in the words of a well-known English collector : " China-collecting is not a mere fancy—it is a complete education."

INDEX